ORAL HISTORY, HEALTH AND WELFARE

Oral History, Health and Welfare highlights the significance of oral history to the history of the development of health and welfare provision in the United Kingdom. By focusing on individual experiences, the human dimension of the history of health and social care is explored. Oral history reveals the personal stories of innovation, policy shifts, training and treatment during a century which has been characterised by both continuity and change.

This book includes discussion of:

• HIV and Aids
• birth control
• the end of the workhouse
• professional education and training of midwives
• the career choices of general practitioners
• pioneers of geriatric medicine
• oral history and the history of learning disability.

Joanna Bornat is a senior lecturer in the School of Health and Social Welfare at the Open University, **Robert Perks** is Curator of Oral History at the British Library National Sound Archive and Director of the National Life Story Collection, **Paul Thompson** is Research Professor of Sociology at the University of Essex and Director of Qualidata, and **Jan Walmsley** is a senior lecturer in the School of Health and Social Welfare at the Open University.

ORAL HISTORY, HEALTH AND WELFARE

Edited by
Joanna Bornat, Robert Perks,
Paul Thompson and Jan Walmsley

London and New York

First published 2000
by Routledge
11 New Fetter Lane, London EC4P 4EE

Simultaneously published in the USA and Canada
by Routledge
29 West 35th Street, New York, NY 1001

Routledge is an imprint of the Taylor & Francis Group

© 2000 for editorial matter and selection, Joanna Bornat,
Robert Perks, Paul Thompson and Jan Walmsley;
for individual chapters, the contributors

Typeset in Baskerville by
The Florence Group, Stoodleigh, Devon
Printed and bound in Great Britain by
T.J. International Ltd, Padstow, Cornwall

British Library Cataloguing in Publication Data
A catalogue record for this book is available from the British Library

Library of Congress Cataloging in Publication Data
Oral history, health and welfare/edited by Joanna Bornat . . . [*et al.*]
p. cm.
Includes bibliographical references and index.
1. Medicine – Great Britain – History Sources. 2. Medical care –
Great Britain – History Sources. 3. Oral history. I. Bornat, Joanna.
R487.073 1999
362.1'0941–dc21 99–20476

ISBN 0–415–19156–4

CONTENTS

CONTENTS

FIGURES AND TABLES

Figures

Tables

CONTRIBUTORS

John Adams is a senior lecturer in the School of Health Studies, Homerton College, Cambridge. He is the consultant editor of the *International History of Nursing Journal*.

Stuart Anderson is a lecturer in the history of pharmacy at the London School of Hygiene and Tropical Medicine. His recent research has involved oral histories of both community and hospital pharmacy practice in Great Britain during the twentieth century.

Dorothy Atkinson is a senior lecturer in the School of Health and Social Welfare at the Open University. Her background is in social work and includes several years' experience of working with people with learning disabilities. She is co-editor of the *British Journal of Learning Disabilities* and author of *An Auto/Biographical Approach to Learning Disability Research* (Ashgate, 1997).

Virginia Berridge is professor of history at the London School of Hygiene and Tropical Medicine, and head of its history group. She is the author of *Opium and the People*, and *Aids in the UK: The Making of Policy 1981–94*.

Michael Bevan was a research officer at the Wellcome Unit for the History of Medicine, Oxford from 1992 to 1995. He is now a research editor with the *New Dictionary of National Biography*.

Robin Dixon retired from the post of academic secretary at the University of Essex in 1992. His thesis, 'Reinterpretation of the Couvade', was awarded in 1997. He now works as a volunteer adviser and employment specialist with a Citizens' Advice Bureau. He has three children and six grandchildren.

CONTRIBUTORS

Rona Ferguson is based at Glasgow Caledonian University where she is a research assistant funded by the Wellcome Trust and a PhD student. She has variously studied art, philosophy and librarianship at Glasgow School of Art, Strathclyde University, Glasgow University and the Open University.

Kate Fisher's DPhil thesis is entitled 'An Oral History of Birth Control Practice *c.* 1920–1950. A Study of Oxford and South Wales'. She is working at the Cambridge Group for the History of Population and Social Structure on a research project: 'Marriage, Fertility and Sexuality, 1900–1950. An Oral History Study'.

Sally French is a lecturer in the Department of Health Studies at Brunel University. She also works as a freelance writer, researcher and physiotherapist. She has written widely in the field of disability studies and psycho-social issues relating to health and illness.

Margot Jefferys After lecturing at the London School of Hygiene and Tropical Medicine, Margot Jefferys moved to Bedford College, where in 1968 she received a personal chair in medical sociology. Since her retirement she has worked on the sociology of ageing, from 1992 at Kings College, London.

Maxine Rhodes is a senior lecturer in social history at Westhill College of Higher Education. Her research interests include the development and status of midwifery knowledge, the experience of childbirth and the expansion of hospital birth in the inter-war period.

Wendy Rickard is a senior lecturer in the Department of Health Sciences, University of East London. She continues to work on the HIV/Aids Testimonies Project upon which this chapter is based and is also undertaking an oral history of prostitution in the UK. Both projects are conducted in collaboration with the British Library National Sound Archive.

Elizabeth Roberts is the director of the Centre for North West Regional Studies in the University of Lancaster. She is also a reader in the history of the family. Her main research tool has been oral history and she used oral evidence extensively in two books, *A Woman's Place 1890–1940* (Blackwell, 1984) and in *Women and Families 1940–70* (Blackwell, 1995).

Neil Small is Senior Research Fellow in the Department of Palliative Medicine at the University of Sheffield, UK. His research interests include the history of hospices and the impact of policy change on service provision for people with chronic and terminal illness.

John Swain is a reader in disability studies at the University of Northumbria, and has contributed to the production of a number of Open University courses in the area of disability studies.

Paul Thompson is a research professor in social history and director of Qualidata at the University of Essex. He is founder-editor of *Oral History* and founder of the National Life Story Collection at the British Library. His books include *The Voice of the Past*, *The Work of William Morris*, *The Edwardians*, *I Don't Feel Old* and *Growing Up in Stepfamilies*.

Jan Walmsley is a senior lecturer in the School of Health and Social Welfare at the Open University, and co-editor of the *British Journal of Learning Disability*. Her main research interests are in the area of learning disability with a particular focus on women's issues.

INTRODUCTION

Paul Thompson

The middle years of the twentieth century, the period on which this book primarily focuses, witnessed an astonishing transformation of both the delivery and nature of health care and of welfare philosophies and organisation in Britain and world-wide. This included the introduction of the National Health Service, the spectacular growth of heart surgery, the development of new diagnostic instruments such as ultrasound and body scanners, and the introduction of new forms of drug treatment for purposes ranging from contraception and inoculation to the curing of syphilis, tuberculosis, mental depression and Aids. From conditions which have dogged societies for centuries to the newest plagues, medical responses have been devised, and the scale of effort devoted to the maintenance of health and the avoidance of premature death has reached a level far beyond that in any preceding era of human history. Over roughly the same period debates concerning the nature of the most appropriate forms of care and support for more vulnerable members of society have provoked impassioned responses. Questions about the forms and philosophies of social welfare provision also raise profound issues about rights and responsibilities, reaching all sections of society.

As far as the history of these two areas is concerned, both so intimately connected to all our lives, development has been uneven. While the same period saw a transformation of the history of health and medicine, there has been much less progress in developing a history of social welfare. Fifty years ago medicine was scarcely recognised as a branch of professional history: very much like local history, it was seen as a backwater, typically colonised by retired doctors with an antiquarian interest in the past of their own profession. Since then, thanks particularly to the generosity and vision of the Wellcome Trust and its advisers,

1

the history of medicine has not only become one of the most vigorous and highly professionalised branches of historical research, but has immeasurably broadened its scope, to the point that its interests now encompass all levels of the healing professions, its concerns are with health rather than merely with curative medicine, and it has become as well known as a form of social history as of the history of science.

This broadening process was well advanced by the end of the 1980s when, again through the initiative of the Wellcome Trust, two further steps were taken. The first was the launching of a research programme intended – and this remains regrettably exceptional among historians more generally – to focus on the most recent decades, through the launching of the History of Twentieth Century Medicine Group in 1990. Led by Tilli Tansey, this group provides a meeting-ground for clinicians, scientists and historians interested in the recent past, and has helped to stimulate a variety of important archival initiatives for the documenting of the later twentieth century, including the holding of 'witness seminars'. The second was the initiation of a series of residential courses on 'Oral History in the History of Medicine', also beginning in 1990 and taught primarily by myself and Rob Perks, which have offered a specialised training ground for those researchers – including several of those whose projects are described here – intending to use oral history methods as part of their research in this field.[1] In contrast to the United States, where the use of oral history sources was already well established by the pioneering work of Saul Rivers on the history of virus research in the 1960s,[2] there had hitherto been a striking neglect of the oral history approach in British work on the history of medicine. This book, like the 'Cradle to Grave: Oral History, Health and Welfare' conference of the Oral History Society in 1996 which was its genesis, is therefore an important reflection of the new atmosphere which was soon generated by these initiatives in the history of medicine. It is the first collection of new British work using oral history in the field: first fruits, we hope, of a continuing rich harvest for the future.

In its own way this book may also be able to influence the direction which a history of welfare takes. In contrast with the history of health and medicine, social welfare has enjoyed a much more highly developed profile, thanks mainly to the historians of social administration since the 1950s who have taken care to identify the twists and turns of the legislative and administrative development of such key aspects of welfare as social security, housing and education. Indeed, in a work such as that of Timmins,[3] the welfare state now has its own 'biography'. In its most public and political sense, welfare already has a well-established history.[4] However, the human side of the social history of welfare has experienced much less in the way of sponsorship, either from key professionals or from historians themselves. Always the poor relation of health, there is no equivalent to the medical hierarchy in social welfare, so that few practitioners have been keen to record their contribution to an area of practice which lacks both the glamour and the prestige of medicine. There have, nevertheless, been some significant changes in recent years which are leading to new evaluations of what may be understood to be a history of health and welfare. Searching for the origins of much of what is often taken for granted as originating with the post-war legislation, historians such as Lara Marks and Keith Laybourn have begun to identify much earlier initiatives for community-based welfare provision in the early twentieth century.[5]

Alongside this more straightforward research endeavour there have been developments in teaching, yielding their own results with a much more historically focused approach to understanding social welfare practice. For more than a decade, academics at the Open University's School of Health and Social Welfare have taken an approach to teaching which has included the voices of both users and practitioners recounting their experience as recipients and as practitioners in social welfare settings. This has led to a series of publications, set texts, which have led student practitioners to follow with their own project work in particular areas of provision, learning disability, mental health and community care.[6]

What then, can oral history contribute to the history of health and welfare? What has been achieved? What is novel in the chapters here? What could we imagine as future possibilities?

To use oral history sources in any field brings three special advantages to historians. The first is to enable us to create a more complex and rounded picture of the past by documenting the lives of people of all kinds, many of whom can rarely be traced through conventional written or printed sources. Hence the direct voices of women, of ordinary working people, of ethnic minorities, and also of many sections of the middle classes who do not often write autobiographies, can be brought into the historical perspective. This potential undoubtedly applies to most types of medical practitioner and equally to the nursing profession, social workers and a whole range of carers and activists engaged in health and social welfare.

The second advantage is to allow us to explore those crucial areas of life which the written record scarcely touches: the private world of family relationships, for example, and all the influences from childhood onwards which go into the shaping of a professional life, and the often crucial support of partner and family through adulthood. Similarly, we can uncover the hidden informal culture of work, the personal relationships which underlie the dynamics of a research laboratory or an operating theatre team, the crucial deals or mutual rewards not mentioned in the formal minutes, and the jokes and play at work which help to make a working life in proximity to suffering and death more tolerable. Oral history can delve into the hidden world of the institution, the clinic or the hospital, revealing the daily experience of routines and treatments as told by the subjects, clients or patients at the receiving end of services.

Third, with the help of oral sources we can re-examine well-documented spheres through new perspectives: just as crime can be seen from the underworld rather than the judge's bench, so welfare or hospitalisation can be witnessed as experienced by the recipient or patient rather than the administrator or doctor. And life stories also enable us to make connections which are possible in no other way. Thus we can follow a migration between two cultures or continents from beginning to end. We could hope to understand far better, for example, the cultural journey undertaken by a Jamaican nurse or an Indian geriatrician working in Britain, and how far their work skills here still draw on their own pasts.

What had been achieved through these approaches up to the mid-1990s, when the first results of the new initiatives began to show? We shall leave aside those not infrequent instances in which a conventional history, for example of a hospital, based almost entirely on documentary records, had been supplemented by informal interviews with some retired practitioners living locally: providing background information which typically is not even directly cited, and leaving a set of untranscribed tapes which were frequently consigned to the dustbin along with the historian's other notes. More significant oral history work can be divided into four broad categories.

The first is evidence for the history of health and welfare produced as an offshoot of a non-medical social history programme.

In Britain, in contrast to the United States, in terms of publications this has hitherto been the most active type of project: a situation which underlines how slow medical historians had been to adopt the technique themselves. For almost all published British oral history work up to the mid-1990s was carried out by social historians, local oral history groups or reminiscence professionals.

A striking early instance was Diana Gittins' *Fair Sex* (1982),[7] in which she was able to show through oral history interviews that family limitation was not, as previous historians had argued, taken up by working-class couples as a result of middle-class influence, but on the contrary, through their own separate networks of information and attitudes; and equally important, that family size did not just depend, as had been assumed, on men's occupations, but equally crucially on women's own work patterns. Another pioneering example was Jocelyn Cornwell's *Hard Earned Lives* (1984).[8] Interviewing men and women about their experiences of health care in the East End of London, she found that at a first encounter people gave 'public' accounts of family life and experiences of health care which were often predictable and stereotypical. In a second interview, more 'private' stories emerged which were often questioning and critical of doctors and other health professionals.

Other local and community-based contributions to an oral history of health and welfare include, Age Exchange, *Can We Afford the Doctor?* (London, 1985); Rachel Adam and Rachel Van Riel, *In Sickness and in Health* (Castleford, Yorkshire Art Circus, 1987); and – to accompany an oral history television series – Steve Humphries and Pamela Gordon, *Out of Sight: the Experience of Disability 1900–1950* (Plymouth, Northcote House, 1992). A more recent addition, Shirley Aucott's *Mothercraft and Maternity: Leicester's Maternity and Infant Welfare Services 1900 to 1948* (Leicester, Leicestershire Museums, Arts and Records Service, 1997) extends the range still further. The lasting value of such work is especially in providing sources from the perspective of lay people and patients.

These were almost typically audio recording programmes focusing on health and welfare at a local level. It is therefore important to remember that there is already a substantial body of oral history material relevant to the field, including some interviews with medical practitioners, which has previously been archived, some of it including memories recorded in the 1970s which go back to the 1890s or even earlier. Thus the 'Family and Work Experience before 1918' national sample of 444 interviews which I used for *The Edwardians* (London, Weidenfeld and Nicolson, 1975) – now held at the University of Essex and also in the British Library National Sound Archive – includes detailed questions on health and welfare provision. So do the 270 interviews at the Centre for North-West Regional Studies at the University of Lancaster which Elizabeth Roberts revisits for her chapter in this book.

Two further types of material have been collected incidentally as part of military history and of women's history. The Imperial War Museum has long had an exceptionally well-funded Department of Sound Records with its own regular recording programme and as part of this produced *War Work 1914–1918: Medicine and Welfare, Industry and Agriculture* (London, 1977). There has also been some recording of interviews with women doctors and health pioneers for work on women's history and biography: examples are to be found in Valerie Grove, *The Compleat Woman* (London, Hogarth Press, 1988), and Rebecca Abrams, *Woman in a Man's World* (London, Methuen, 1993). There have not as yet, however, been any British studies to compare with the systematic oral history work on women in medicine in the United States, such as Gwendolen Safier's pioneering *Contemporary American Leaders in Nursing: an Oral History* (New York, McGraw Hill, 1977), or subsequently Regina Morantz, *In Her Own Words: Oral Histories of Women Physicians* (New Haven, Yale University Press, 1986) and Karen Brodben Sachs, *Caring by the Hour: Women, Work and Organizing at Duke Medical Centre* (Champaign, University of Illinois Press, 1988).

The second main category is the collecting of oral history source material with the deliberate intention of creating resources for future historians of medicine. An unusual instance is the audio archive of St George's Hospital Medical School which was created by Dr Bryan Brooke as Emeritus Professor of Surgery, consisting mostly of interviews with retired doctors, who were astonishingly candid to their genial colleague in describing sensitive issues such as deliberate social and racial bias in the selection of students, personalities, conflicts between rival hospital firms, alcoholism, and other recreations in the hospital including shooting. Not surprisingly, this is a confidential collection with access controlled by the hospital's archivist.

Another form is that of the 'witness seminars' which as already mentioned were initiated by the History of Twentieth Century Medicine Group. Since 1993 some twenty meetings have been recorded at which key participants are invited together to discuss issues which have ranged from 'The early history of renal transplantation' to 'Oral contraceptives' and 'Drugs in psychiatric practice'. Edited transcripts of these discussions are now being published in a new series, *Wellcome Witnesses to Twentieth Century Medicine* (London, Wellcome Trust, 1997).

A parallel approach of equal importance is the full life story interview with significant individuals, which ideally traces the life from childhood and family background, through education and training, to professional career, later family life and leisure. In this type of recording each subject is approached in a particularly flexible spirit to respond to different careers and personalities, while ideally always aiming to draw out a personal interpretation, highlighting crucial influences, turning points and obstacles, and providing details of important interpersonal relationships, and the assumptions, culture, and atmosphere of particular times and institutions. The objective is a rounded individual portrait which reveals both the driving forces behind achievement and the human oddities and relaxations that went with it. Because medical practitioners and scientists, in contrast to those leading figures in politics or the humanities, have rarely been autobiographers, this is a much-needed form of resource. Moreover especially when on video it has a special potential because of the compelling intimacy with which it can convey the key emotional significance of moments of change in medical knowledge and practice over the past fifty years.

The first British video collection of this type was a programme initiated in 1983 by Harry Bradford, Professsor of Neurochemistry at Imperial College, jointly with the Biochemical Society: altogether some twenty interviews with scientific pioneers, usually interviewed by fellow scientists.[9] There is also a substantial audio collection developed since the late 1980s held by the Royal College of Nursing (with copies at the British Library National Sound Archive). The most substantial programme, however, began with the audio recording of senior Fellows of the Royal College of Physicians from 1969 at the instigation of its librarian, Dr Charles Newman. During the 1980s this blossomed into a joint video programme led by Dr Max Blythe of Oxford Brookes University, who went on to record the history of the Wellcome Institute itself. Nearly half of the 200 interviews from this programme are now fully transcribed, and the material is available for consultation both in Oxford and at the Royal College of Physicians.

The third category of work is the thematic analytic historical study which draws upon oral interviews as a major source, but interprets them in the broader historical context of other sources, ideologies and social structures. This is the most central for the interpretation of the history of medicine, yet had been the rarest type of oral history work in the field until the mid-1990s.

A notably early instance of this approach was by Virginia Berridge, whose research with Stuart Anderson on community pharmacists is represented here. Already in the late 1970s she was interviewing older lay people as part of her study of the former widespread use of opium in the Fenland area of England.[10] Two other pioneering researchers who combined oral and written sources were both at the Wellcome Institute at Oxford. Jennifer Beinart interviewed retired anaesthetists for her *History of the Nuffield Department of Anaesthetics, Oxford 1937–87* (Oxford, Oxford University Press, 1987), while Elizabeth Peretz recorded early local authority maternity workers for her thesis on the development of community health care between the wars.[11]

Parallel with this, and perhaps most significant for a political perspective, there is oral history work which has sought to change understandings of health and welfare. Teaching initiatives such as those developed at the Open University mentioned earlier were in part spurred by the personal stories and criticisms of disabled people or users of welfare services seeking to centre their experience in accounts of welfare provision. These include residents of mental handicap hospitals, as was shown by Maggie Potts and Rebecca Fido, *A Fit Person to be Removed: Personal Accounts of Life in a Mental Deficiency Institution* (Plymouth, Northcote House, 1991) but are mainly individual accounts such as George A. Cook, *A Hackney Memory Chest* (London, Centerprise, 1983); Ernest (Tom) Atkins, *One Door Closes: Another Opens – A Personal Experience of Polio* (Waltham Forest, Waltham Forest Oral History Workshop, 1994); David Barron, *A Price to be Born* (Harrogate, Mencap Northern Division, 1996). To include a user's perspective of health and welfare in today's practice of oral history is not simply a question of adding a complementary source to match documentary evidence, it is more likely to challenge and subvert understandings of care and control, the boundaries between health and welfare, the location of centres and margins and notions of status and eligibility in all sectors of society and conditions of life.

Finally, it has been important overall that throughout the past twenty years and more, *Oral History*, the journal of the Oral History Society, has played a consistent part in publishing the fruits of much of this research and writing. From the mid-1970s issues and articles have ranged widely, including birth control, opium use, dental history, childbirth and death, older people's remembering and special issues on health and caring in 1989 and 1995.[12] All these helped to lodge health and welfare research firmly within the repertoire of oral history and to promote a more questioning approach to its place within social history more generally.

If we turn now to this current book, it is immediately evident that it combines developments from the first, third and fourth approaches to the use of oral testimony. There are contributions which spring from the earlier broad interests of oral historians in the social history of health and welfare, rather than from the more recent branching out of the history of medicine. This is most notably true of Elizabeth Roberts' chapter drawing on her own earlier interviews in north Lancashire towns on work, family, and community; and the influence of the main current of oral history work is equally clear in the chapters focusing on people with learning difficulties or with HIV/Aids, in which the focus is not on the professionals or on medicine, but rather on the experience of those who have such conditions, and how it shapes their personal lives and feelings. This is especially true of the chapter by Sally French and John Swain on the education of partially sighted girls, for this represents the important oral history tradition of encouraging self-advocacy for groups who have been marginalised or whose personal history of health and welfare is a story of oppression and stigmatisation.

Most of the chapters in this book are, however, based on thematic studies within the history of health and welfare, examples of the third of the oral history approaches mentioned earlier. This is especially true of the first part of the book, which focuses on health professionals, where three of the papers are the outcome of important new projects initiated through Wellcome Trust funding.

Of these, Michael Bevan's chapter draws on a major new collection of interviews with GPs who started work just before and just after the setting up of the National Health Service in 1948. This is a rich quarry now available to other researchers at the British Library National Sound Archive, and Bevan's chapter gives some hints of the fascinating information which it can yield. He looks at the family backgrounds and training of these doctors, and why they chose general practice for their career. Quite contrary to the widespread myth that doctoring is either a career already followed in the family, or a calling to heal the sick felt from childhood, it turns out that only a quarter of these GPs came from medical families, or felt any sense of vocation in their choice of career. Nevertheless family looms large in these accounts, with references to networks of support and motivation. Bevan shows that these GPs' attitudes to medicine were also very different from those of their patients, and suggests that these findings may help to explain some of the widespread problems of general practice reported by contemporary surveys in the 1950s and since.

The chapter by Stuart Anderson and Virginia Berridge is from a double study of the role of pharmacists in medicine, both within hospitals and outside where they are known as 'chemists'. Here the authors describe the changing role of the community chemist as remembered by their interviewees. Throughout this century chemists' shops have served as primary points for medical advice, and often also as first-aid stations. Chemists would weigh babies and are still key suppliers of baby food. They also have a continuing role in sexual health, which has extended from their earlier selling of contraceptives and abortifacients to the treatment of venereal diseases and to pregnancy testing. With tobacco, by contrast, as with opium, they have switched from being suppliers to supporting the cessation of use.

Margot Jefferys also offers some first findings from a third project, on the development of geriatric medicine as a new specialty, which are again available in the British Library National Sound Archive. Looking at a cohort of men, principally, who were at the point of seeking medical posts following war service during the Second World War, she too found that it was most often chance, and the difficulty of getting work in more prestigious spheres of medicine, which led doctors into working with older people, and thus eventually a pioneering concern with developing new medical approaches to their care.

John Adams, on the other hand, although also concerned with the history of geriatrics, approaches it from another direction. He is someone with a background in the nursing care of older people who has played an important role in pioneering the therapeutic practice of reminiscence work. Here he argues that the history of geriatrics has overemphasised the pioneering work of doctors. Poor Law Officers have attracted consistent criticism from Charles Dickens' *Oliver Twist* to Peter Townsend's *The Last Refuge*, and have been regarded as at best unimaginative drudges keeping a complex and distasteful system working. Using interviews with retired workhouse masters, he argues that there is a case for their defence to be heard, and that there was a significant minority among them who, despite lack of resources, did struggle to innovate and improve the care of older people.

Two other chapters in this section focus on the role of midwives and nurses in the community. Through a study of midwives who later practised in Hull, Maxine Rhodes explores how midwives acquired their professional skills using a combination of formal courses and learning on the job. She also discusses the relationships between midwifery and nursing. Rona Ferguson has been recording retired district nurses in Scotland for a project launched by the Queen's Nursing Institute Scotland, which has also been supported by Wellcome. Although working in the community, district nurses were trained with hierarchical severity and most of the older generation of women midwives remained unmarried, giving their lives to their profession. They were also strikingly unconcerned with the financial returns of their work even in the pre-NHS period, and worked very much on their own with little supervision from GPs, whose medical instructions they could sometimes even regard as 'interference'. Since outside the main cities they also took on the functions of midwives, district nurses held for many decades a central social position in rural Scottish communities, the confidante of people of all ages, who also often functioned as a home help and cook for the sick: 'a Jenny-a'-thing'.

The second section of the book focuses on the care of people who have been socially marginalised. Sally French, who is herself visually impaired, contributes with John Swain a challenging critique of earlier accounts of segregated education for the blind or 'partially sighted', together with an inside account, based on her own memories and interviews with other girls, of the residential Barclay School in Berkshire which she attended. She vividly conveys the rough and uncaring regime in which they were treated like delinquents, deliberately cut off from their families, and given little encouragement towards positive self-development. This is essentially an autobiographical chapter reinforced by testimonies from others who have shared many of her experiences and also share her views: it is a powerful piece of self-advocacy which conveys the strong but rarely heard feelings of a marginalised group.

The chapter by Dorothy Atkinson and Jan Walmsley reviews the way the history of learning disability has been studied and demonstrates through detailed examples the contrasting accounts by two different stakeholders – a retired Mental Welfare Officer and a former resident of a mental handicap hospital. They argue for a plurality of voices to be heard, recorded and incorporated into the developing knowledge of this once neglected subject area.

Elizabeth Roberts writes more broadly of those in the population who have been marginalised by poverty. She draws on her Lancashire interviews to explore the conflict in attitudes among working-class families between, on the one hand, their beliefs in self-help and independence, and on the other, their common need for help from either charities or the Poor Law at critical stages in the life cycle, especially when they had large numbers of dependent children or in old age and sickness. This is a characteristically sharply observed piece by one of Britain's most experienced oral historians, whose work includes her classic book on the same group of Lancashire families, *A Woman's Place* (Oxford, Blackwell, 1984).

Lastly, Wendy Rickard draws on a project interviewing people with HIV/Aids to provide direct accounts of the impact of the illness on their lives. She explores in particular the significance of other aspects of their lives, including both their earlier experiences of other traumas, and the self-reflection and determination to make the best of what is left of life which underlies much of their resilience. Paradoxically, her chapter emphasises the ways in which a group whose members may be thought of primarily as exceptional and marginalised have in fact led a great variety of lives, some not at all exceptional, and she is therefore able to point to a kind of work which could be usefully done with others.

The final section of the book explores the impact of health caring at the beginning and the end of the life cycle. Kate Fisher contrasts the documentary record of the birth control movement in South Wales during the 1930s, in the main supplied by its leaders, with evidence from working-class people. She shows that few working-class women had heard of birth control clinics, most remained suspicious of the caps and sponges favoured by birth control campaigners and, most strikingly, few saw any moral distinction between contraception and abortion. Robin Dixon's chapter, which is based on interviews in Essex, looks at the changing role of fathers in childbirth itself, both emotionally and as a practical help for a partner. He links the emotional needs of fathers to the couvade, men's pseudo-maternity behaviour, and suggests that in accommodating to fathers' needs midwives may be acting as 'mid-husbands' to couvading fathers. Finally Neil

Small provides some initial findings from another Wellcome-funded project on the history of the hospice movement. Hospices have both reflected and contributed to new social attitudes towards death and dying, and have provided a key scenario for the development of a new specialty of palliative medicine.

The work presented in this volume demonstrates a striking advance over the past five years. Much more remains to be explored. Indeed it is possible to envisage, as Ludmilla Jordanova did in 1993,[13] a much more important future role for oral history in the history of medicine or in social welfare: no longer largely supplementary, but as a key catalyst in reshaping future practice and policy. Let us consider this from three perspectives: first, health and welfare as practice; second, as part of daily life; and third, ideas and images of health and welfare as part of our culture.

The history of medicine first developed as the history of medical science, and then of medical institutions, but it still needs to encompass the history of medical practice. For the twentieth century, which has seen such fundamental political changes in the delivery of services as well as such proliferation in curative technology, this is a crucial area. Although we have already lost the chance to study the impact of the state intervention launched in 1911, oral sources could still give us access to these changes from the 1930s onwards – and indeed the interviews collected for the GP project, as also some of those collected from projects on nursing and the workhouse, are important new resources of precisely this kind waiting to be compared and fully analysed.

Studying medical practice provides a measure of how far innovation really affected everyday treatment. It can allow us to see more clearly how and why there were striking local variations from the often misleading models provided by professional textbooks – a point which Kate Fisher's chapter here on contraception also highlights. It also helps us to plot the shifting boundaries, again varying by place as well as time – as Rona Ferguson's work on district nurses indicates – between professionals and para-professionals, indicating what each group was expected and allowed to do, and their privileges, bars and restrictions: and beyond this, help towards understanding how far this changing division of labour reflects the growth of knowledge as well as political and group pressure. How do we explain, for example, the shifts in nursing role between the administration of treatments and domestic functions such as bed making or washing and comforting patients?

Such a perspective can also open the way to a new and richer form of institutional history. A hospital's history, as shown by the examples of the Littlemore in Oxford and St Richard's Hospital in Chichester,[14] can be written not only from its administratively controlled official record, but from the bottom of the hierarchy too, introducing the perspectives of the radiotherapists and dieticians, the boilermen and porters, and the dynamic interactions between such groups and the more prominent medical professionals. In the same spirit, the experiences of the patients can also be introduced, allowing not only insights into their own feelings about hospitalisation, but also details of the parts played in the handling of their illnesses by staff such as cleaners and chaplains, and, equally important, by their own kin.

We have now an inspiring instance of the historical richness which such an approach can bring in Diana Gittins' *Madness in its Place: Narratives of Severalls Hospital 1913–1997* (London, Routledge, 1998). Gittins not only offers us a fascinating documentation of the interactions between patients and staff at all levels in this giant mental hospital on the edge of Colchester, which at its peak housed over 3,000 patients, and for which many local families had provided generations of staff. She forces us to think again about the social meanings of madness. And she also reflects fascinatingly on the strengths and weaknesses of different kinds of historical record, and how it is only through comparing them, and through testimony from as wide a variety of viewpoints as possible, that some secrets hidden from the official records – such as the illicit experiments which were being carried out through operations on patients – can begin to be disentangled.

If so much of fundamental interest can come from the story of one relatively unusual hospital, the potential fruitfulness of more multi-layered institutional work of this kind is manifest. It could indeed be argued that a true social history of late twentieth-century health and welfare should be conceived, not so much as being broadened to include patients, but as starting from them: from the typical experience of health and welfare of the British population in our time.

This would immediately draw attention to another important issue: the growth of alternative medical practice outside the officially recognised system. The study of the community chemists and the alternative therapies explored by those with HIV/Aids are steps in this direction, but far more remains to be done. Professional medical anxiety about various forms of rivalry goes back a long way – some forms of 'quack' or 'healer' have been vigorously denounced. Nevertheless the growth of osteopathy, chiropractic, massage, acupuncture, health diets and so on has gone forward unabated, while their social and medical implications and practice remain little understood.

As with health and medicine, so also with aspects of welfare practice. Accounts of the emergence of social work as a profession are still rarely found and the boundaries between voluntary and paid social work have only been in part located as particular organisational histories come to be written. The poor reputation which social workers enjoy in the late twentieth century deserves an historical probing which only the personal histories of practitioners, and the users of provided services can supply. For example, has the scope and role of workers with responsibilities for children, mental health service users, older and disabled people changed over the past fifty years? And how did ideas of community and community work emerge and change, from the first settlement projects of the early part of the century, through the work of wartime pacifists through to the Community Development Units of the 1960s?

Just as health has its alternative and lay approaches, so too has welfare, and a focus on user movements, including tenants' associations, claimants' unions, movements of unemployed people, civil liberties struggles, refuges and shelters would help to shift stereotypes of the deserving and undeserving poor and perhaps relocate social welfare practice, hauling back to the social and collective and away from the individual and a culture of blame.

The market in alternative medicine and a focus on social action can also be seen as part of our second perspective, health and welfare as part of daily life. Health has its place in the high street consumer culture, but there has also been a striking growth at the same time in the number of places in which official medicine is available. Health visitors, once viewed as interfering busybodies, are now accepted along with trained midwives as part of the normal process of childbirth. Children at school are given medical tests; and schools also refer children for psychological problems to both health and social services. Bereavement and marriage counselling are now recognised as necessary and helpful interventions. The spread of travel, both for work and holidays, has brought much wider direct knowledge of the dangers of exotic tropical diseases and the inoculations and precautions needed for self-protection against them. More dramatically, as a consequence of the threat of Aids, any sexual relationship now develops in the shadow – whether accepted or defied – of government-backed medical recommendations.

More and more then, in varying forms, medicine has infiltrated our daily lives. Most strikingly of all, as is reflected in our concluding section in this book, it frames their beginning and ending. Whether births are at home or, as most often, in hospital, the controlling presence of midwives and of doctors is almost always crucial. We need to know more about the social handling of childbirth by these key professionals: for example, what midwives chose to wear or to eat while at work, how they cope with the death of a baby, whether they came from generations of midwives, and so on. Death too has increasingly taken place in hospitals, and even its timing increasingly depends on decisions taken by a medical team. There has been some historical study[15] of how the management of dead bodies and of funerals, formerly centred on neighbourhood and home, became fully professionalised in parallel: but almost none of the changes in the process of dying. This makes the study of the hospice movement reported here particularly welcome. But much more is needed on these themes.

Welfare issues too have become a feature of daily life and daily debate. Single parents, drug abusers, asylum seekers and homeless people are readily portrayed not only as failures of a welfare system but also as somehow without a history in the twentieth century. Oral history might help to change these perspectives by opening up opportunities for the telling of stories of life on the margins of society and in so doing make connections across the years and across social boundaries. Welfare histories within lives, connecting events and the impact of particular policies on individual life histories are beginning to emerge, most notably in the area of learning disability. Here research by Jan Walmsley, Dorothy Atkinson and colleagues is identifying the impact which changes in the law have made to the boundaries between institutional and community care and consequently to the life chances of those identified as in need of care. Other areas, for example changes in the provision of income and benefits, fostering and adoption, mental health after care and family law, await systematic investigation.

Our third perspective, the ubiquity of health and welfare ideas and images in our culture, is in one sense a consequence of this ever-extending presence of medical and social welfare issues in our intimate everyday lives. New medical technologies have shattered centuries-old concepts of conception and fertility, birth and death. Even the difference between a dead person and a live person is an issue for debate. Ideas about the location of parental responsibility are being tested with, on the one hand night-time curfews for children, while on the other hand ideas of fatherhood are challenged by a feminised family form. How people work their way through family change, adapting and developing their own moralities, is a recent area of interest but one where an oral history approach could play an important role.

There has, of course, always been a widespread folklore about health and illness. This is in itself another area too little studied: how have patients' own beliefs about their illnesses been changing? And how does this relate to the development of medical knowledge? The growth of alternative medicine suggests that there may be many different and often contradictory belief systems. There is also a complex relationship between religion and medicine, going back to the founding of the nursing orders and medical missions to the British empire, which needs unravelling for the twentieth century.

Perhaps the most distinctive feature of contemporary culture, however, is the ability of the mass media to make available medical ideas and images along with others in a standardised form to entire populations. This can result in striking changes in ordinary social behaviour: the decline of smoking among men, for example; or changes in eating habits, both long-term and as a result of media-propelled panics about contagion, such as the flight from British beef following the emergence of 'mad cow disease'. It would be useful to compare such changes, and the handling of those who resist them, with earlier instances: is being a recalcitrant smoker today akin to being a Victorian anti-vaccinator?

The idea that welfare is something which is done to other people is deeply ingrained in society. The stigma of being a recipient, poor or needy, is absorbed as personal failure. To what extent, mid-century, this was overcome through a social contract which bridged class and generation is a story yet to be told at personal and community level. Who gets access to health care and how may depend as much on people's social history as on their medical history. In exploring the complexities of human need and obligation oral history is able to play a key role, for example in challenging those negative and marginalising stereotypes which have dogged the lives of welfare recipients. It could do this by identifying the resources which different families and communities have offered to members, exploring the response to challenging individual conditions and investigating how people cope with change and loss in their lives as resources and policies are successively withdrawn or replaced.

Each age also has its most-feared disease, its victims vulnerable to social stigma as well as sickness itself. Cholera was succeeded by tuberculosis from the mid-nineteenth century; and in our time, by Aids. Comparison will again help us to understand the feared diseases of both centuries. We need to contrast the folklore about such diseases with official professional opinions, and relate both to the other social priorities of the time. Fear of tuberculosis was a form of fear of the poor; fear of Aids is the Achilles' heel of a society which vaunts sexual fulfilment among its highest priorities.

Medical ideas, in short, are intertwined with our fundamental concepts of good and bad societies. Universal health is today one of our utopian social goals. And conversely, when speaking in criticism we point to a 'sick society' or a 'sick environment'. Oral history can offer one vital means of access to this changing cultural interpenetration of ideas and images. This book, in short, marks an important step forward, a first step in a path which can lead to a more profound reshaping of the field. For with the help of oral history we can both situate the history of health and welfare more firmly within the wider contexts of social history and the social construction of knowledge, and also demonstrate how fundamental these dimensions are to the history of the twentieth century as a whole.

Acknowledgements

While the compilation and editing of the chapters in this book has been the work of the four people whose names appear on its title page, this work would not have seen the light of day without the support throughout of Brenda Corti of the Department of Sociology at the University of Essex and Robert Wilkinson, Planning and Economic Development Department, London Borough of Waltham Forest. The editors would also like to thank Christine Finch of the School of Health and Social Welfare at the Open University for her help in preparing the manuscript.

Notes

1 This introduction in part is adapted from a booklet specially produced for that course (Thompson, P. with Perks, R., *An Introduction to the Use of Oral History in the History of Medicine*, National Life Story Collection at the British Library National Sound Archive, 1993.

2 Rivers, S., *Tom Rivers: Reflections on a Life in Medicine and Science: An Oral History Memoir*, Boston, MIT Press, 1967; essay by Rivers, S., in Clarke, E. (ed.) *Modern Methods in the History of Medicine*, London, Athlone Press, 1971, pp. 286–305.

3 Timmins, N., *The Five Giants: A Biography of the Welfare State*, London, Fontana Press, 1995.

4 See for example from varying perspectives: Titmuss, R., *Essays on the Welfare State*, London, Allen & Unwin, 1958; Fraser, D., *The Evolution of the Welfare State*, London, Macmillan, 1973; Donnison, D., *The Politics of Poverty*, London, Martin Robertson, 1982; Thane, P., *Foundations of the Welfare State*, London, Longman, 1982; Cootes, R.J., *The Making of the Welfare State*, London, Longman, 1984; Means, R. and Smith, R., *The Development of Welfare Services for Elderly People*, London, Croom Helm, 1985; Williams, F., *Social Policy: A Critical Introduction*, Oxford, Polity Press, 1989; Lowe, R., *The Welfare State in Britain since 1945*, Basingstoke, Macmillan, 1993.

5 Marks, L., *Model Mothers: Jewish Mothers and Maternity Provision in East London, 1870–1939*, Oxford, Oxford University Press, 1994; Laybourn, K. (ed.) *Social Conditions, Status and Community, 1890–c.1920*, Stroud, Sutton, 1997.

6 Atkinson, A., and Williams, W. (eds) *Know Me as I Am: An Anthology of Prose, Poetry and Art by People with Learning Difficulties*, Sevenoaks, Hodder & Stoughton, 1990; Read, J., and Reynolds, J. (eds) *Speaking our Minds: An Anthology of Personal Experiences of Mental Distress and its Consequences*, Basingstoke, Macmillan, 1996; Bornat, J., Johnson, J., Pereira, C., Pilgrim, D., and Williams, W. (eds) *Community Care: A Reader*, London, Macmillan, 1997 (second edition).

7 Gittins, D., *Fair Sex: Family Size and Structure 1900–1939*, London, Hutchinson, 1982.

8 Cornwell, J., *Hard-earned Lives: Accounts of Health and Illness from East London*, London, Tavistock, 1984.

9 Bradford, H.F., '"Telling It How It Was": recording the oral history of biochemistry in the UK', *Biochemist*, 13, 1, 1991.

10 Berridge, V., 'Opium and oral history', *Oral History*, 7, 1, 1979.

11 Peretz, E., 'A maternity service for England and Wales: local authority maternity care in the inter-war period in Oxfordshire and Tottenham', in Garcia, J., Kilpatrick, R., and Richards, M. (eds) *The Politics of Maternity Care*, Oxford, Clarendon Press, 1990; and 'The professionalisation of child care', *Oral History*, 17, 1, 1989.

12 See Gittins, D., 'Married life and birth control between the wars', *Oral History*, 3, 2, 1975, pp. 53–64; Gittins, D., 'Women's work and family size between the wars', *Oral History*, 5, 2, 1977, pp. 84–100; 'Women's History' issue, *Oral History*, 5, 2, 1977, passim; Berridge, V., 'Opium and Oral History', *Oral History*, 7, 2, 1979, pp. 48–58; Chamberlain,

M. and Richardson, R., 'Life and death', *Oral History*, 11, 1, 1983, pp. 31–43; Mourby, K., 'The wives and children of the Teesside unemployed 1919–1939', *Oral History*, 11, 2, 1983, pp. 56–60; Roberts, E., 'The working class extended family; functions and attitudes 1890–1940', *Oral History*, 12, 1, 1984, pp. 48–56; 'Oral History and Community Projects' issue, *Oral History*, 12, 2, 1984, passim; Coleman, P., 'The past in the present; a study of elderly people's attitudes to reminiscence', *Oral History*, 14, 1, 1986, pp. 50–59; Wright, M., 'Priming the past', *Oral History*, 14, 1, 1986, pp. 60–65; Frostick, E., 'The use of oral evidence in the reconstruction of dental history at Beamish Museum', *Oral History*, 14, 2, 1986, pp. 59–65; Atkinson, E., '"Strict but not Cruel": living in Children's Homes 1903–1943', *Oral History*, 15, 2, 1987, pp. 38–45; 'Health and Caring' issue, *Oral History*, 17, 1, 1989, passim; 'Reminiscence' issue, *Oral History*, 17, 2, 1989, passim; 'Health and Welfare' issue, *Oral History*, 23, 1, 1995, passim; Atkinson, D., 'Autobiography and learning disability', *Oral History*, 26, 1, 1998, pp. 73–80.
13 Jordanova, in Thompson and Perks, 1993, op. cit.
14 Goddard, J., *Mixed Feelings: Littlemore Hospital – An Oral History Project*, Oxford, Oxfordshire County Council, 1996; Bailey, C.H., *St Richard's Hospital and the NHS: An Oral History*, Chichester, Phillimore, 1998.
15 See Chamberlain and Richardson, 1983, op. cit.; Richardson, R., *Death, Dissection and the Destitute*, London, Routledge and Kegan Paul, 1988; Roberts, E., 'The Lancashire way of death' in Houlbrooke, R. (ed.) *Death, Ritual and Bereavement*, London, Routledge, 1986, pp. 223–47.

1

FAMILY AND VOCATION

Career choice and the life histories of general practitioners

Michael Bevan

During the early 1950s a series of investigations took place into the state of general practice in Britain. In 1950 Joseph Collings, a Research Fellow from Harvard, produced a highly critical report which caused a considerable stir when it was published in *The Lancet*. His findings led the British Medical Association (BMA) and the Nuffield Foundation to organise their own inquiries which resulted in the report of Stephen Hadfield, published in the *British Medical Journal (BMJ)* in 1953, and Stephen Taylor's book *Good general practice*, which appeared a year later.[1] These reports mainly concentrated on the organisation and running of practices, on the physical conditions under which medicine was practised, and on the level of service offered to the patient. However, little or no attention was given to the effect that the personality of the individual doctor could have on the health and welfare of patients. It could not be said that this element of general practice went unrecognised by contemporaries. Collings himself wrote that general practice was:

> a unique social phenomenon. The general practitioner enjoys more prestige and wields more power than any other citizen, unless it be the judge on the bench. In a world of ever-increasing management, the powers of senior managers are petty compared with the powers of the doctor to influence the physical, psychological, and the economic destiny of other people.[2]

Later, the BMA was to express its view as to the qualities required by the ideal family doctor. After putting a sense of vocation at the top of the list of desirable attributes, it went on to list the other personal qualities enjoyed by the ideal general practitioner (GP):

> He should have inexhaustible tact, wisdom, patience, discretion, and that 'imperturbability' which Osler placed in the forefront of the qualities of a physician or surgeon. He needs to be gentle, yet firm in speech and action, and his manner must inspire confidence and trust. He should have a kindly, humane approach to his patients and, however pressed he may be for time, each patient should be made to feel that his illness is of real concern to the doctor. The general practitioner needs a deeply imagina-tive sympathy which enables him to understand his patients' fears and anxieties, pain and discomfort. . . . The general practitioner is all things to all men; he is guide, philosopher, and friend to patients of all classes, and shows himself equally at ease with the duke and the dustman, the bishop and the boiler maker.[3]

Obviously, this is an ideal which few, if any, doctors could have lived up to. Nevertheless, these statements indicate the importance which the personality of the GP was felt to have in his or her relationships with patients. The extent to which the GP was able to meet these expectations is an interesting question. And, given that the personality of the doctor was believed to be so crucial to the influence he or she had in dealings with patients, it is some-what surprising that the issue was not given greater consideration in the discussions about the work of the GP in the various reports on general practice.

Someone who did give the problem some thought was the psychoanalyst Michael Balint (1896–1970). In his book *The doctor, his patient and the illness*, published in 1957 but drawing on research begun in 1950, Balint wrote that the seminar he organised for GPs on the topic of the drugs prescribed by general practitioners soon came to realise that 'by far the most frequently used drug in general practice was the doctor himself, i.e. that it was not only the bottle of medicine that mattered, but the whole atmosphere in which the drug was taken'.[4] However, he noted that the drug 'doctor' was not having the intended effect. 'Why', Balint asked, 'does it happen so often that, in spite of earnest attempts on both sides, the relationship between patient and doctor is unsatisfactory and even unhappy?'.[5]

As it was generally agreed during the early 1950s that the standard of general practice in Britain left much to be desired, and also that the personality of the individual GP played an important part in general practice, it is interesting to explore the degree to which the two elements may, to some extent, be connected. How far might the unhappiness which Balint identified in doctor–patient relationships be attributed to the background and character of those who became the nation's GPs? I intend to go some way to answering this question by presenting evidence gathered from a series of life history interviews with general practitioners; concentrating on what they had to say about their upbringing and about their decision to become a general practitioner.[6] These personal testimonies show how important the family was in shaping an individual's career in medicine. In addition to actually influencing a child to choose medicine as a career, the family had other contributions to make in the formation of the future GP: it was the main site for the transmission of values and beliefs, some of which might remain with the individual, to a greater or lesser degree, throughout his or her life; it could help determine the selection of medical school and to influence the decision to enter general practice; and it could be the provider of resources in the form of finance, support and possibly, access to a network of family connections, in universities or hospitals, for example, which could be useful in furthering a career.

Social origins of general practitioners

I will begin by providing a rough outline of the social origins of the GPs who were interviewed. For the purpose of this chapter I have looked at a sample of forty-one out of a total of seventy interviews carried out with general practitioners who qualified between 1923 and 1955.[7] Thirty-three of the forty-one are men, and eight are women. Their dates of birth range between 1899 and 1932.

In terms of social class it should not come as too much of a surprise to find that most GPs had middle or lower middle-class backgrounds. A third of the GPs in my sample had fathers who were shopkeepers or merchants of some sort. Teachers are well represented, while other paternal occupations include bankers, farmers, civil servants and artists. The fathers of eleven GPs were medical practitioners of some type: six were themselves GPs, two were pharmacists, the others were a dentist, an ophthalmologist, and an osteopath. The traditional professions other than medicine, the law and the church, are not represented at all.

Again, it will cause no surprise to learn that working-class families did not tend to provide many members of the medical profession. Among the fathers of my GPs probably only two (the children of a railway worker, and of a weaver) might be designated working class. These figures seem to be in line with statistics published in the *BMJ* in 1944 which claimed that social classes III, IV and V supplied only 5 or 6 per cent of the profession.[8]

As regards maternal occupations, almost half of my informants had no knowledge of their mother working outside the home. Of the rest, teachers and, in very general terms, textile workers of one sort or another dominate. Some of these women ran or helped to run a family business, others were ladies' maids, piano teachers and office workers. Many of these women gave up working outside the home after marriage.

If we turn to grandparents we find that only four informants gave their paternal grandfather's occupation as doctor and only two had maternal grandfathers who were doctors. A career in medicine therefore involved a degree of upward social mobility for most of my informants.

The parents of my group of GPs had an average of around three children per family. Interestingly, in seventeen of the forty-one families at least one other of the children, in addition to my informant, went on to work in medicine in some way. In eleven cases a sibling underwent full medical training. This mainly applied to the male siblings. Female siblings who worked in medicine were more likely to work in one of the auxiliary occupations such as midwifery or nursing.

A little under half of the male GPs were educated at public school, and the rest were mainly grammar school boys. Three of the eight women were educated at boarding schools.

As regards religious affiliation, eighteen of the sample described themselves as being brought up in the Church of England, and the rest as Catholic, Methodist, Jewish, Presbyterian, Congregationalist or Parsee.

When questioned about their parents' political views eighteen of the forty-one considered their fathers to support the Conservative Party, ten the Liberals and two the Labour Party. The remainder had no memory of their parents' political views. I should perhaps stress that these political affiliations are mostly those of the father. In many cases informants told me that their mother took no interest in politics or informants assumed that their mother held the same views as their father. However this probably tells us more about gender relations than it does about maternal political affiliation.

This is a very general guide to the social origins of the group of GPs dealt with in this chapter. I now move on to look at how some of the GPs themselves remember their upbringing and explain how they came to choose general practice as a career.

Family

As stated above, the family was the main location where values were instilled into children. Most of the GPs interviewed shared common memories of the values imparted to them by their parents. Obedience, hard work, integrity, honesty and fair play in dealings with others, were regularly singled out as being the important values in their parents' lives. 'Doasyouwouldbedoneby', from Charles Kingsley's *The water-babies* (1863) was quite frequently remembered as being a parental motto.[9] All of these would have been common to a lot of middle-class families, and especially, perhaps, in those who owned their own businesses and came into contact with the public in the course of their work, where the virtues of hard work, honesty and fair play would be vital. Robert Andrews' parents, who owned a butchery business, are a good example. Andrews recollected that 'the standards they set me were the standards of example, in terms of integrity and honesty, and playing fair with others, and the strength of the family'. Of his father he said, 'I admired and respected him, because he knew his job, and because he didn't care what hours he worked, providing that the job was done right'.[10] Henry Taylor, whose father was a manager of an Edinburgh building company, was taught that 'there was to be no nonsense, no stealing or anything. You did a fair day's work in return for a fair day's pay',[11] while James Harrison, the son of a Lancashire weaver and osteopath, recalls that his parents set great store by keeping their word and in never being in debt.[12] Many other similar examples can be found in the stories of other GPs interviewed.

Another common memory among the GPs was that they were expected to do well at school and were encouraged to better themselves. With this in mind many parents set their children the goal of joining a profession. This desire for their children to have a better job and lifestyle than they had themselves led some parents to make a considerable investment in their children's education. In families where money was tight the child would often become aware both of the sacrifices made on his or her behalf and of the need not to make unnecessary demands on parents' pockets. This put pressure on some to win scholarships, to pass exams at the first attempt, and to start earning as soon as possible. As the only child of a small wholesaler Anne Finch knew that a large proportion of her parents' resources were put into her education, and she was keenly aware that she was, in her words, 'the only egg in their basket'.[13] Family fortunes could also be affected by the loss of a parent. Following the death of his doctor father Charles Williams' family 'had a rough time from then on, we had very little money and we were in straitened circumstances . . . it behove us to get on'.[14] Occasionally relatives might relieve the burden on parents. Charles Newton remembered that 'I had a godmother aunt who was very well off, and had no children. She gave herself the job of financing my education. So father was able to concentrate on educating the others.'[15] Mary Barber's father worked as a cotton-broker in Liverpool. Money became short at the beginning of the war when the cotton trade was disrupted, but it remained important for them to maintain a middle-class way of life:

> I think my mother had got a struggle, because we must keep up appearances. I can remember going to the Co-op each week, on Friday with the order. And the order always had to come to 19/6d, and if it was 19/7d then the list was gone through, as to where we could save a penny by buying something less.

In the event Barber's education was paid for by a wealthy great-aunt.[16]

Of course, not all GPs came from backgrounds where money was short. John Wright and Edward Littleton, both doctors' sons incidentally, came from relatively prosperous backgrounds and were protected from the money worries that affected the families of some other informants. But if Wright and Littleton did not experience pressure arising from having to fulfil family ambitions with limited resources, they did have other burdens to bear.

Though their fathers' work dominated the family life both felt distant from them. Littleton's memory was that 'I was rather in awe of my father. I had the impression that his temper was a little . . . he was rather on a short fuse at times. And I think I wasn't as close to my parents as other children.'[17] John Wright, brought up on the south coast in the 1930s, gives us a fuller picture of his childhood:

Certainly days would pass when one wouldn't see my father at all. And hours would pass, perhaps a whole day when we wouldn't see my mother. I mean, there was a nursery nurse, and a nanny. There was a groom/chauffeur and life just ticked on. I don't remember him [his father] ever once coming to any kind of event at my prep school. I remember it being said that one time he was asked, he didn't know what public school I was at. So there was that degree of remoteness. It probably explains the way one ticks. But it perhaps makes for a curious background, you know curious approach. But again, is that what turns one into a general practitioner?[18]

Wright's and Littleton's backgrounds made them, in different ways, conscious of their own class position and of class differences. Littleton said:

I suppose I was a bit sensitive. You see my parents wanted me to do all sorts of things like swimming lessons, and riding lessons. Well in order to get from Billingham to this riding school, you go through Middlesbrough and the Tees, and I would go in a bus, with jodhpurs on, right through depressed parts of Teesside. I felt terribly sensitive about that. You could see people who were poor, and here I am in this riding kit. I didn't like that at all.[19]

Unlike Littleton's parents, John Wright's mother did not feel this seeming indifference in matters of class:

My mother certainly regarded anybody who worked, and was not in a profession, as being 'the others' – working class. So that you had to make it clear that you'd been to a good prep school and that you could go into one of the professions, or the services, or, perhaps, be 'something in the city'. But certainly, you wouldn't look at doing any kind of occupation that were the correct province of the working classes.[20]

Jean Adams, brought up on the Isle of Skye, was conscious of how the doctor's family was set apart from the local community:

> I was fairly aware of the fact that nobody came to our house without first knocking at the door. When you went to visit a house, they put out the cups and saucers, and took you into an unused front room, so that I always felt accepted if I was taken into the kitchen and given a cup of tea in a mug. [She nevertheless found it hard to make friends.] It was difficult to become really close friends. For one thing, we had books, and we spoke English at home, and they didn't. I never really felt I belonged there.[21]

Examples such as these seem to bear out Richard Hoggart's remark in *The uses of literacy* (1957) that GPs were seen by the working class as being part of 'Them' – the section of society consisting of bosses and public officials who had the ability to order one's life.[22] The awareness of class amongst doctors' children is not found to the same extent amongst informants from non-medical families, but even with this group we find that many middle-class children had little contact with children from outside their own class.

Family tensions are a not uncommon feature in my informants' stories. Fathers were often portrayed as absent or distant figures. Edward Littleton was not alone in being afraid of his father. Henry Taylor's father was 'a bit firm. I was little scared of him. I could get what I wanted from my mother, but not from him! He was very upright.'[23] Likewise, David Monck: 'I was a bit frightened of my father, and I wasn't frightened of my mother. And I think I regarded my mother as an ally.'[24] John Dyer's father:

> was really quite brutal, and used to inflict corporal punishment on us to the extent that he used to keep two large leather straps which were brought out at a small excuse and wielded with some ferocity. I think he was a difficult man to get the best out of. He went for long periods, terribly long periods, sometimes two or three months at a time, without speaking to any of us. It was really . . . absolutely shattering.[25]

James Harrison's father, a frustrated doctor at heart, was, his son remembered:

a self-made man . . . a very independent man, and people like that have tremendous ambition, and they tend to be, not exactly selfish, but they don't get involved with emotions too much. He was too busy getting somewhere. You know whenever you talked to my father, he told you what he was doing, not what you were doing. You couldn't get through to him.[26]

Mary Barber realised when her parents separated that it was important for a woman to be able to be independent and earn her own living. Until then she had been closer to her father than to her mother but the separation changed matters:

I'd put my father on a pedestal until he was away from home. I found that I had to mend my own punctures on the bicycle, and change electric plugs. Previously when I had a puncture I had to hold this, and I had to do this, and I was shown how to do it, but I was never allowed to do it. When he had gone I suddenly thought 'I mended that puncture by myself' and 'I put that plug in'. It doesn't need a man to do that.

She felt her father was a little afraid of her enquiring mind and encouraged her to be passive, a result, she said, of his being a weak man in a family of strong women.[27]

Other informants had more ambivalent feelings about their mother. Thomas Cole's is an extreme case. His mother came from a well-connected French academic family, and following the death of her mother she was brought up in the household of prime minister Gaston Doumergue (1863–1937). She had great ambitions for her children and this led to problems for Cole:

My mother really was a nitwit. You know what ignorant people are, they're terribly conceited, and consider that their children carry on the tradition of the family and of course they don't. I suppose I was the only one that gave my mother any satisfaction at all, because I took up medicine. She was such a snob.[28]

He seems to have had a strange relationship with his mother. An aunt advised him to break away from his mother because she was ruining him. He agreed, 'she ruined me. And when I look back

29

at myself, at the age of fifteen, sixteen, seventeen, I must have been a filthy little bastard.' A few years later Cole advised his father to leave his mother, which he did.[29]

Edward Rushton's view of his mother stemmed from over-hearing a conversation as a small child:

> My mother was a very strict but kind woman. She didn't have any of the bohemian attributes which my father had. I was far closer to my father than my mother, because of that, I think. And I can remember when I was a little boy of about four, my mother had a friend in for tea, and they were gossiping together, in front of the coal fire. And I was playing with my little toy motor cars near them, and I can remember my mother saying to this friend, 'He wasn't planned'. I'll never forget that. 'He wasn't planned'. But what she meant was, I wasn't expected, and I wasn't wanted.[30]

It is, of course, difficult to speculate as to how upbringings such as these might have affected GPs' work. Wright, for one, was aware of how his upbringing might have led him to a career in general practice. Dyer was also sure that his relationship with his father affected his approach to his patients and his own children. He spoke of how he 'always felt how important it was that I didn't become like my father. And I think there's no doubt that a lot of my approach has been absorbed from him, nevertheless.'[31] These two were aware of how their early experiences may have had some influence on the way they practised medicine. At the very least it does seem from the oral evidence that family backgrounds and relationships of GPs led some of them to take an interest later in life in the dynamics of the family; precisely the sphere of influence of the general practitioner. Another point worth considering is how the future GPs' approach to their patients was formed to some extent by being brought up in hierarchical institutions such as the household and the British public school.[32] Later, many informants also spent time living and working within the hierarchies of the armed forces. And what influence may have derived from being brought up in a lower middle-class household, which perhaps ran a family business, valued independence, self-reliance, thrift and hard work, but which was, in the words of two informants from that background, 'the most reactionary of classes'?[33]

Vocation

On the basis of this type of evidence, especially that of the sons of doctors, it is not too Freudian to see the choice of a career in medicine as being, in some cases, a way of winning the approval of a father who was possibly absent for a lot of the time, frequently bad-tempered or who was an awe-inspiring figure. The GPs themselves do not present their choice in these terms. Nor should we expect them to. In some cases, especially where doctors' sons are concerned, following their father into medicine was hardly a conscious choice. Edward Littleton was, he said, 'always interested in medicine, particularly the personal side of medicine [but] I wasn't aware of any pressure to do medicine, I rather enjoyed the idea of it, but I wouldn't say I had an absolutely burning, thrusting desire to do medicine'.[34] Alan Baker's parents (his father was a doctor) 'were hoping that I would take up medicine, and I rather drifted in from there'.[35] John Wright has a similar recollection: 'I didn't decide. One just drifted in.'[36] So too has David Monck, another doctor's son: 'I don't think I ever thought of anything else. But I observed what his life was and it didn't upset me. Medicine was not so much a pressing vocation.'[37] It was even possible for someone from a non-medical background to stray into medicine. Michael Bruce 'decided to do medicine basically because I had three good friends who went into medicine, and they all went into the medical sixth, and I was half inclined to go on and do history. And then I thought, well, I don't know. My friends are doing medicine. So that's really how I decided to do medicine.'[38] For these there was no 'burning desire' to have a career in medicine, and, apart from Bruce, becoming a doctor was, for these men, a seemingly natural passage following in their fathers' wake.

Medicine was also a natural choice for two other doctors' children, but for quite different reasons. Security, status, and tradition were the attractions for Charles Newton: 'It seemed to me that it was a career that was a fairly safe one, and an honourable one, and one's family had done it before.'[39] Charles Williams had concentrated on Classics at school but the death of his father made it imperative that he should help support his family as quickly as possible. Following his late father into medicine was an obvious choice.[40]

It was not only those from a medical family for whom a career in medicine did not pose a dilemma. These informants, however, could not remember a time when they did not want to become a doctor. Anne Finch, knew 'from the time I was about five years old, I was never going to do anything else but be a doctor. I think it was born in me.'[41] Similarly, Robert Andrews could 'never remember any other time when I hadn't wanted to do medicine, from cutting up a goldfish when it died when I was six years old'.[42] Neither came from a medical family. For Thomas Cole it was almost predestined that he should have a medical career: 'I was going to be an engineer and I chucked that up. I had a feeling that I had to do medicine. I was a born doctor. And my mother had a friend, who was a fortune-teller, and she told her when I was the age of nine I was going to be a doctor.' The truth of this story is beside the point. The interest lies in the fact that it forms part of Cole's own narrative of being a 'born doctor'. It was a calling he could not avoid.[43]

For those for whom fate did not play a part the local doctor could be a source of inspiration. In some cases the local GP appeared to be a glamorous figure, who had both status in the community and an enviable lifestyle. Robert Blair was the son of a Scottish headmaster. His father was friendly with the local doctor (these two, plus the local minister, would have been the three authority figures in the local community of Fraserburgh). Blair described his local doctor as being 'not a wealthy man, but he behaved as if he was. He dressed in the most odd way. He got up at all hours. And he lived a life that just seemed so different from the staid life that everyone else had.' A church elder, who was well read and well educated, the doctor was different in character as well from his own father who had, as he put it, 'a more rigid personality'.[44] John Dyer's mother and their GP were close friends, and Dyer appears to have compared him favourably with his own father. In addition the GP had a son at medical school whom Dyer considered to be a 'very glamorous figure'.[45] Henry Taylor was also influenced by his family GP: 'There was an elderly doctor, who was held in great respect, in our area, and I sort of thought, "Now, there is a man I could admire". He was our doctor.'[46]

In the eyes of many children and adolescents in this period the job of a doctor would have seemed to offer glamour and the more solid prospects of status and a secure career. These assets, combined with the chance to exercise a sense of duty, must have made medicine an attractive proposition.

David Silverman's account of his route into medicine is an example of how family relationships and values could work to motivate someone to become a doctor. Silverman came from a Jewish family from Leeds. His father was an unsuccessful shop-keeper who later became a factory worker. His mother's family ran a successful tailoring business. Silverman's father valued education and regretted that he had not done more with his life. This led to conflict with his wife's family who were business oriented:

> My mother's family despised my father's family, because it was working class and poor, and also they thought that his attitude towards education and culture was getting above yourself. So there was a lot of tension there, and I can remember, as a child, having to make up my mind which side I was on. It was really a moral conflict. But there was never any doubt in my mind, because as my mother had made the mistake of marrying someone like my father, she was always treated with contempt by her family. And I can remember going with my mother to visit my grandmother on her side, and her coming home in tears because they had spoken to her so contemptu-ously. And so I thought, 'Well, there's not much cop in this, is there! So I'm not ever going to be somebody who wants to make a lot of money, I'm going for the moral side of life.'[47]

Silverman originally wanted to become a scientist but his parents:

> brought a lot of pressure to bear on me to become a doctor, because, they said, 'Jews won't get a job easily in science', and they had lots of stories about how Jews were discriminated against, and would never get a job, whereas you can always be a nice Jewish doctor. And my father of course was keen on me to be a doctor, because that was dutiful, you were doing good to humanity. Being a doctor united their two views of what life should be about.

Medicine was a career which united duty with money-making.[48]

Motivation for a medical career might also stem from religious belief or a family tradition of public service of some kind. For example, the Primitive Methodist family of Thomas Russell stressed the importance of service.[49] So too did the family of Edward Rushton, whose father worked as a fund-raiser for the

League of Nations and for various charitable organisations. Rushton, too, had a Primitive Methodist family background.[50] A tradition of religious and public service was also apparent in Charlotte Smith's family. Her father was a high-level civil servant in the Home Office, and two of her brothers went on to become Catholic missionaries while the other became a doctor.[51]

For some women medicine was not the career which sprang immediately to mind. Charlotte Smith's first impulse had been to become a nurse, and it was only following the death of a family friend from TB while nursing which prompted her to become a doctor. Sarah Egerton's father had once owned his own shop in Liverpool but he had been reduced to running a market stall, and was never in constant employment. Sarah had

> vaguely thought of being a doctor, because my grand-father had been a doctor, and my father should have been a doctor, if he'd been able to attend school better. And then [I had] a vague idea, but I thought it wouldn't be possible. And then I thought about teaching as a possibility. And then I saw an advertisement in the paper in 1909, and they wanted female sanitary inspectors. And I decided this was a thing I could manage to do.

As it turned out, medicine became a possibility only when her aunt's family agreed to finance her university course.[52]

Finally, Mary Barber was persuaded by her headmistress to consider medicine rather than zoology as a career. It is worth noting that Barber had to go to a local boys' school to receive teaching in the sciences.[53] It seems that most of the women doctors interviewed were poorly taught when it came to science. This left one informant at a disadvantage when she began her medical training. Anne Finch left school:

> never having done one bit of science in my life. And can you imagine what the first MB was like? I had no idea where to begin. I shall never ever forget my first biology class, which was a botany one, and there was a sheet of paper provided, with the instructions, 'Cut a section of the stem provided.' And I just looked at the paper, and [thought] 'what on earth does this mean?'. I had no idea what it meant. Can you imagine what the demonstrators were like? I lived through absolute hell that first year.[54]

So far I have focused on the family background of the GP and on the relationships within their families. To recap, in some cases medicine was the only choice, whether through the pressure to carry on a family tradition in medicine or through a sense of vocation. For others medicine appealed because it offered status and security and upward social mobility. Within the family, relationships with parents, attitudes about class and social hierarchy, social values about work and service to others, for example, all played a part in the making of the future GP. Not all values, beliefs, experiences would remain with them into adult life and into their dealings with patients, but I think we can be certain that vestiges of them would endure and surface in their dealings with patients, many of whom would have value systems and backgrounds very different from their doctor. This is not to claim that the negative aspects of a childhood would necessarily lead to problems when it came to dealing with patients. As John Wright remarked, the recognition of the inadequacies of their own family life could lead to an interest in families, their problems, and the link between family relationships and ill-health in its members. In fact an awareness of the difficulties of family life must surely have been a benefit when dealing with patients. And, of course, not all doctors had turbulent childhoods. Anne Finch and Charlotte Smith, amongst others, both recall having a happy childhood, and they may have brought experiences from theirs, along with some of the attitudes and values passed on to them during their upbringing, into their later work. Then again, we need to keep in mind the comment of Dyer, that aware as he was of the need to be different from his father, it was impossible for him to shake off his father's influence entirely – in which case the inheritance from an unhappy childhood with difficult family relationships may have been detrimental to the relations he had with his patients.

Training and career

The family continued to play a part in my informants' accounts once they had decided upon a medical career. Training had, of course, to be paid for. In most cases the cost fell on parents but, as with Sarah Egerton, other family members sometimes paid for the education of a relative.[55] Once again, the sacrifices made by the family to do this often put pressure on the student to work hard, to limit his or her social life, and to avoid the extra time and expense involved in retaking exams. As Alan Baker said, 'I hadn't got the money for the high life, because it was a sweat for my parents to put me through'.[56]

Money was not the only resource available from parents or other kin. A family network often came in useful when it came to deciding where to study medicine. Two main factors can be seen as influencing the choice. First, a family tradition might have been built up at a hospital or university. The attendance of a family member in the past was useful when it came to coping with entrance procedures. George Stevens left his home in Devon in about 1927 to study at St Mary's where two or three of his uncles worked, St Mary's other attraction being its convenience for those travelling from the West Country into Paddington. Even so, Stevens found St Mary's 'decadent, shabby and most depressing'.[57] Charles Newton trained at Guy's 'because father was there, I had uncles who were there, I had aunts who had been there'.[58] John Wright trained at St Thomas's, as had every other doctor in the family. In his case, 'there was a very brief interview, it was mostly the Dean talking. I mean, I don't think I was asked any question very much. It was just "When are you starting?", you know, and "Where are you going to live?". There was no question of any kind of interrogation as to one's suitability at all. It was just . . . "You're coming, aren't you?".'[59] When David Monck was interviewed at St Thomas's he was asked if he had any family connection with the hospital. When he replied that his family had been trained at Edinburgh and St Bartholomew's the interviewer was mystified as to why he wanted to train at St Thomas's.[60] This family link with a particular medical school was the prime factor behind the choice of university and hospital for many of those from a medical background. Once attached to an institution it then became possible to use contacts made there when the time came to look for jobs following qualification. Personal contacts, whether of family or medical school, turned out to be in the course of the interviews a very common way of finding jobs of all sorts from house jobs, to locums, to introductions to partnerships in general practice.

The other major factor behind the choice of medical school was its close proximity to home. For families making a financial sacrifice to send a child to medical school, having the student live at home or with a relative made it possible to save on accommodation and other living expenses. Charles Williams went to Birmingham University 'chiefly because of the financial situation. My uncle was in practice in Walsall, and I was able to travel from

Walsall to Birmingham, and lodge with him.'[61] Charles Newton lived at home most of the time while he was at Guy's.[62] And even when he was away from the family home in Devon, George Stevens was able to draw on the support of his relatives in London who kept an eye on him and found him suitable digs in a Quaker establishment.[63] For whatever reason, many chose to remain near the family home. Anne Finch from Worcester studied at Birmingham,[64] Robert Andrews went to his home-town university of Sheffield,[65] Russell[66] and Littleton[67] from the north east trained at Durham, and so on. Whether because of finance or other family circumstances, the student did not usually travel far to train, the exceptions usually being when there was a family tradition or when the university involved was either Cambridge or Oxford.

Where our future GPs were to be trained was therefore almost universally determined by family tradition or circumstances. The standard of training available at the university or hospital hardly ever came into play when the choice of medical school was made. Instead the deciding factor was the existence of a family network which could facilitate entry into university or teaching hospital or which could provide support during the period of training when family resources would be stretched.

The image of general practice

Many GPs remarked during the course of an interview that once they had embarked upon their medical training their intention was to become a specialist of some type. Very few, except perhaps the children of GPs who were able to join the family practice, intended to become general practitioners. This is not especially surprising. General practice was, after all, not looked upon as a good career for an aspiring medic. At medical school GPs were often scorned as being 'failed consultants'. According to Joseph Fawcett, who qualified in 1947 after training in London: 'You didn't get a lot of encouragement in those days. It was very much, "well, if you can't think of anything else to do, you can always do general practice".'[68] David Silverman remembers that:

> General practice wasn't a popular choice then. It was, to use a famous phrase, falling off the ladder. If you had any kind of ambition, you hoped to stay in your medical school and go on to be a specialist there, because that's where all the big prizes were, in money and social prestige.[69]

When John Wright was training general practice was considered 'Second best. If you couldn't get into a speciality, you dropped into general practice.'[70] GPs were, said Henry Taylor, '"Also rans", you see the lads who set out to be an ophthalmologist, and didn't make it dropped into general practice'.[71] To be a general practitioner meant leaving the hospital-based career structure where the stages for advancement were set out. It was possible for the specialist to progress. General practice meant entering a career where no such structures existed and apart from financial differences the most junior GP was on a par with the most senior. Realistically GPs remained on the same level for the rest of their career.[72]

These factors led to many GPs having a self-image of being intellectually inferior to their hospital-based colleagues. They dealt with the routine and the mundane while specialists and consultants dealt with the intellectually challenging work. Alan Baker, for example, felt that he 'wasn't good enough to go into anything else. You've got to be pretty bright to go into a specialty. I mean general practice is the obvious thing unless you're a high-flyer.'[73]

The criticism of the general practitioner which took place during the training of medical students took a more formal shape in the non-teaching of general practice. Most, if not all of my informants qualified without receiving any training in general practice. Two examples will suffice: 'There was no teaching of it at all', recalls David Silverman, 'I think we had a visit from a GP who came in and talked to us in an amiable sort of way, for a lecture, and that was it.'[74] A few years earlier Michael Bruce's time at Durham had involved 'absolutely no training for general practice at all. You didn't know what it was like. You had no lectures on general practice. You didn't even really know a GP. It was still very much the old apprenticeship system, where people would go and practice as a locum or assistant, and you would pick it up as you went along.'[75] The hospital bias of training could mean that students would qualify without coming across some of the illnesses most commonly dealt with by GPs, no doubt helping to confirm some consultants' views of the general practitioner.[76]

Entry into general practice

Why then, given the image of general practice in large sections of the profession, did medical students come to choose general practice as a career? As we have seen, for some it was a case of following a father into practice – a move which was felt to be acceptable, on a par with entering an established family business. For others it was the fulfilment of a childhood dream.

This leaves us with those who had different routes into general practice. Once again the family has an important part to play in their decision. Often the family could not afford to finance the child for any further training or to supplement income while he or she worked in a series of poorly paid hospital jobs. David Moss qualified in 1935 but had no intention of becoming a GP.

> I think I would have preferred to have specialised, but my father wasn't prepared to fund me any more. He said 'Well, I think you should get into practice now'. And then, of course, along came the War. That tore a big hole in my life, because that's another five years gone. And by the time the War had ended, I didn't want to start specialising then, I wanted to get settled down.[77]

George Stevens, who qualified in 1936, confirmed the need for extra income to go on to specialise:

> In those days a fair amount were expected, by their parents, to take over their father's practice. Quite a lot of them did. And I got the impression they did it in a rather half-hearted manner. They weren't always very keen. A certain number went on for higher medicine. It's nice to specialise, but fewer people specialised. I think it was a question of LSD, you see. I mean if a man wanted to go in for medicine, someone had to find the money. And it usually fell to a lot of parents. Well, I was the oldest of five, and father had to provide for not only me but three daughters, and a son who was ten years younger than me. So it was rather imperative to get into general practice and earn one's own living.[78]

Others tell their story as one of failure to pass the Fellowship exams and a struggle to survive. Failure meant more time spent struggling on a low income. General practice offered the chance to start earning immediately. Henry Taylor, for one, gave up trying for the FRCS (Fellow of the Royal College of Surgeons) after failing an exam. Taylor recalled that:

I came out of the army, and went to do the FRCS course, and discovered that I couldn't keep up with the other boys, who had not been in the Forces, and who had got themselves jobs as demonstrators in anatomy, in medical schools. I felt a bit disappointed that it was obviously not going to be. But then it occurred to me that, even if I did persist, and even if I did get an FRCS, I wouldn't get a job. There were surgeons in their forties, if I was twenty-two or twenty-three, there were surgeons of forty-two, forty-three, looking for jobs.

This, said Taylor, led some men leaving the army to go straight into general practice without first taking the usual house surgeon/ house physician post, 'because they needed the money. They had a wife and kids and they wanted the money.'[79]

For those who wanted to marry it was necessary to earn a better income than that available to those starting on the first steps towards becoming a consultant. For many young doctors an ambition in this direction would usually have meant delaying marriage. In some cases the impossibility of carrying on to become a consultant became obvious after marriage. John Dyer wanted to do paediatrics:

> but it fairly quickly became obvious to me that I couldn't afford to specialise, because I had a wife and a child to support, and there was no way in which I could survive otherwise, so I had to get a job as quickly as possible. [As a houseman Dyer received £300 a year less £100 for his keep.] And we had to maintain a flat and my wife and baby to be clothed and fed, and this is why I couldn't contemplate carrying on there, in hospital. I mean, there were times when my wife couldn't afford to eat, or to have the Tube fare to come up to see me.[80]

General practice was the only alternative for David Silverman:

> I was married, and we were going to have a child, so there wasn't any question of living in an attic and writing poetry, and being airy fairy, not with the influence of my father and his moral systems, I couldn't have done that. So I knew I had to practise whether I liked it or not. And I thought, 'I can't stand the hospital, (a) because I'd never

have a career, because I'd always be quarrelling with authority and (b) I just don't like big institutions.'[81]

In other cases general practice began to appeal to informants while they were in hospital jobs. Charlotte Smith considered working in paediatrics but found aspects of the work difficult to cope with: 'I thought of doing paediatrics, because of loving children and so forth, [but from] working in a paediatric house job, I knew that it wasn't for me. It was very hard to get penicillin, you had children dying of many diseases on the wards, there was very little you could do for them.'[82] Thomas Russell discovered that he *needed* to work in general practice during his period working in paediatrics: 'Donald Court[83] wanted me to stay in paediatrics, but I really felt that I wanted to do more than that. I wanted to see people, I wanted to see whole families. To have a baby in, and then a week later, hand it back to its parents was not enough. I needed to know about the parents, and I needed to know about the family.'[84]

In these cases the decision to enter practice was made because their route into another career was blocked or because they realised that they would be happier working in general practice. Although it is hardly ever explicitly stated, one does get the impression that many GPs did feel themselves to be failures in some way. Sometimes this was felt to be because of a personal failing of their own (not passing the required exams) but mainly a failure because family circumstances had made it impossible for them to follow their preferred direction.

If the family was felt by some GPs to have been a hindrance and diverted them from their first choice career it could also have its positive aspects. The family network could help in finding a way into practice by facilitating introductions to potential partners or finding locum work. Families might also lend the necessary money to start a practice. Or indeed for the children of general practitioners, they could supply a ready-made position in the family practice.

For married women working in general practice could prove particularly difficult. Combining work with bringing up a family meant that some were forced to leave the irregular hours and immense demands of general practice for the regular hours of local authority clinic work; work which GPs often considered as being of lower status than their own. Margaret Bishop explained that she 'was going into general practice, but then I became pregnant, and I felt that I could only do a job that was sort of nine-to-five, part-time, when I had the baby'.[85] It was also difficult for a woman to enter practice after the War. Jean Adams had always wanted to follow her father into general practice. However, there were problems:

> There were a lot of men coming from the Forces, and they'd only take a woman on very poor wages. You could be a sort of slave and do all the chronics, and all the gynaecology, which one tended to do anyway. In fact I just found it more convenient to do infant welfare. In fact when I first got married [to a GP], for six months, I didn't work. I nearly went mad![86]

If the woman did continue working it could lead to tensions within the family. Sarah Dixon had been diverted from general practice into family planning work which she combined with running the home and looking after her GP husband and their children. She remembered being:

> Fed up sometimes. Possibly at times resentful, because if you've got a busy husband, and one who'd never in his early years, ever done anything, well, I mean the gentleman who's just come in and sit down, and even though you've been out to work, you did the evening meal and that sort of thing. But it was just the accepted thing. You got mad at times like we all do.[87]

Margaret Bishop avoided going into general practice because she realised that she would not be able to combine work and family arrangements, being aware that having both partners working 'caused tremendous strains in the marriage. It is a form of jealousy. They don't like the attention which comes, particularly if the other person, in whatever their job, does well.'[88] Whether the GPs were male or female, the decision to start their own families was one which could significantly affect the course of a career.

Conclusion

We have seen from the evidence presented from the life histories of my informants that the family looms large in their stories of how they came to become general practitioners. It could provide motivation, financial support, and, sometimes, access to a network of contacts which could be used to help advance a career. In some cases, the family supplied an inheritance, in the shape of a father's practice. Alternatively, the family could prevent an individual from fulfilling his or her own ambitions. Some did have a vocation for medicine and for general practice. Others felt they were expected to follow their fathers into medicine and general practice but had no real desire to do so. Still others entered general practice because, often for family reasons, they were unable to continue to work towards a consultantship. Hence, they felt that the only alternative was to become a GP and work in an area which they had through their training been taught to think of as being inferior to specialist medicine. Once there they perhaps found that being a doctor did not carry with it the status they believed it to possess when they had chosen medicine as a career. And, as we have also seen, the family was the source of a person's earliest principles, values and beliefs.

Is there anything here which could account for the unhappy relationship between doctor and patient which Michael Balint observed? I would suggest that possible explanations for the failure of the drug 'doctor' to work during this period, if it had ever done at all satisfactorily, may have originated from a background in the home and school which commonly instilled into them the values of individualism, self-reliance, order, hierarchy and service which may have been brought increasingly into question in post-war British society, especially by a working class about whom many of my informants knew little and with whom they had very little contact until they reached adulthood. With the introduction of the National Health Service in 1948 the whole nature of the doctor–patient relationship underwent a fundamental change.[89] A perceived loss of independence under nationalisation and the elimination of the majority of private practice brought about a huge change in the financial and personal relationships which many doctors had with their patients. In a sense the world had turned upside down for the doctor, with a decrease in professional freedom and increased power for the patient who had access to a 'free' medical service. This must surely have led to difficulties for those who had been taught to respect self-sufficiency, authority and deference. In addition to this we have seen that although many GPs remembered having a happy childhood a large proportion had mixed feelings about their early life. How much this may have influenced their relationships with patients is difficult to say. But, given the emphasis placed on the personality of the doctor in the work of the GP, it is plausible that doctor–patient relations were affected by these early experiences. We may consequently point to part of the problem of general practice in the early post-war years as resulting from the presence of a number of GPs who regretted not being able to follow a specialist career and who felt they were working in an inferior occupation and were finding it difficult, through no fault of their own, to be in sympathy with the needs of their patients.

I would like to conclude by making it clear that I am in no way condemning all GPs, or even all the GPs who were inter-viewed, as bad doctors. I am convinced that many did their best for their patients. The problem lay in the idea that the GP should be 'all things to all men (and women)': possibly too much was expected by patients and practitioners of the GP. Given what we know about the backgrounds, upbringing, and career path of the GPs studied, it was impossible for them to meet such demands. What I have tried to suggest is that the way GPs thought about and performed their work was shaped by factors in their back-grounds and family life as well as by other forces. In any event, I would argue that focusing on the history of the individual general practitioner can help us to begin to understand the origin of some of the problems recognised by those mid-century investigations into general practice.

Notes

1   J. S. Collings, 'General practice in England today: a reconnaissance', *The Lancet*, 25 March 1950, pp. 555–85; S. J. Hadfield, 'A field survey of general practice, 1951–2', *British Medical Journal*, 26 September 1953, pp. 683–706; S. Taylor, *Good general practice*, London, Oxford University Press, 1954.
2   Collings, 'General practice in England', p. 555.
3   British Medical Association, *General practice and the training of the general practitioner*, London, BMA, 1950.
4   M. Balint, *The doctor, his patient and the illness*, 2nd edition, London, Medical Publishing Co., 1964, p. 1.
5   ibid., p. 5.
6   These interviews were undertaken as part of a project entitled 'The Oral History of General Practice in Britain, 1935–52'. The master tapes of these interviews are held at the British Library National Sound Archive; copies are held at the Contemporary Medical Archives Centre, Wellcome Institute for the History of Medicine, Euston Road, London. Some informants have requested that their interviews should remain closed to the public for a number of years.

7 The size of the sample was determined simply by the number of interview transcripts available at the time of writing this chapter. I have no reason to believe that my findings would be considerably different if I had been able to draw upon a transcript from every interview.

8 P. D' Arcy Hart, correspondence on the 'Social background of the future doctor', *British Medical Journal*, 9 September 1944, p. 356.

9 C. Kingsley, *The water-babies: a fairy tale for a land-baby*, London and Cambridge, 1863.

10 Oral History of General Practice (OHGP), C/22. The names of all informants have been changed.

11 ibid., C/30. Interview closed.

12 ibid., C/38.

13 ibid., C/6.

14 ibid., C/18. Interview closed.

15 ibid., C/12.

16 ibid., C/34.

17 ibid., C/13.

18 ibid., C/23. Interview closed.

19 ibid., C/13.

20 ibid., C/23. Interview closed.

21 ibid., C/31. Interview closed.

22 R. Hoggart, *The uses of literacy. Aspects of working class life with special reference to publications and entertainments*, Harmondsworth, Penguin, 1957, chapter 3.

23 OHGP, C/30. Interview closed.

24 ibid., C/27.

25 ibid., C/25. Interview closed.

26 ibid., C/38.

27 ibid., C/34.

28 ibid., C/14.

29 ibid.

30 ibid., C/35. Interview closed.

31 ibid., C/25. Interview closed.

32 Many informants grew up in households which employed servants; but this is not to say that the family itself is not an hierarchical institution.

33 Comments made by informants David Silverman and Michael Bruce.

34 OHGP, C13.

35 ibid., C/21.

36 ibid., C/23. Interview closed.

37 ibid., C/27.

38 ibid., C/29. Interview closed.

39 ibid., C/12.

40 ibid., C/18. Interview closed.

41 ibid., C/6.

42 ibid., C/22.

43 ibid., C/14.

44 ibid., C/11.

45 ibid., C/25. Interview closed.

46 ibid., C/30. Interview closed.
47 ibid., C/17.
48 ibid.
49 ibid., C/2.
50 ibid., C/1.
51 ibid., C/9.
52 ibid., C/37.
53 ibid., C/34.
54 ibid., C/6.
55 ibid., C/37.
56 ibid., C/21.
57 ibid., C/19.
58 ibid., C/12.
59 ibid., C/23. Interview closed.
60 ibid., C/27.
61 ibid., C/18. Interview closed.
62 ibid., C/12.
63 ibid., C/19.
64 ibid., C/6.
65 ibid., C/22.
66 ibid., C/2.
67 ibid., C/13.
68 ibid., C/4.
69 ibid., C/17.
70 ibid., C/23. Interview closed.
71 ibid., C/30. Interview closed.
72 This and other matters relevant to understanding the way the medical profession is organised can be found in Clifford Geertz's, 'The way we think now: toward an ethnography of modern thought', in his book *Local knowledge. Further essays in interpretative anthropology*, New York, Basic Books, 1983, pp. 147–63.
73 OHGP, C/21.
74 ibid., C/17.
75 ibid., C/29. Interview closed.
76 The lack of training for general practice is confirmed by Michael Weller in his autobiography, *You've got cancer doctor*, Royston, Herts., Ellisons' Editions, 1991, p. 40.
77 OHGP, C/8.
78 ibid., C/19.
79 ibid., C/30. Interview closed.
80 ibid., C/25. Interview closed.
81 ibid., C/17.
82 ibid., C/9.
83 Donald Court (1912–1994) was Reader in Child Health at the University of Durham at the time. He later became Professor of Child Health at the University of Newcastle.
84 OGHP, C/2.
85 ibid., C/20.
86 ibid., C/31. Interview closed.
87 ibid., C/15.

88 ibid.

89 The correspondence columns of the *British Medical Journal* in the years leading up to the introduction of the National Health Service and immediately afterwards are useful for learning about GPs' attitudes in these matters. The general history of the peiod is dealt with by Peter Hennessy, *Never again, Britain 1945–51*, London, Cape, 1992; John Stevenson, *British society, 1914–45*, Harmondsworth, Penguin, 1984; Arthur Marwick, *British society since 1945*, Harmondsworth, Allen Lane, 1982; Paul Addison, *The road to 1945*, London, 1975; idem, *Now the war is over: a social history of Britain 1945–51*, London, BBC, Cape, 1985; P. Clarke, *Hope and glory: Britain 1900–1990*, Harmondsworth, Penguin, 1997. For general practice and the health service see Charles Webster, *Problems of health care: the National Health Service before 1957*, London, HMSO, 1988; Frank Honigsbaum, *The division in British medicine. A history of the separation of general practice from hospital care, 1911–1968*, London, Kogan Page, 1979; Rosemary Stevens, *Medical practice in modern England. The impact of specialization and state medicine*, New Haven, Conn., Yale University Press, 1966. I. Loudon, J. Horder, and C. Webster (eds), *General practice under the National Health Service, 1948–1997*, London, Clarendon Press, 1998, appeared after this chapter had been written.

2

THE ROLE OF THE COMMUNITY PHARMACIST IN HEALTH AND WELFARE, 1911–1986

Stuart Anderson and Virginia Berridge

Introduction

The role of professions is well represented in historical writing about health and welfare, particularly with regard to the medical and nursing professions, and to a lesser extent of the professions supplementary to medicine, such as chiropody, optics and physiotherapy. There has also been significant interest, particularly through oral history, in the continuing role of lay care, in the growth in use of complementary medicine, and in the role of non-medically qualified practitioners in health and welfare. Yet the role of the pharmacist in this area has been surprisingly neglected. Pharmacists in the community, or 'chemists' as they were always known, both by themselves and the public,[1] have long occupied an indeterminate terrain in health and welfare, falling somewhere between business and professionalism, and between professional care and lay care – tensions which remain largely unresolved to this day.

Throughout the twentieth century, local chemists have had strong links with the traditions of lay care and with popular medicine: they have been a readily accessible and unpaid source of health information, advice and support. They have been available in most communities throughout Great Britain, over extended hours and without appointment, providing advice on a wide range of health matters without charge. Most of them were men.[2] The chemist has rightly been characterized as the 'poor man's doctor'.

But during the course of the twentieth century the role of the retail chemist has undergone enormous change. At the beginning of the century, many chemists were involved in secondary occupations, such as dentistry or optics. These formed a vital part of the chemist's business, but such combinations of activities slowly died out as these occupations became professionalised in their own right.

Before the welfare state, chemists also played an important part in the care of patients and in the promotion of health. Most of their shops were used as first-aid stations, for everything from minor cuts and bruises to serious lacerations to arms and legs. This use of the chemist died out with the implementation of the National Health Service (NHS) in 1948, following the passage of the Act in 1946. This gave patients free and ready access to doctors, as well as access to hospital accident and emergency services. Mothers with small babies frequently used the local chemist as a welfare centre, where the babies would be weighed, welfare foods obtained, and advice on teething, wind and sleeping sought. Again, these welfare activities of the chemist died out following the establishment of child welfare clinics. Retail chemists found themselves in the middle of a shifting relationship between self-help and lay care on the one hand and state provision of services on the other.

The most important factor affecting the role of the chemist was the inexorable increase in the number of prescriptions written by doctors. Substantial numbers of prescriptions reached chemists' shops for the first time following the National Health Insurance (NHI) Act of 1911. But the most dramatic change came with the implementation of the NHS on 5 July 1948: the number of prescriptions presented for dispensing increased almost fourfold, from 70 million per year in 1947 to 241 million in 1948.[3] Almost overnight chemists migrated from the front of the shop to the back to keep up with demand, and it is only in very recent years that they have re-emerged to reclaim their place as adviser to the public on medicines.

Perhaps the greatest impact of this change was the contribution of dispensing to the chemist's income. At the beginning of the century no more than 5 per cent of the chemist's income was derived from the dispensing of publicly funded prescriptions; by 1990, this figure had risen to over 70 per cent. In 1900, over 50 per cent of the income of some chemists came from dental work; by 1950 this source of income had completely disappeared.

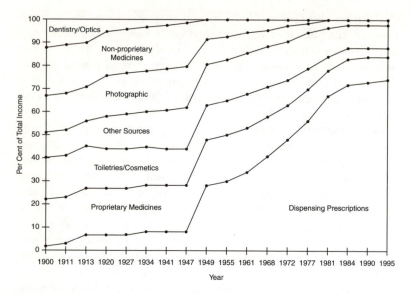

Figure 2.1 Sources of income of independent community pharmacists, 1900–1995

Changes in the average income of pharmaceutical chemists during the course of the twentieth century are illustrated in Figure 2.1.

In this chapter we explore how the main activities of the chemist in the field of health and welfare have changed during the course of the century, based on the oral testimony of fifty retired retail chemists.[4] We use this testimony to illustrate three of these changes: the shift by which the taking on by chemists of secondary occupations moved from being the norm to being the exception, as these activities became professionalised; the shift away from home remedies towards manufactured products; and the impact of the growth of the welfare state. We suggest that these changes contributed, at least in part, to the erosion of the traditional role of the chemist; but that developments in recent years represent a limited return to this traditional role.

The demise of the chemist's secondary occupations

The origins of pharmacy, from spicers and grocers to apothecaries and chemists and druggists, have been well documented in the history of pharmacy literature.[5] The growth of professionalism in

50

pharmacy during the nineteenth century has been extensively explored by Crellin,[6] and more recently by Burnby.[7] Larkin has described elsewhere the emergence of other health occupations as 'professions' during the course of the twentieth century. These follow a common pattern of formation of a society of existing practitioners, mandatory training and examination, and ultimate registration with a professional body. Larkin documents the formation of a British Optical Association in 1895, a Society of Chiropodists in 1912, and Societies of both Physiotherapists and Radiographers in 1920.[8] But the emergence of these professions over a period of years meant that it was often possible to practise one or other of them while being formally trained and qualified in another.

This was certainly the case with pharmacy. Pharmacy had a distinct advantage at the turn of the century in having already undertaken many of the steps towards professionalisation during the second half of the nineteenth century. As Larkin puts it: 'occupations such as pharmacy or dentistry accompanied, rather than post-dated, the occupational ascendancy of medicine'.[9] But many pharmacists continued to practise secondary occupations well into the twentieth century, most notably dentistry, optics and chiropody.

The chemist-dentist

The pharmaceutical dentist of the nineteenth century has been described by Hillam.[10] It is clear that, throughout that century, many pharmacists provided dental services from their premises, as is indicated by the following complaint which appeared in *Forceps* in 1844:

> How repeatedly we see a chemist or apothecary add to his other occupation that of dentist, and exhibit in his window a label announcing that teeth are extracted. Some persons are induced by the show cards to entrust their jaws to the tender mercies of the pseudo-professor, who manages – by extreme manual exertion – to drag teeth out.[11]

Ross reports that, in Scotland, the chemists and druggists were the main purveyors of dental treatment, practising dentistry as a secondary occupation principally in rural areas.[12] He indicates that a similar situation existed in England at that time, and continued well into the twentieth century. Indeed, before the 1921 Dental Act anyone with only the most basic of training could set themselves up as a dentist, and many chemists did so. While most restricted their activities to the extraction of teeth, others attended short courses to enable them to undertake fillings and to make crowns. According to Holloway, 'when the first edition of the [dental] register appeared in 1879 it contained the names of 5,289 persons of whom 2,049, or well over one-third, were registered as combining the practice of dentistry with that of pharmacy'.[13]

Evidence in support of the contention that the secondary occupation of the chemist continued well into the twentieth century is available from the oral history study. In the late 1940s Basil Trasler worked as an 'improver' (someone who had completed an apprenticeship but was not yet registered as a pharmaceutical chemist) in a long-established business in a midlands town, with an elderly pharmacist who was one of the few remaining members of the Chemists' Dental Association (CDA). He was still actively practising as a dentist, and Basil Trasler assisted him in this work:

> There was a reasonably well-lit dental surgery, plus a small separate waiting room, directly alongside the shop. It was a typical dental surgery – nice and clean. Most dentistry was still done in the sitting position. He had a modern cord-driven electric drill, but he also retained a cast-iron treadle foot drill. He was conscious that most of the pain was generated by heat. When he had trouble he switched over to the slow foot-drill. I sometimes operated the foot-treadle for him. The business was half and half dentistry and pharmacy. I assisted him when he needed an extra pair of hands, extracting teeth, filling them, supplying and fitting dentures.[14]

He remembers when the first acrylic powders were introduced for denture plates, and recalls the impact they had on the business. His boss was still also supplying vulcanised ones:

> He had this little vulcaniser. It was heated by a Bunsen burner. It was always on when I was having my lunch. The boss would say 'keep an eye on it – switch it off in twenty minutes.' After the introduction of acrylic dentures he used the services of a dental mechanic. He'd been

practising for many years before the advent of the Dental Act of 1921; he was fully qualified to register under the Act. He was President of the CDA for about three years in the late 1920s.[15]

The Chemists' Dental Association had been formed before the First World War because the government of the day was thinking of establishing a register of dentists. 'So many pharmacists were practising dentistry in their shops during those years that an Association was formed to protect the interests of these chemists during the passage of the legislation.'[16] By the late 1940s the numbers had dwindled – there had been no newcomers since 1921. 'My boss went to the winding up meeting of the CDA in 1949: by that time the number of members had reduced to five.'[17]

The chemist-optician

In the early part of the century it was also quite common for chemists to undertake some very limited supplementary training in order to practise as opticians, and the tradition of the chemist-optician continued until recently, when optics became a degree course in its own right. Alan Garrett, who practised in Enfield, Middlesex, had qualified as a chemist in 1935, but he felt that he wanted to keep up to date, and one way of doing this was to study optics. 'I wanted to advance myself, and to make some profit.' So he became a Fellow of the British College of Opticians in 1938, which involved taking a postal course over one year, and then spending time with another optician, who was a friend, and taking a not very difficult examination. However, he practised as an optician from home. 'It was a very simple business, and I saw lots of private patients.'[18]

Alan Dickman's shop in Berkhamsted, Hertfordshire, still displays a sign over the door saying 'Chemist and Optician'. His father had qualified as an optician in 1934, although he had practised optics before that during the period when no qualification was required. 'People would come in privately to have their eyes tested, and so on. It was done upstairs in another room, which is now a hairdressers.' His father gave up eye-testing following the introduction of the NHS in 1948, although he did some NHS work for a short while. 'From 1948 you could get specs on the NHS for nothing – it more or less killed his private work.' The optical trade was clearly a profitable part of the business. 'People were always coming in with busted frames, which we had to send off for repair – very profitable.'[19]

Although the chemist-dentist ceased to exist after 1949, the association between pharmacy and optics continued for several more decades, although the numbers of dual practitioners (who had mainly qualified before the war) slowly diminished. However, a number of pharmacists continue to qualify as opticians also, and there is a Chemists' Opticians Association still in existence today (1998). But this occupation underwent great change in the mid-1980s following deregulation of the optics business, and the withdrawal of free eye tests for all. This led to the proliferation of opticians on the high street, including their appearance in department stores. Boots (who run a large chain of chemist's shops throughout the United Kingdom) introduced in-store opticians in 1987, thus reverting to the situation of having a pharmacy and opticians under the same roof. This time, of course, the pharmacist and the optician were usually different people.

Other secondary occupations

Although dentistry and optics were the commonest forms of secondary occupation undertaken by pharmacists, individuals undertook a variety of additional activities. Alan Garrett remembers that in Essex 'many pharmacists also took up chiropody. They had so much spare time before the war.'[20] Some chemists at the beginning of the century also practised not only as dentists but as veterinary surgeons. Thus, Burnby and Rawlings refer to one Alfred Lamery Smith, of 37 Milk Street, Bristol, who in 1900 described himself as a chemist, dentist and veterinary surgeon.[21] Individual chemists appear to have practised any combination of these occupations. Ronald Benz, who was born in 1910, recalls his early childhood living above his grandfather's chemist's shop in Eastbourne around 1915:

> My maternal grandfather had a pharmacy in Eastbourne. He seemed to be a man of many hats. He also did optics. He also did dentistry. He had a dental surgery in the back, and he used to do fillings using a rather archaic method. He had a treadle thing to work the drill. He used to treadle it with his foot, and hold the drill with his hand. And as a small boy I can remember hearing cries of anguish and pain, because the patient was not anaesthetised in any way.[22]

One by one, chemists' involvement in these supplementary occupations – at least in significant numbers – slowly died out, as each became regulated as a profession in its own right. But the tradition of combining work as a chemist with another trade or commercial activity in order to maintain the viability of a business continued, so that there are many examples of chemists' shops combined with tobacconists, off-licences, or post offices. Geoffrey Knowles, for example, owned a small private chemist's in a tough area of Ellesmere Port on Merseyside in the mid-1950s. He spotted an advertisement to provide the service when the local sub-post office closed. 'The one down the road was vacant, so I put in for it. I applied to Post Office headquarters in Liverpool. They did a cursory interview – as a pharmacist you were considered to be a safe bet.'[23] He was awarded the contract and used one side of the shop as a sub-post office. 'It was jolly hard work for what you got, but it enabled me to make a reasonable living, which I would not have done otherwise.'[24]

In more recent years, the trend has been to combine pharmacy with one or other of the complementary medicine occupations. Today, a number of pharmacists also practise herbal medicine, homeopathy, aromatherapy, and acupuncture. But such pharmacists are now the exception, while earlier in the century chemists with a secondary occupation were commonplace, as a result of practices largely established in the nineteenth century.

From home remedies to manufactured products

The largest part of chemists' non-dispensing business – certainly until the NHS Act of 1946 was implemented in 1948 – was the sale of home remedies, and of preparations made to their own formulae, such as mixtures to cure a cough, diarrhoea or indigestion. The availability of free medicines under the NHS impacted on the chemist's business in three main ways: the numbers of doctors' prescriptions being presented at chemists' shops increased dramatically; the numbers of private prescriptions written by doctors and presented at chemists' for dispensing diminished greatly; and the demand for over-the-counter medicines reduced, as patients could – at least initially – obtain whatever medicines they needed free of charge from the doctor. But this downward trend in the sale of proprietary medicines was short-lived, first as a result of the introduction of prescription charges in 1951, which discouraged at least some patients with minor ailments from visiting the doctor, and later as a result of the post-war increase in the advertising of proprietary medicines, particularly on television.[25]

Home remedies

Before the advent of the National Health Service, people would often have their own family remedies for a whole range of ailments.[26] Alan Kendall undertook his apprenticeship in a small chemists' shop in Shipley, Yorkshire in 1938:

> A lot of home recipes were brought in. In the winter time, the main one was three penny worth of chlorodyne, and three penny worth of liquorice. [This was] mixed together and made up into an eight ounce bottle. This was more or less Mist. Tuss. Nig. [black cough mixture] wasn't it? And then there would be variations on that. Things like 'All Fours', which was a combination of, I think, honey-seed oil, with tincture of opium, I believe, and peppermint oil, and possibly another of the aromatic oils, I am not sure. Paregoric [camphorated tincture of opium] often went with people asking for linseed as well, a mixture of ... they used to boil their own linseed up to make a mucilage from it, and then mix that with either paregoric or liquorice, or sometimes chlorodyne.[27]

The trade in home remedies clearly altered with the seasons, and the items requested were not always for medicinal purposes, as Alan Kendall recalls:

> Christmas time was the worst time of the year for these sort of things, because several times a day people would come in with their own pet recipe for ginger wine essence, which always had a slight variation on the amount of tincture of capsicum in it; also strong tincture of ginger and citric acid, and then some would want raspberry flavouring, and others would want lemon flavouring, and others would want orange flavouring. It was the bane of our lives as apprentices, because we always had to do this sort of thing, you see.[28]

Part of the seasonal variation was due to differences in the occurrence of particular minor ailments, such as coughs and colds. Alan Kendall continues:

> I can't remember what was needed during the summer months on these recipes, but everybody had their own pet remedy for colic. Colic was tincture of rhubarb and syrup of ginger, I think it was, which they used to take. Sweet nitre was also a popular thing (spirit ether net.) which we used to sell in winter time, because of people with a cold – a heavy cold – and they used to want to sweat it out, and so would take the sweet nitre in a hot drink.[29]

People used a wide range of home remedies, and some of the formulae were treated with great secrecy. They were often handed down from one generation to the next, occasionally even skipping a generation. Often the variation from a standard theme was quite minor, with perhaps something omitted or something extra added in order to change the colour or the taste, or perhaps even to reduce the cost.

However, not all the ingredients bought at the chemist's for a penny or tuppence were designed to be used in home remedies. Some were more concerned with folklore than folk medicine. Michael Peretz, who undertook his apprenticeship in Guernsey in the Channel Islands in the 1930s, recalls:

> The country cousins who would come in on a Saturday from the outlying districts of Guernsey would speak in patois – Guernsey patois – still in those days. They would speak English, but heavily accented English; and they had some pretty ancient ideas about medicine too, you know, they still believed to some extent in witchcraft, just to take one example. So that you would get requests for half an ounce of dragon's blood, and a small tiny bottle of quicksilver; which took me a long time to work out what all that was about. But apparently in the country districts, and I'm now talking about 1934/35, the girls would believe that throwing dragon's blood into the fire, and chucking quicksilver into the fire as well, they would see the face of their husband to be.[30]

Nostrums

Although home remedies remained popular until the introduction of the NHS in 1948, it was certainly much more common for the public to rely on the advice and expertise of the local chemist. For minor complaints, and sometimes more serious ones, they would present their symptoms at the pharmacy. Before the Second World War, patients would occasionally request an advertised product, but more often than not they would seek the advice of the pharmacist. John Cave, who was undertaking his apprenticeship in Guildford, Surrey, in 1936, recalls:

> Patients very seldom asked for a named preparation, unless it was Andrews Liver Salts, Beecham's Pills or something like that. . . . They would come in and say, 'I want something for my cough', and nine times out of ten we would make them up something special, because it did them a lot more good than if they bought something off the counter, or so they thought.[31]

Many pharmacists did good business in the sale of these 'nostrums', or preparations to their own formula, which would be labelled as their own brand. Nostrums were normally made up (usually by the apprentice) in batches of a few gallons at a time, packed and labelled ready for sale. But later changes in legislation eventually brought about the demise of the nostrum. Geoffrey Knowles managed his own pharmacy in Hoylake, on the Wirral, until he retired in 1984. He remembers:

> I continued to make a few nostrums until I retired. But new regulations had been brought in following the Medicines Act [1973], which made it more difficult. There were regulations about how you must label them – they had to be labelled in the dispensing manner rather than the commercial manner . . . and you were not allowed to keep any stock in hand. The Pharmaceutical Society Inspector rapped my knuckles once or twice because he saw a little stock waiting to be issued.[32]

Proprietary medicines

Although nostrums remained popular with the public, especially older people, until the 1970s, their place had largely been taken by heavily advertised branded products. A significant shift in the public's preference occurred in the early 1950s, as Christine Homan, who undertook her apprenticeship with Boots in Lambeth, London, recalls:

> Initially people came in asking for something for a cough, or whatever. The trend towards asking for branded products by name came towards the end of my two years with Boots [in 1954] . . . Gilbert Harding [TV personality] was advertising Macleans Indigestion Tablets on television. It started a trend for asking for named brands. People came in and started asking for 'Gilbert Harding Tablets'. Prior to that people were not really aware of brand names.[33]

Since the 1950s, the sales of proprietary over-the-counter medicines have risen steadily and consistently, eventually displacing both home remedies and chemists' nostrums.[34] The thirty-year period between the 1930s and the 1960s therefore witnessed the transfer of responsibility for the making of medicines, initially from the family to the chemist, and later from the chemist to the manufacturer. It has also witnessed the depersonalisation of the medicinal product, with the chemist no longer making something 'specially for them'.

At the same time the number of outlets for over-the-counter medicines has increased greatly, such that they are now to be found on the shelves of every supermarket. By 1995 the value of the over-the-counter medicine market in the UK, through both pharmacy and grocery sales, was over £1.25 billion.[35]

The sale of non-medicinal products

Throughout the century chemists have been involved in the sale of a wide variety of merchandise, much of which has had little to do with remedies or medicines. Many sold a range of chemicals and poisons for specific purposes. There were also many commodities for which, at least in the early part of the century, the pharmacist was virtually a monopoly supplier, but for which in the second half of the century specialist suppliers have taken over much of the market. Examples include photography, with developing and printing, where chemists were seen as the natural suppliers because of their scientific training (some even undertook developing and printing on the premises) and the supply of health foods and complementary medicines, with many chemists involved in the sale of herbal remedies. But as the market for these items increased, particularly after 1945, the chemist lost market share to specialist shops and suppliers, including specialist photographic shops, developing and printing shops, and specialist health food shops. Various attempts were made to restrict the range of merchandise which could be sold through chemists, with a view to raising the professional image of the pharmacy, but in each case these were defeated by the chain stores.

The sale of tobacco

The chemist's business has also changed in a number of ways as a result of changes in social attitudes to various substances, and of changes in their control through legislation. For example, at the beginning of the century many chemists were also tobacconists, selling a wide range of cigars, cigarettes and snuff. But the cigarette has moved, during the course of the twentieth century, from being seen as a product with potential health benefits to one perceived as a danger to health. At its meeting in March 1987, the Council of the Royal Pharmaceutical Society of Great Britain decided that 'members be informed that they should not sell tobacco or tobacco products, including cigarettes containing tobacco, from registered pharmacy premises'.[36]

By the early 1990s, however, chemists were presented with a new and profitable way of merchandising nicotine, packaged, not in the form of cigarettes, but as nicotine replacement therapy (NRT); this followed its change in legal status from being available only on prescription to being available for sale through pharmacies.[37] Alcohol also underwent a change of status. During the first half of the twentieth century many chemists obtained wine and spirit licences and sold not only alcoholic tonic wines, but also a wide range of wines and spirits. Chemists combined with off-licences continued until the 1980s.

In some parts of the country chemists with integral off-licences and tobacconists were seen as natural partners. In 1971, as a newly qualified pharmacist, Jennifer Andrews worked in such a shop owned by Barnsley Cooperative Society in Yorkshire. 'People would come in and ask for a bottle of Benylin [cough mixture] for my cough, and twenty Benson and Hedges [cigarettes], please, without seeing any connection between the two.'[38]

Complementary medicines

It was only later, with the Nuffield Report in 1986,[39] that the potential of the chemist as a source of health promotion was fully recognized, and initiatives to develop further the so-called 'extended role' were taken.[40] For some chemists the extended role has included greater involvement with alternative therapies. But what we now call complementary medicine was in fact part and parcel of the chemist's normal business earlier in the century. Even in the 1920s there were some chemists whose businesses involved the sale of significant amounts of herbal and homeopathic remedies. Rex Howarth undertook his apprenticeship in a small private chemist's in Bournemouth, Dorset, during the 1920s:

> I seem to remember that in the mid-1920s we had a full range of homeopathic remedies. They were common medicine in those days. My mother brought me up on homeopathic remedies – Belladonna, Aconite, Rhus tox. – I can remember all those things. And we had the full range, such as it was. I would imagine about 30 to 36 products, made by Ashton and Parson. And they were in a little tube in a small square long carton, and were six pence a time. And they were very commonly asked for. Homeopathy was quite acknowledged, and used in those days. You may also say that aromatherapy was, the number of essential oils we bought for this, that and the other. There was nothing new about it all, and it was the poor man's medicine – homeopathy.[41]

Generally speaking, however, homeopathic and other medicines which today we consider to be complementary medicine, usually just made up a small part of the chemist's business, as even in the early 1900s this demand was largely met by specialist homeopathic pharmacies.[42]

Promoting health in the community

We consider now some of the wider health issues traditionally addressed by the retail chemist prior to the introduction of the NHS in 1948: these included the use of the pharmacy as a first-aid station; advice on the care of children; and guidance on issues of sexual health. The use of hospital outpatient departments as the first port of call for poor patients before the days of free access to a general medical practitioner has been discussed elsewhere.[43] But chemists also played an important role as a source of medical advice and assistance, and people regularly used the local chemists as a first-aid station. Many chemists report a steady stream of butcher's boys with badly cut fingers, casualties from nearby road traffic accidents, and mothers bringing in young children with everything from cuts and bruises to bites and stings. Alan Kendall recalls working in a chemist's in Shipley, Yorkshire, around 1938:

> We did quite a lot of cuts and bruises. Treating minor injuries as well, and people with things in their eyes. You know, sort of dust in their eyes, that was a daily occurrence, several times a day, often. The streets nowadays must be very much better swept than they were in those days, because in my latter years in pharmacy it was rarely that anybody came in with anything in their eyes. But it was a daily occurrence in the 1930s for people to do that.[44]

Several pharmacists also recalled that casualties from nearby road traffic accidents were brought to the chemist's for immediate attention and to await the arrival of the ambulance.

Advice on the care of children

Chemists usually built their businesses around the needs of the local population. Where there were young families, chemists generally provided a wide range of baby requisites, and some even went as far as packing their own baby foods into tins. Most chemists supplied baby soothers (dummies), and many did a good business in teething powders, in gripe waters, and in ointments and creams for nappy rash. Many chemists also provided a baby weighing service, with mothers frequently coming into the shop every week to have their baby's weight checked, and carefully entered onto a card. Jack Maskew, who as an apprentice worked in a small pharmacy in the suburbs of Liverpool in 1943, remembers doing good business in baby weighing at a penny a time. 'People couldn't afford their own scales. The staff weighed the babies. [The scales] had a wicker basket and blanket; together they weighed two pounds. We also gave general advice.'[45]

There were other reasons why women might prefer visiting the chemist's rather than the welfare clinic. Clinics demanded that babies be undressed before being weighed; at the chemists mothers did not need to undress them.[46] By the 1950s most mothers were left to weigh their babies themselves. Peter Homan, who undertook his apprenticeship with Boots in Chelsea, recalls that even in 1960 'branches of Boots had blue and pink record cards which were left next to the weighing scales for the mothers to write down the weights. There was no charge, but they had a one penny weighing machine for adults as well.'[47]

Some even had baby scales which they rented out, for mothers to weigh their babies at home. Edith Spivack ran her own business in Kingsbury, North London, in the 1940s:

> Yes, I rented out baby scales, and I still today meet the babies that the mothers say 'Miss Spivack supplied the baby scales when you were born'. I still meet that today; the kids that are getting married. I had about six or eight sets of scales, and they'd have them for two or three months, and paid me so much a month for them. Bring them back, and they would go to somebody else. I did quite a big business in that. That brought on other baby business.[48]

Pharmacies were also major centres for the distribution of baby milk. Jack Maskew, talking about the pharmacy in Liverpool where he worked in 1944, remembers having a big turnover in National Dried Milk. 'They were big grey and blue tins of powdered milk. We were distribution agents for it, it was a wartime thing. People held vouchers for it. There was also National Orange Juice (concentrated), also Rose Hip Syrup in five ounce bottles.'[49]

Sometimes mothers would not have the money to pay for baby milk, and the pharmacist might be asked to supply it 'on account'. Reginald Scott-Wood undertook his apprenticeship in his father's shop in Nottingham during the mid-1930s. He recalled how mothers would obtain Glaxo baby food from the chemists' by pawning goods – usually pots and pans – and then coming in later in the week with the money once the husband had been paid.[50]

Sometimes the chemist was the only person mothers felt they could turn to for support and advice, particularly when their child fell ill. Often the assistance required went beyond the supply of thermometers and hot water bottles. Grace Goodman was undertaking her apprenticeship in a private chemist's in Bedford in 1942:

Another incident I remember was, a lady whose child –
a boy I think it was – was suspected as having TB, I think.
And the doctor told her to take his temperature every
morning, as part of the diagnosis I suppose, and she
couldn't read the thermometer. So every morning she
used to come in, having taken his temperature, and then
we had to read the thermometer! I mean, what happened
to it in the meantime, I don't know![51]

Guidance on matters of sexual health

Between the wars ignorance about sexual matters among newly
married couples was very common, and this meant that the
chemist in popular honeymoon spots, such as seaside resorts,
sometimes had to provide some basic lessons in sex education.
Ronald Crisp, as a newly qualified pharmacist in the early 1930s,
worked for a number of years in a chemist's shop in Torquay,
Devon:

In those days, I mean you had young couples come to you,
and they would walk past, up and down; and eventually
came in to find a man there, and they would ask him all
sorts of questions. I have advised – when I was a young
man – I have advised many a person about when they
have come down on honeymoon to Torquay, what to do.
Remarkable! Absolutely remarkable! People would come
down, and they didn't know what the devil it all meant![52]

Sometimes, requests would be received by the chemist for
materials which could be used to perform an illegal act, such as
abortion. Such requests presented considerable difficulties to pharmacists, particularly in those cases where the material concerned
might have equally legitimate alternative uses. This was certainly
the case with regard to Slippery Elm Bark, which had an entirely
legitimate use as a health food. The advice to members of the pharmacy profession from its professional body was perfectly clear. 'If
it is suspected, even on the most slender of evidence, that the pur-
chaser requires a particular substance for this purpose (i.e. to bring
about the miscarriage of any woman), then the only possible action
on the part of the seller is the refusal of the sale.'[53]
Evidence gathered in this study suggests that a great deal of
ingenuity went into the procurement of such agents, that a wide

range of materials were used for this purpose, and that chemists were only too willing to supply them. A woman would never, of course, request such an item on her own behalf. The messenger was sometimes a man, frequently a child, and occasionally an older woman. In some areas, such requests would be surprisingly frequent. As an apprentice in 1939, Brian Hebert worked in a small chemist's in a working-class part of Portsmouth, Hampshire:

> Oh yes, and I mean the big joke – well I don't know if it was much of a joke, but we thought it was funny at the time. Slippery Elm was the requested item, and of course we followed the Pharmaceutical Society's instructions of breaking it up into, I think it was described as less than two inch lengths then, but certainly short lengths. You break it all up, and sell it to the child. It was always a child who would come in for it. And, er, sure enough, within two minutes the child would be back and say 'mummy says have you got the bigger pieces?' and that was common place, quite common place. And then Penny Royal pills, and all the rest of it, were asked for.[54]

This level of unwanted pregnancy was, of course, a reflection of the level of ignorance at the time about sexual matters in general, and about contraception in particular.

Although the sheath (or French letters as they were generally known earlier in the century) was available, there were three major barriers to their regular use even when their existence was known about: first, they were expensive, costing two shillings and sixpence for three in the 1930s, compared with around £1 for three in the 1990s; second, they were never on display, so customers had to ask for them by name; and third, even if a customer had plucked up courage to ask for them, the disapproval of the proprietor would often be apparent. Jesse Boot's Methodist principles, for example, meant that the sheath could not be sold through any Boots' branch, supposedly to avoid embarrassing the staff, a policy which was reversed only in the 1960s. Peter Homan worked as a pharmacy manager for Boots in the early 1960s:

> Boots only sold contraceptive pessaries. There were not many requests for the sheath – most people seemed to know that Boots didn't sell them. But occasionally we would get requests. They would come in and say 'packet

of Durex please'. You would say 'sorry, we don't sell them'. They would ask 'why don't you sell them?' And we would say that the company doesn't allow us to sell them. 'Why's that then?' 'Because they feel it's embarrassing for the staff.' 'Well, it's a darn sight more embarrassing for the staff when I come in here and ask for them and they have to explain to me why they can't sell them' . . . that's the sort of reaction you would get. So [the policy] was a lot more embarrassing for the staff. At least [if you sold them] you could slip them into a bag and pass them over the counter; it is a lot less fuss than trying to explain why you couldn't sell them in the first place.[55]

Many independent pharmacists followed Boots' example in not getting involved in the supply of the sheath. As a result much of this business was lost to the local barber shops. Those chemists which did supply them did so very discreetly. Brian Hebert, working in a chemist's in Portsmouth in 1939, recalls the sale of French letters:

Oh, very, very, under the counter. Only the pharmacists sold them. I wasn't allowed to sell them [as an apprentice]. In fact, I was not shown where the Durex was kept. They were in a drawer. I discovered that because I could go anywhere I liked, but I discovered those on my own. That was rather like the whole conception of birth and everything between parents and their children. You sort of grew into the knowledge, and my apprentice master very much followed that. And no one sold Durex to the customers except the pharmacist. The customers would come in and say 'may I see Mr Elder, please?' or 'may I see the pharmacist?' Of course, every member of the staff knew exactly what they wanted, but that was the attitude. Very much under the counter.[56]

This attitude was reinforced by directions from the Pharmaceutical Society, which stated that where contraceptives were sold, only a small sign saying 'family planning requisites' could be displayed.[57]

The dispensing of prescriptions

The principal activities of the chemist, in terms of those to which he devotes most time, have changed considerably during the course of the twentieth century. In the early 1900s, chemists' businesses consisted largely of the sale of over-the-counter medicines, nostrums made to their own formulas, a few pennyworth of ingredients for home remedies, and packs of domestic necessities such as Epsom Salts and Glauber's Salts. They also carried out a wide range of supplementary activities, from the weighing of babies and the treatment of minor injuries to the putting down of small animals and the syringing of ears. The impact of the growth of the welfare state during the twentieth century on the chemist's livelihood was considerable, and it was also a double-edged sword: on the one hand, a number of activities traditionally undertaken by the chemist were now undertaken by the state: on the other hand, prescriptions written by doctors reached chemists' shops in substantial numbers, and represented an increasing proportion of their income.

Before the National Health Insurance Act of 1911, most chemists rarely saw a prescription written by a doctor as the bulk of dispensing was done by the doctors themselves.[58] The 1911 Act created the first legal distinction between the prescribing and dispensing of medicines; and it was Lloyd George himself, as the Minister of Health at the time, who was keen to separate the two

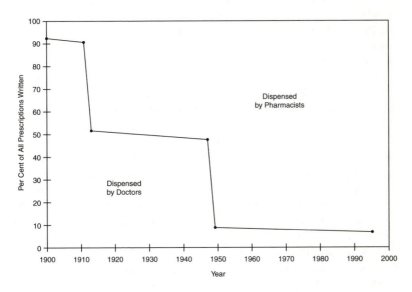

Figure 2.2 Proportion of all prescriptions written and dispensed by doctors and pharmacists, 1900–1995

functions between the medical and pharmaceutical professions.[59] Even at the time of the passing of the National Health Service Act in 1946, much of the dispensing was still done by doctors, many of whom employed dispensing assistants. Only with the NHS did the balance change in favour of the chemists; by 1948, when the NHS Act came into force, 94 per cent of the population were obtaining their medicines from registered pharmacies. In 1946, 23 per cent of prescriptions presented to chemists in England were for private patients (i.e. those able to pay directly the doctors for their consultations and the chemists for their medicines),[60] and in Scotland 65 per cent of prescriptions were private. After 1948, only 6 per cent of prescriptions were private.[61] The proportion of prescriptions written by doctors in Great Britain between 1900 and 1995, and dispensed, respectively, by doctors and by pharmacists, is shown in Figure 2.2.

Indeed, at the turn of the century it was only chemists in the big towns and cities – and to a lesser extent in seaside towns – who did much in the way of dispensing. Prescription numbers did increase substantially following implementation of the 1911 NHI Act, from around 20 million a year in 1910 to around 50 million by 1920.[62] But it was only after implementation of the NHS Act of 1946 that the dispensing of prescriptions came to dominate the working day of the chemist. Between 1946 and 1949, the number of prescriptions dispensed in England increased almost fourfold, from nearly 70 million a year to over 240 million. These trends are illustrated in Figure 2.3.

When the NHS was introduced in 1948 the majority of prescriptions still needed to be made up individually, resulting in the preparation of large numbers of mixtures, ointments, creams, lotions and so on. These tasks were undertaken with great skill and pride, and once finished the product would be wrapped carefully and sealed with red sealing wax. The result of this enormous increase in dispensing was that the chemist migrated almost overnight from the front of his shop to the back – a situation which the pharmaceutical profession is even now still trying to reverse. The enlargement of dispensaries, the appointment of dispensing assistants, and competition for many areas of the chemists' traditional business all reinforced perceptions of the chemist as little more than a dispenser of prescriptions during the 1950s and 1960s. The impact of these changes has been discussed more fully elsewhere.[63]

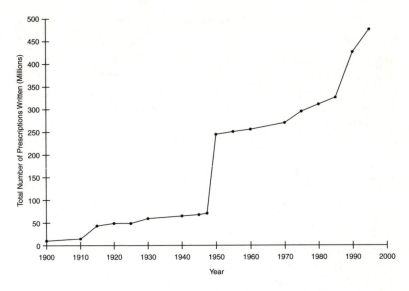

Figure 2.3 Number of prescriptions written by doctors in Great Britain, 1900–1995

Conclusion

In this chapter we have attempted to illustrate some of the wide range of health and welfare activities with which chemists have been involved during the course of the twentieth century. The changing role of the chemist has reflected changes in society as a whole, particularly the growth of the welfare state, and especially the enormous increase in prescription numbers which followed introduction of the NHS in 1948. Their role in sexual health, for example, has extended during the course of the twentieth century from the sale of abortifacients and aphrodisiacs to the supply of the Pill and to pregnancy testing. In tobacco use, the role has changed from the supply of cigarettes and tobacco in the first half of the century, to providing support for those who wish to stop smoking in the second. At the same time, the sale of opiate-based medicines has given way to the provision of needles and syringes to drug misusers.

Change

The evidence presented in this chapter suggests themes around two main axes: boundaries and time periods. The boundary changes revolve around occupational differentiation (secondary occupations as dentists and opticians); around self-help and commercialisation (home remedies versus proprietary medicines); and around relationships with medical practice (the division of labour between prescribing and dispensing). Three periods of change are suggested by the evidence: the period between 1911 and 1920, during which the National Health Insurance Act (1911), the Dangerous Drugs Act (1920), and the Dental Act (1920), were enacted, and major changes occurred in the supply of proprietary medicines as a result of investigations by the BMA;[64] the introduction of the NHS in 1948, resulting in the almost fourfold increase in the number of prescriptions reaching chemists' shops; and a period from 1948 until the 1970s during which chemists were preoccupied with the dispensing of prescriptions and largely invisible to the public, while slowly losing many of their traditional areas of trade.

Continuity

But although much has changed during the course of the twentieth century, some things have stayed the same. The local chemist has remained a readily accessible source of health advice and support. Such assistance has been available during normal shopping hours, with no appointment necessary; the advice has been available without charge, and where medication has been recommended, low-cost medicines have generally been available. The oral history of health professionals provides us with a unique opportunity to discover what individual practitioners, usually working alone and often in professional isolation, actually did, what goods and services they provided to their local communities, and what their contribution to health and welfare has been. In this chapter we have shown that chemists have made a significant contribution, not only by the dispensing of medicines and the giving of a wide range of health advice, but in the provision of a variety of health and welfare services in the community. The chemist has played a key part in mediating at the boundary between professional and lay care.

The future

Today, promotion of the pharmacy as the 'first port of call' for health services, and encouragement of the public to 'ask the pharmacist' in relation to minor ailments, all represent at least a partial return of pharmacists to their historic role in the community. These changes, promoted and supported by the profession, have been facilitated by a series of policy documents and the freeing up of controls on medicines.

But such developments have resulted in a number of innovations which directly impinge on the role of the chemist, such as nurse prescribing and the emergence of the nurse practitioner.

The loss of retail price maintenance on proprietary medicines, and their sale from supermarkets at substantial discounts, will further erode traditional areas of the chemists' business. The outcome is likely to be the closure of a number of pharmacies, particularly in areas where the business is already marginal; and yet further reliance on the dispensing of state prescriptions by those pharmacies which remain. The early part of the twenty-first century seems likely to see the rapid growth of pharmacies in supermarkets, accompanied by the steady dominance of chemists' chain stores on high streets and in shopping malls. Traditional independent proprietor chemists, providing an important and valued service in the community where they live and work, seem likely to follow the ranks of other small shopkeepers, and disappear from the local shopping parade. But the new corporate pharmacy will be tailored to meet the increasing demands of the public for advice on self treatment and for a wide range of services. The chemist of the twenty-first century may resemble the chemist of the twentieth century rather more closely than might be expected.

Acknowledgements

The oral history of British community pharmacy practice study was supported by a project grant from The Wellcome Trust, awarded to Professor Klim McPherson and Professor Virginia Berridge at the London School of Hygiene and Tropical Medicine. All quotations are taken from interviews recorded by Stuart Anderson during 1995. The assistance of Miss Helga Mangion in the compilation of the figures is gratefully acknowledged. Much helpful advice from the editors is also gratefully acknowledged.

Notes

1 The words 'pharmacist' and 'pharmacy' came into common usage only after the Second World War. In this chapter we use the word 'chemist' to denote a pharmaceutical chemist or pharmacist, and the word 'chemist's' to describe the retail premises where they practised.

2 In 1920 only 7 per cent of the names on the pharmaceutical register were those of women: this had risen to over 15 per cent by 1941, and to 18 per cent in 1953. By 1964 it had reached 26 per cent, and by 1984 it was 36 per cent (S.W.F. Holloway, *The Royal Pharmaceutical Society of Great Britain 1841–1991: A Political and Social History*, London, The Pharmaceutical Press, 1991, p. 268).

3 Ibid., p. 345.

4 The study involved recorded life story interviews with 50 retired retail pharmaceutical chemists, representing a variety of location (from inner city to rural), of ownership (from independent proprietors to large companies), and of customers (from the very poor to the very rich); eleven participants were women, and the sample included representatives of the Jewish, Polish and Asian communities, from England, Scotland and Wales. Quotations are used and interviewees are identified by kind permission.

5 J. Grier, *A History of Pharmacy*, London, The Pharmaceutical Press, 1937; L.G. Matthews, *History of Pharmacy in Britain*, London, E. & S. Livingstone Limited, 1962; Holloway, *The Royal Pharmaceutical Society*.

6 J.K. Crellin, 'Pharmaceutical History – The Growth of Professionalism in the Nineteenth Century', *Medical History*, 1967, vol. 11, pp. 215–227.

7 J. Burnby, 'The Professionalisation of British Pharmacy', *Pharmaceutical Historian*, 1988, vol. 18, pp. 3–5.

8 G.V. Larkin, *Occupational Monopoly and Modern Medicine*, London, Tavistock, 1983.

9 Ibid.

10 C. Hillam, 'Pestle and Forceps: The Pharmaceutical Dentist of the Nineteenth Century', *Pharmaceutical Historian*, 1988, vol. 18, pp. 2–3.

11 Editorial, 'Chemist-Dentists', *Forceps*, 1844, vol. 1, pp. 74–75.

12 R. Ross, 'Chemist-Dentists', *Dental Historian*, 1995, vol. 3, pp. 31–45.

13 Holloway, *The Royal Pharmaceutical Society*, p. 261.

14 Interview with Mr Basil Trasler (retired pharmacist from Northampton, born on 13.5.22) recorded on 8.8.95 (Pharmacy In Practice PIP/03), 2B, 107–125.

15 Interview with Mr Basil Trasler, ibid., 2B, 125–153.

16 Interview with Mr Basil Trasler, ibid., 2B, 153–164.

17 Interview with Mr Basil Trasler, ibid., 2B, 164–171.

18 Interview with Mr Alan Garrett (retired pharmacist from Enfield, Middlesex, born on 27.6.11) recorded on 16.6.95 (Pharmacy In Practice PIP/05), 1B, 355–368.

19 Interview with Mr Alan Dickman (retired pharmacist from Berkhamsted, Herts, born on 15.5.15) recorded on 13.10.95 (Pharmacy In Practice PIP/34), 1B, 150–163.

20 Interview with Mr Alan Garrett, op. cit., 1B, 368–384.

21 J.G.L. Burnby and F. Rawlings, 'Pharmaceutical Dentists', *Dental Historian*, 1994, vol. 27, p. 16.

22 Interview with Mr Ronald Benz (retired pharmacist from Eastbourne, East Sussex, born on 17.6.10) recorded on 2.8.95 (Pharmacy In Practice PIP/18), 1A, 39–48.

23 Interview with Mr Geoffrey Knowles (retired pharmacist from Hoylake, Wirral, born on 10.12.19) recorded on 17.10.95 (Pharmacy In Practice PIP/36), 2A, 290–296.

24 Interview with Mr Geoffrey Knowles, ibid., 2A, 297–304.

25 C. Fitzsimon, 'The PAGB and the Regulation of Advertising', *Proprietary Medicines Supplement to the Pharmaceutical Journal*, 1994, vol. 252, pp. M7–M11.

26 V.S. Berridge, 'Opium and the People', *Oral History*, 1979, vol. 7, pp. 48–58.

27 Interview with Mr Alan Kendall (retired pharmacist from Stockton on Tees, Teesside, born on 16.2.20) recorded on 5.12.95 (Pharmacy In Practice PIP/48), 1B, 78–92.

28 Interview with Mr Alan Kendall, ibid., 1B, 119–131.

29 Interview with Mr Alan Kendall, ibid., 1B, 132–145.

30 Interview with Mr Michael Peretz (retired pharmacist from Chichester, West Sussex, born on 17.11.16) recorded on 29.6.95 (Pharmacy In Practice PIP/07, 2A, 1–41.

31 Interview with Mr John Cave (retired pharmacist from Harlow, Essex, born on 14.5.19) recorded on 6.7.95 (Pharmacy In Practice PIP/10), 1B, 178–194.

32 Interview with Mr Geoffrey Knowles, op. cit., 2A, 141–163.

33 Interview with Mrs Christine Homan (retired pharmacist from Epsom, Surrey, born on 17.3.38) recorded on 24.11.95 (Pharmacy In Practice PIP/46), 2A, 76–92.

34 C. Fitzsimon, 'The PAGB and the Regulation of Advertising', 1994, op. cit., pp. M7–M11.

35 *Annual Report 1998*, Proprietary Association of Great Britain, London, PAGB, 1998, p. 20.

36 *Medicines, Ethics and Practice – A Guide for Pharmacists*, London, Royal Pharmaceutical Society of Great Britain, 1989, no. 3, p. 91.

37 P. Mason, 'Action on Smoking – Can Pharmacists Make a Difference?', *Pharmaceutical Journal*, 1996, vol. 256, pp. 263–265.

38 Interview with Mrs Jennifer Andrews (practising pharmacist from Peterborough, Cambridgeshire, born on 22.10.47) recorded on 6.9.95 (Pharmacy In Practice PIP/25), 1B, 281–295.

39 *Pharmacy: A Report to the Nuffield Foundation*, London, The Nuffield Foundation, 1986.

40 *Pharmaceutical Care: The Future for Community Pharmacy*, London, The Royal Pharmaceutical Society of Great Britain, 1992.

41 Interview with Mr Rex Howarth (retired pharmacist from Southbourne, Dorset, born on 13.10.10) recorded on 6.10.95 (Pharmacy In Practice PIP/32), 2A, 289–308.

42 I.F. Jones, 'Community Pharmacy and The National Health Service', *Supplement to the Pharmaceutical Journal*, 1998, vol. 261, pp. NHS24–27.

43 I. Loudon, *Medical Care and the General Practitioner, 1750–1850*, Oxford, Clarendon, 1986.

44 Interview with Mr Alan Kendall, op. cit., 2A, 48–63.

45 Interview with Mr Jack Maskew (retired pharmacist from Liverpool, born on 21.4.26) recorded on 20.10.95 (Pharmacy In Practice PIP/39), 2A, 69–84.
46 V.A. Fildes, L. Marks and H. Marland (eds), *Women and Children First: International Maternal and Infant Welfare*, London, Routledge, 1992.
47 Interview with Mr Peter Homan (retired pharmacist from Epsom, Surrey, born on 2.9.38) recorded on 30.6.95 (Pharmacy In Practice PIP/08), 1B, 352–367.
48 Interview with Miss Edith Spivack (retired pharmacist from Hendon, North London, born on 21.1.11) recorded on 29.8.95 (Pharmacy In Practice PIP/22), 3B, 50–68.
49 Interview with Mr Jack Maskew, op. cit., 2B, 134–148.
50 Interview with Mr Reginald Scott Wood (retired pharmacist from Reigate, Surrey, born on 19.9.08) recorded on 12.1.98 (Pharmacy in Practice PIP/13), 2A, 243–256.
51 Interview with Mrs Grace Goodman (retired pharmacist from Canterbury, Kent, born on 5.12.25) recorded on 12.10.95 (Pharmacy In Practice PIP/33), 3A, 57–72.
52 Interview with Mr Ronald Crisp (retired pharmacist from Exeter, Devon, born on 24.4.14) recorded on 4.8.95 (Pharmacy In Practice PIP/19), 1A, 119–136.
53 M. Delevigne, *Pharmacy Law*, London, Pharmaceutical Press, 1936.
54 Interview with Mr Brian Hebert (retired pharmacist from Bletchingley, Surrey, born on 1.11.19) recorded on 1.9.95 (Pharmacy In Practice PIP/23), 1B, 147–163.
55 Interview with Mr Peter Homan, op. cit., 1B, 368–381.
56 Interview with Mr Brian Hebert, op. cit., 2A, 345–357.
57 J.R. Dale and G.E. Applebe, *Pharmacy Law and Ethics*, London, Pharmaceutical Press, Fourth Edition, 1989.
58 J. Anderson-Stewart, 'Jubilee of the National Insurance Act', *Pharmaceutical Journal*, 1962, vol. 189, pp. 33–35.
59 Holloway, *The Royal Pharmaceutical Society*, p. 342.
60 Before 1948 free medical services were available under the National Health Insurance Act only to working men earning less than an income limit, which was increased to £420 per year in 1942. By 1946, 24 million workers were covered, representing about half the British population. For non-hospital care their dependants usually relied on self-help or lay care, although some belonged to clubs into which they paid a small amount each week and had their doctors' bills paid when necessary.
61 Holloway, *The Royal Pharmaceutical Society*, p. 261.
62 Ibid., p. 342.
63 For a more detailed account of these changes see S.C. Anderson, 'Community Pharmacy in Great Britain: Mediation at the Boundary Between Professional and Lay Care 1920 to 1995', in T. Tansey and M. Gijswijt-Hofstra (eds), *Remedies and Healing Cultures in Britain and the Netherlands in the Twentieth Century*, Amsterdam, Rodopi Press, in press.
64 *Secret Remedies: What they Cost and what they Contain*, London, British Medical Association, 1909. *More Secret Remedies: What they Cost and what they Contain*, London, British Medical Association, 1912.

3

RECOLLECTIONS OF THE PIONEERS OF THE GERIATRIC MEDICINE SPECIALTY

Margot Jefferys

It fell into two classes. There were those who said: 'This
is what we need. I'm glad you're doing something about
it' and others who said: 'There's no such thing as
geriatrics. Talking nonsense of rehabilitation.'[1]

In Britain, formal recognition of the need for a medical specialty
in the care and treatment of older people came in the decade
after the Second World War. However, the decision to provide
consultant posts in geriatric medicine was not taken without some
controversy and opposition, and the British example, in the main,
has not been followed elsewhere. This chapter draws on a selection
of interviews which were carried out with more than 70 men and
women who pioneered geriatric medicine in the early years of the
National Health Service.

I begin with a brief description of the organisation of medical
care of older people in the pre- and post-war period and then go
on to sketch in the social and medical backgrounds of the interviewees and what led them to gravitate towards care of elderly
people. I then consider their accounts of the kind of medical care
which hospitalised older people could expect to receive in the
1940s and 1950s. Next I describe the impact which the pioneering
work of Marjory Warren, generally acknowledged as the major
innovator in the field, had on them and on the development of
a medical specialism concerned with treating older people. The
interviewees' accounts of the reactions of physicians and others

not engaged in geriatric medicine to that development follows. My final section deals with some of their comments on the impact of the development of which they were a part on the present and future medical care of older people.

The context of medical care for older people

At the start of the National Health Service in 1948 medical care provision for older people was operating within a particular historical context. Hospitals divided into two types, predominantly. By the end of the 1930s the voluntary hospitals were admitting almost exclusively those patients who needed acute medical or surgical treatment. Those who were viewed as chronically sick or incurable, as well as those with highly infectious diseases, were deliberately excluded. Those labelled 'chronic sick' were mainly cared for in large local authority hospitals which, until 1929, had been the poor law infirmaries. The majority of the 'chronic sick' were poorer old people. Younger people tended to be allocated to local authority fever hospitals or to tuberculosis hospitals.

The predominant view, one shared by the public as well as the majority of the medical profession – most of whom would have been trained in the high prestige voluntary hospitals – was that sickness in old age could not be cured or treated. Care was characterised by what later came to be described as 'warehousing'.[2] As I have described it elsewhere, 'the pre-1948 legacy . . . has resulted in a predominantly segregated service where old, frail individuals could at best expect benign guardianship until they died rather than active treatment aimed at their ultimate discharge'.[3]

The situation was confronted by two people, Marjory Warren and Lionel Cosin, who challenged these segregating and denying practices. Both were superintendents of poor law infirmaries where they had medical responsibility for chronically sick patients. They initiated treatment regimes for elderly patients which, astonishingly innovative at the time, involved a thorough medical examination and diagnosis with a programme of rehabilitative activities. By monitoring these interventions they were able to show that patients could recover some of their physical and mental capacities. Moreover, many regained an interest in their own personal hygiene and appearance and took an interest in once again managing tasks of daily living. Some were able to return home, while others became fit enough to go into residential care where medical care was not provided.

There were class as well as age implications to be drawn from such findings. Warren and Cosin went on to argue against pre-NHS practices which segregated older people, in particular lower-class older people, from active medical treatment. They could show that medical interventions in old age were justifiable. The early geriatricians therefore aimed to bring the medical care of older people into the general hospitals. In doing so they were combating the ageism of the medical profession as well as dealing with the fears of older people who had seen their own parents die in hospitals where no treatment had been available. Warren and Cosin argued for the appointment of consultants who would have specific responsibility for geriatric medicine. Debates about how exactly responsibilities should be worded run through the proceedings of the annual conferences of the Medical Society for the Care of the Elderly which was founded in 1947 (in 1959 this became the British Geriatric Society). In general the outcome was that two routes into the geriatric specialism emerged. In some cases Regional Health Authorities (RHAs) appointed general physicians with a special interest to district general hospitals which had originated in the voluntary sector. Other RHAs gave consultant status in geriatric medicine to those who had been medical superintendents of old poor law infirmaries, hospitals which had always been in the public sector.

The brief account I have just outlined draws in part from accounts provided by the pioneer geriatricians we interviewed. This is a story of a specialty which has struggled for recognition, against both medical and social prejudices. In telling their stories, many of our interviewees were recalling their own awakening as well as a life of professional campaigning against inequality and exclusion in health care provision.

The interviewees: social and medical backgrounds

In searching for interviewees we[4] were conscious of the fact that we would be looking for people who were already in retirement, members of a relatively low status specialism, some of whom might have worked in obscurity, only a minority of whom would be better known. We started work in 1989 searching the relevant medical and social policy journals of the period immediately before and after the Second World War. We examined the records of the British Geriatric Society (BGS) and its predecessor, the

Medical Society for the Care of the Elderly, as well as official documents lodged at the Public Record Office. The BGS records were particularly helpful because they contained a so-called 'Hall of Fame' file. This included biographical details of many past and present members of the Society and we used it to compile a list of those geriatricians whom we intended to ask for interviews. To this we added a number of medically qualified individuals who had questioned in print the wisdom of developing a new medical specialty. We also decided to approach one or two politicians who had important decision-making roles in the early days of the specialty as well as a senior medical civil servant whom we knew had played an important role in promoting it. We also included a few nurses, social workers and therapists who had played a prominent part in the early years of the developing specialty.

In all, during 1991, we interviewed 72 people.[5] In writing this account, I am using 23 of the transcripts of the interviews. The individuals concerned can be regarded as survivors of the earliest cohort of geriatric consultants. They were born before 1921, qualified just before or during the Second World War and obtained consultant posts in geriatric medicine in the 1940s, 1950s and early 1960s.

They all were recognised by their peers then, or by their successors subsequently, as having made a significant contribution to the developing specialty. Of course, since they are the survivors of a much larger number of pioneers, we cannot claim that their experiences and views were representative of the entire first generation. Nor can we overcome the possible distortions which partial memory and hindsight combined may give to their recollection of events and motivations. We were impressed, however, by the general consistency of their accounts of the medical arrangements which existed in the early years of the NHS, of the respect which those working with older people and their patients could expect from fellow doctors and the public, and of the steps which were taken to establish the legitimacy of the new specialty. Background information as to their family origins and early experience of work as doctors provides some helpful clues as to the status of medical care of older people and of the professional hierarchy within which the geriatric specialty developed.

Of the 23 whose accounts I draw on here, six were born and qualified in Scotland, three in Northern Ireland, and three overseas, the last requalifying in this country after he had fled from Nazi Germany in the 1930s. Of the remainder, one was a

Mancunian and another a Yorkshire man, qualifying respectively at Manchester and Leeds. Two were Londoners and the rest were born in various places in the midlands and south of England.

In the absence of information about the generation of newly qualified doctors to whom they belonged, it is equally difficult to discern any particular social or personality characteristics which marked them out from their medical contemporaries. Impressionistically, however, there may well have been fewer among them whose fathers were doctors (only one in this sample; see also Michael Bevan's chapter in this book) and fewer too whose parents were well-to-do business people or members of the learned professions. Several had teachers as parents, and others, shopkeepers. No-one's father was a manual worker. All of those brought up in the UK went to grammar-type secondary schools, either as fee-paying pupils or on state scholarships.

All had parents who were ambitious for them, wanted them to have 'a career' and 'security'. One, for example, talked about his father as 'a frustrated doctor' and many mentioned a relative – a cousin or uncle – who had been a doctor, dentist or pharmacist, as having played a part in steering them towards a career in medicine. Only one spontaneously mentioned religious belief or values inculcated during childhood as being important in the choice of medicine as a career.

What was fairly clear from all the interviews was that hardly any of our 23 interviewees had developed a strong inclination to enter a specific branch of medicine or surgery by the end of their medical training. This was understandable for those who qualified just before or during the Second World War. Several had ambitions to become surgeons. They knew, for the most part, however, that they had to join the forces and hence had to postpone any decision as to their future career in civilian life. But even those who had qualified well before 1939 seem to have drifted rather aimlessly after their initial posts as dressers in hospital or assistants to general practitioners, rather than follow certain well-defined objectives.

One Londoner with ambitions to become a surgeon began on such a career in the mid-1930s, but found the competition too fierce. He joined a doctor in general practice as an assistant, and stayed there until he was recruited to join a surgical team in a suburban London municipal hospital (erstwhile poor law infirmary). This had emptied all but two of its many wards of long-stay chronically sick patients and a maternity unit in order to accommodate expected military casualties. In the event, after a flurry of military admissions following the Dunkirk evacuation in 1940, most of the casualties it received in the next few years were East End Londoners, victims of the Blitz. His own duties in the hospital, largely self-determined it seems, became more and more administrative and by 1944 he had been appointed medical superintendent of the hospital and began to turn his clinical gaze (to coin a phrase) on the occupants of the long-stay wards.

Only one other of our interviewees had a pre-war or war-time experience of working in the non-voluntary hospital sector. To work in a municipal hospital was almost the equivalent of working with patients labelled chronically sick, the majority of whom were elderly. On the appointed day – 20 July 1948 – at the start of the NHS, both these men were medical superintendents and in the course of time were given the new status of consultant physicians.

The six Scots among them had all held posts in local authority hospitals either before or after the appointed day. Given the distribution of patients between voluntary and municipal hospitals, this inevitably exposed them to older patients so frequently labelled, whatever the overt reason for their initial admission, as chronically sick. It seems that they were less likely than their English counterparts to consider such posts as evidence, if not of failure, at least of second-class status.

Impressionistically again, the three Ulster men among our interviewees seemed less conscious than the English of the symbolic status of different specialties. Our three immigrants, on the other hand, indicated that they were aware of the prevailing pecking order; but the effect on them was perhaps to persuade themselves that, as incomers, they were more likely to succeed and make a mark in their adoptive country in a field which was not too competitive.

Among the English – other than the two who had backgrounds as medical superintendents – the typical progression seemed to be from a recognition that they were likely to find it a hard struggle to obtain a consultantship in a preferred medical specialty (cardiology and general medicine were each mentioned more than once) and did not want to become general practitioners, to a realisation that they stood a good chance of advancement in a field where the need for medical concern was becoming recognised but the response from the profession itself was muted.

Medical provision for older people: accounts from the interviews

With the backgrounds just described, the interviewees provide insights into the nature of medical provision from the period before the war and afterwards during the early years of the NHS.

Comparatively few of our interviewees had worked in wards for the chronic sick before the Second World War. I was somewhat surprised, however, that the comments of those who had done so painted a reasonably favourable picture of what they found as did those whose first experience was during or immediately after the war.

It seems that part of the legacy of the poor law infirmaries – since 1929 re-designated as local authority public health institutions – was a benign paternalism. At least that is an impression that I got from our interviewees – two out of the four, let it be noted, coming from north of the border:

> In those days, Glasgow had a very good service for the elderly, which incidentally was abolished when the NHS came out. It had public health clinics and it had full-time doctors attached to them. Their reputation was varied but most of them were kindly in the extreme and one or two of them were excellent. Anyway, in Glasgow if somebody was in a model lodging house, which we had plenty of in those days, there was a duty on the keeper if the man was ill and he had the power pretty well to get them in within 48 hours because the corporation hospitals were very well run.[6]

From the midlands, another commented:

> Well the staff at the institutions were all resident, all the doctors were resident and the lay staff – clerks – were all resident, the labour masters, so-called, who would look after the able-bodied, were all residents. So living in the place they had their own snooker team. I played football every Saturday, but the thing is they knew the patients so that the question of the personal knowledge of the patients was possibly more in those days than later when all the resident posts went by the board.[7]

It was with some insight, therefore, that one informant suggested:

So without our workhouses and municipal hospitals, which were also based originally on workhouses, I don't think we could have set up this sort of system.[8]

A more expected response came from another informant who had worked in London:

> In some hospitals the young chronic sick were all amongst the elderly patients. But the LCC had grouped them all together because they had such a lot. A lot of them were treating the hospital as a hotel really.[9]

While the structure of provision tended to be recalled in positive terms, the quality of care and of access to medical treatment was less glowingly recalled. For several of the sample their first exposure to the chronic sick wards of erstwhile poor law infirmaries was during or immediately after the war when the old workhouse system had been taken over and the early years of the NHS were bringing changes possibly rather too rapidly. One, for example, told us that, while still a medical student:

> They shoved me in charge of what they called the 'chronic sick' wards. These were mostly fairly elderly people, not always because some had MS and were younger, but they were people about whom they said: 'We can do no more for him or her – she's just got to exist here until she dies.' So I saw rank upon rank of chronic sick wards in East London with people lying in bed all the time. They never had day rooms, they had occasionally a chair beside the bed, they had minimal medical facilities and they were just waiting for the end. Absolutely nothing going on and no comfort and no activities and no physiotherapy and nothing of that sort.[10]

Another described his experience in Leeds:

> At St James, which was a municipal hospital before the NHS came in, with a large department – I can only describe it as for 'derelict' people. Nobody knew what to do with them – old people, incapacitated people.[11]

Another had his first experience in Enfield:

I went to this chronic sick ward in the long-stay section of the hospital and when I got there I found the most remarkable place. There were all sorts of people for all sorts of reasons: some of them needed to be there, some didn't, none of them had been properly diagnosed and very few had any, any form of meaningful treatment.[12]

Yet another, when asked if he witnessed neglect, replied:

Not exactly left without treatment, no. It's without, shall we say, too active an approach towards rehabilitation. They were all well treated; there was no neglect in that sense.[13]

One graphic picture was drawn by a Mancunian:

Well old people were not treated: if you were old you were regarded as sick, and if you were sick and old you were to be nursed.[14]

The pressure for change began in the post-war years, but those early advocates who were appointed as consultants in the first post-NHS decade described the conditions they had to confront. Their accounts were graphic, as were the steps they took to try to improve and innovate:

No patient was ever out of bed and the first thing I had to do was to convince one nursing sister that people could get out of bed. . . . And from then on people got better. When people were taken out of the so-called chronic sick wards and given active treatment they could be discharged.[15]

Another, in outer London told how:

It was an infirmary ward and was really typical of all that was wrong with the care of the elderly in those days. When I went, there were 200 beds stuffed into every nook and cranny in two buildings. Beds were absolutely close together, you could hardly get between them. There were masses of cot-side beds with people lying between the sides like cages. The bedpans were washed in the bath.[16]

At Crumpsall in Manchester an informant described conditions in 1952, when:

> One set that had come were all chipped bedpans which had been condemned as of no further use from the so-called acute wards in the other part of the hospital.[17]

The most detailed and graphic account came from the consultant appointed to a Bradford hospital in 1953:

> So I had to look after these 750 patients in seven hospitals single-handed. When I went round they had absolutely no notes. They had a sort of card on which was written particulars for identification, and what their father had been and what their religion was, but as for medical notes there was nothing at all.
>
> And these chronic sick wards, so called, were of a very tumble-down nature. Three of them were single-storey buildings made of match-boarding. And they had four ranks of patients, 48 patients per ward, anyway, down each side of the ward near the windows, and then in the middle there were two ranks head to head all the way down the middle. The light wasn't good, the plumbing was absolutely deplorable and the roofs leaked. . . . And before I got there they said, 'There's a new physician coming, he'll want good, sound, safe beds.' So they equipped two of the four wards with deep cot-sided metal bedsteads like children's cots only 6 feet 6 inches long with high sides which clattered as you put them up and down and they imagined that I was going to keep my patients in these for ever! And they said 'They'll at least be safe!' Well, this really wasn't good enough particularly since the temperature in the ward – I suppose this was mid-winter – had fallen to something like 35 degrees F. And one patient died that night, and it so happened that the young house physician I had helping me had been a paratrooper and was a tough egg, and said, 'I'm going to certify this case as dying of neglect.' So I said, 'Hang on a minute' and rang the secretary of the Bradford A group and said 'We've got a case here which is going to be certified as dying of neglect.' He said 'Oh my God, stop him doing that! Give me ten minutes and I'll be back to you.' So ten minutes later I

was rung up by the Chairman of the Group saying 'It'll be dreadful for the reputation of the Group if this man is certified as having died of neglect. Can't you stop that?' And I said 'I might be able to persuade this young man, but my conditions for doing so are that you put men on the roof and make it watertight, that you put a steam heating pipe up and down the ward and that you do so in the next 24 hours.' And he said 'Right doctor, I will do that.' And he did. But this was sheer blackmail and we had quite often to use these sorts of methods to get proper care, basic care, even temperature and leaking roofs for elderly people in those days.[18]

From another interviewee we learned that it was not only older patients who were treated as second-class citizens. The new geriatricians themselves did not get VIP treatment:

So I came here in '51, and was given a little back bedroom in the Corporation Hospital with a kitchen table, a rickety chair and a single-bar electric stove which didn't throw out much heat, although I didn't need it because I was above the kitchen and the smell of stale cabbage was terrible. . . . Everything was old, old rubbishy beds, everything, and the staff – I don't know where they found them. Any odd-bods they took on.[19]

That was a Scot speaking, and another was sure that initially the NHS brought no improvement in that country:

There had been a large number of beds in the Poor Houses (Workhouse in England and Wales), with no bad medical attention, but you must remember that, by that time, the Public Health clinics had been abolished because the NHS was coming in and the district medical officers were abolished too. So, initially, all the hospitals became acute hospitals and wanted acute patients and the old people went into a trough of despond because nobody wanted them.[20]

An informant from Liverpool made the point that a good deal of the pressure to admit older people to long-stay wards came from relatives, not from consultants with beds in acute wards:

The waiting list at this time was between 300 and 400 and sometimes rose to 500. Nevertheless admission was obtained usually by means of pressure from the GP or other sources such as frequent phone calls. . . . The patients who came in first were those who had the largest families, because they were the ones who could phone most frequently, whereas the elderly people living alone were the ones who died on the waiting list. . . . The hospital was very much a 'cinderella' hospital. It was a dumping ground. If they became too much trouble they'd be dumped in the hospital![21]

Marjory Warren: geriatric specialist pioneer

The development of geriatric medicine as a specialism is generally agreed to have been inspired and led by one woman, Marjory Warren (1897–1960),[22] who began her pioneering work in the 1930s when she became Deputy Medical Superintendent at the West Middlesex County Hospital. She was supported by Lord Amulree, a hereditary peer who, acting first as a professional civil servant in the Ministry of Health and later as a consultant at University College Hospital London, linked a small but growing band of practitioners and advocates. Revolutionising the care of older hospitalised patients was already being seen as a feasible objective for the NHS on vesting day in 1948. The interview data provide interesting and illuminating insights into Marjory Warren's campaigning style and her qualities as a colleague and leader, recollected some 40 years on.

All the interviewees were asked whether they had known Marjory Warren and if so what sort of a person she had seemed to them. Ten of our 23 pioneers gave us vivid accounts of someone who, by any standards, must be regarded as a charismatic personality.

Only one of the ten had anything at all derogatory to say about her. He was himself an important figure in the development of geriatrics and his comments could be interpreted as reflecting a certain amount of rivalry: 'I think because of her status of having started geriatric wards (she was) somewhat rigid and authoritarian. I think that's all one can say.'[23]

Another, who later became another legend in the specialty's history, was also a little guarded:

And I was of course captivated . . . I think she was the sort of person whom I believe people could take a dislike to because she was very forthright; but she was a wonderful woman. She saw her way absolutely clearly; she saw no obstacle in her way, she knew what she wanted. She worked like anything on earth and inspired countless people. She wasn't well regarded in her own hospital because they hadn't the insight to see what a brilliant woman she was. And I think she incurred a lot of jealousy among her fellow physicians because she was really, in my view, outstanding, outstanding.[24]

A third, a Manchester man, was also a trifle ambivalent:

She was a forceful personality. I thought she was sometimes hard on the patients. You know, sort of bullied them. I mean, you, 'walk' and 'you've got to get going' and so on, but a little bit hard, I thought. But she was a great pioneer, of course.

When further asked whether she bullied her colleagues and juniors, he replied: 'No I don't think so, no, no. She was a very good, a very good person, and what was needed at the time.'[25]
A fellow Mancunian also thought:

She was a bit hard at times, but she certainly paved the trail for mobility and an enormous amount of good started to be done as a result of her efforts, you know. Marjory, bless her heart, wasn't a brilliant academic doctor, but she had a philosophy about the care which she pushed over and it really helped the whole movement.[26]

Other brief comments were 'Very forthright, no nonsense. You wouldn't argue with her at all. She was very much on the ball' (our only woman informant[27]) and: 'She was a very tall, dominant-looking woman. She was actually very nice, a very sweet woman.'[28]
Three of our interviewees had personal reminiscences of working with Marjory Warren, including one who worked in the midlands:

She came to Birmingham. She was staying in a hotel and rang me up. I was just getting out of bed about seven in the morning, and she said 'Can I come to see the hospital?' I said 'Of course, when would you like to come?' She said 'Now!' Seven in the morning! I said 'Give me a chance to shave, Marjory and then I'll come down.' She said 'I'll be there in twenty minutes.' No she didn't ask permission. She gave orders. She was like a ship in full sail. She came down the corridor, master of all she surveyed – yes with her coat tails flapping in the breeze. I rang up the Matron and said 'Miss Thomas, we are in trouble. We have got Marjory Warren coming and she's coming now!' She knew of course that it was the worst possible time because it was chaos at seven in the morning with all the incontinent patients, and all the over-crowding, and the smell of urine that we had in those days.'[29]

An Indian doctor was the only one of the interviewees who had actually worked in her department as a registrar. This was after a stint in the army. He had this to say:

Working with Marjory – it was almost like another regiment! She worked so hard and worked everybody hard too. (*He wanted time to study and thought about resigning.*) The superintendent, a Scotsman – a very nice man – said 'Why don't you want to continue working?' So I looked at Dr Warren and said 'Well, I don't want to complain, sir, and I find the job very interesting but it's a very busy job, I don't find time to study.' I can't imitate his Scottish voice. 'All right, laddie' he says, 'Yes of course you will have time. Marjory can you draw up an agenda for that?' She then gave me a half-day. Of course she had to stand up to all those high-powered specialists. I must say for a woman it would have been difficult. These senior consultants would come along and say 'Dr Warren what about seeing my patient?' And she would say all right and point out what the difficulty was: 'Why can't you discharge this patient yourself? Why do I want to take them over? You're an orthopaedic surgeon. You just haven't got the right kind of stick. It's not the right height.' And they felt stupid. She said 'You should be able to do it yourselves I'll advise you, but don't ask me to take over.' . . . She had faith in people and enthusiasm. And she was a mother in one sense. She would say 'Come on, calm down boys, don't be so depressed.' And in the beginning it was very necessary.

Marjory suffered two things: (a) she was a woman in a jungle of men and (b) she did not have membership of the Royal Colleges. If she had been a member she would have got an honour earlier, much earlier and much more than what she got.[30]

Three of our interviewees were Marjory Warren's self-styled 'disciples', she was their 'guru'. In the early 1950s all three had obtained posts as geriatric consultants, in Belfast, in Cornwall and in Dundee. As one of these explained, 'She called us her "three boys". She had been invited to prepare the agenda for an international conference on geriatrics to be held in London and formed a sub-committee of herself, George, Tommy and myself (Ossie).' The last described their work:

So about 3 in the afternoon we said 'Marjory, we must have something to eat.' She never noticed time. We'd work to 8 o'clock and I'd take us to her home in Isleworth. . . . And we'd talk to maybe one or two in the morning. Sunday morning, first thing, all day. But we were always so devoted to her. She was inhuman, in that she never felt heat or cold or hunger or anything.

She was probably one of the few people in this life who had no faults. She didn't drink or smoke. She never spoke badly of people. She could, she walked any place – the Royal College, House of Lords – and she treated everybody alike. (*In response to a question did she bully you?*) Yes, but in such a subtle way you never felt you'd been bullied at all. She ruled by inspiration not by dictat. And you felt she really believed every word she said, like nobody else you'd met.[31]

Her heroic stature was emphasised by another of 'her boys'. Talking about her death in a car accident in France, he said:

She had been down here staying with us just a week before. She and Enid (her sister) came down. On the way they stopped at Bude and had a swim. It was only afterwards they told me that Marjory had nearly drowned. She was swept out. She got back but she was very short of breath. She'd obviously been inhaling a bit of sea water. She never mentioned it to us.

Summing up her significance he said:

> She was a remarkably capable woman. She puts me in mind of Margaret Fry who was the one who revolutionised the approach to prison treatment and care. She did the same thing for the elderly sick.[32]

Opposition and support

What was the reaction of other physicians and what was the climate within which Marjory Warren and the other pioneers were working?

Fifteen of our 23 interviewees talked to some extent about the reaction of other consultant physicians and surgeons to their appointments as geriatric consultants and their plans for developing their work. Relatively few of them spoke of overt hostility. Some described the reactions in the main as those of disdain or indifference. Given our coverage of medical journals – including correspondence columns – we had expected to find individuals experiencing more difficulty than was admitted to in these interviews.

From the interview data it seems that other physicians were likely to be divided in their attitudes and often individually ambivalent. They might not see the need for a specialism, but then as specialists themselves or as generalists, they greeted geriatric medicine with some enthusiasm, seeing it as possibly relieving them of patients whom they had no interest (or could see no point) in treating. The next five quotations illustrate these conflicting responses:

> A lot of general physicians were very much against it. All they wanted – I think some of them still do – was someone to take from their wards the patients they didn't want. Simple as that. (To them geriatrics was) a 'dustbin specialty'.[33]

> Quite a lot of physicians have said to me in the past: 'Well diseases are diseases, they don't change with age.' But in fact they do.[34]

> The general physicians weren't interested. There was no money in it. They equated old age with poverty and

that was of no interest to them. In the beginning they were actively obstructive. Later on they just let us be and didn't take much notice of us. It was my first business to sort this out and establish a geriatric unit, of course against the wishes of the general physicians who wanted to keep their hand in, and very much in favour of the orthopaedic surgeons and psychiatrists who felt rather lumbered with these people and didn't quite know what to do with them.[35]

Difficult to pinpoint what the resistance was, but it was basically that the upper echelons didn't really see the need. First of all, they'd no experience of it. They had not been involved in public assistance institutions or the chronic sick hospitals. It was unusual for a consultant physician to set foot in a chronic hospital. That was one thing the health service did – it opened up the nooks and crannies of the old chronic sick hospitals to a sphere of medicine which they had never experienced before. There was not a lot of money around. There was a lot of competition from other branches; but . . . one often got more support from the lay members of authorities than from the medical fraternity.[36]

And the physicians they didn't really have a tremendous interest in the elderly; their efforts were all for the younger sick and people they could do something for.[37]

The ambivalence which was a frequent experience of this pioneer generation was well expressed in two other comments:

Oh yes, they welcomed it. They were defending their own beds because otherwise they would get cluttered up with people they couldn't get out. They were an odd lot. Most of them have died now, but at one time a lot of physicians did not talk to one another. They all ran independent units and quite often they would all go on holiday together and leave me to run the whole hospital![38]

I think they were all very supportive. Indeed we used to get on very well together. When they had squabbles among themselves they always used to call me in to adjudicate. All the same there was one physician at Withington (Manchester) who didn't think there ought to be any geriatrics. He used to say 'General physicians can look after them just as well as you.' But of course they *didn't*. They just let dreadful things happen.[39]

Awareness of the status and pecking order in the profession and the way in which geriatricians derived part of their low status from treating a clientele with low social status – from among the old and the poor – emerged in one or two comments. For example:

> It was mainly, I think, uppishness on the part of the old-fashioned consultant physicians who felt themselves rather superior to people in geriatric medicine, and instead of treating you as an equal they would tend to try to push the work on to you that they didn't want. There was a certain snobbery because you were doing work with the poor. But there were some very outstanding physicians who were quite the opposite – including of course Sheldon (of Wolverhampton) and C. T. Andrews of Truro.
>
> And he, (the interviewee's London chief) like so many older physicians, was terribly superior about these places and would feel that any doctor who worked in them (the poor law infirmaries) rather soiled his hands. . . . You see the conditions of the medical service were so bad that no sensible doctor would ever have put in for them.[40]

And another comment from north of the border:

> I think there was a wee bit of a prejudice against people working with old folk. The temptation was to regard anybody who worked with the elderly as in some way second rate.[41]

Views of the future

Towards the end of our interviews we generally asked our informants to tell us how optimistic they were about the future of the specialty and the medical care of older people. The comments frequently concerned longer-term trends in health care provision, including the gradual secular trend to reduce long-stay hospital facilities which particularly affected older people. However, they were also more specifically concerned with the controversy within medical circles as to the desirability of a separately designated geriatric specialty.

The large-scale discharge of older patients from fast disappearing hospital beds into expanding private sector nursing homes was at the centre of many comments:

> I'm not very fond of nursing homes. Some of them may be good but I think that some of them lack a standard which should be kept.[42]

> Nursing homes. Yes. That is going to compound a felony in my view and create what we set out in 1947 to resolve. Because how do you ensure uniform standards of nursing and medical care and physiotherapy and so forth from multiple little nursing homes all round the country-side?[43]

> The hospital had and still has a place to play in the care of the long-term invalid. I regret the way in which long-stay wards have been closed down, the emphasis being on getting old people out of hospital into long-term care in the private sector. . . . Once they are in a nursing home you are unlikely to get a regular review.[44]

> Well, I'm a bit scared that a vulnerable group like the elderly sick might not benefit as much as they should. In fact, I think they might be neglected again. Our work has been let down a little bit because hospitals are so quick, so busy doing routine operations which they get paid a lot for rather than looking after strokes and other problems in the elderly.[45]

Two comments dealt more specifically with the future of the specialty.

> But I do think possibly that the trend now for geriatricians to take a commitment in the acute general medical service may be too much for them, and it may mean that they will forget their long-stay commitment. I know it's going to have difficulties, but I hope it's here to stay. The present resource problem will make it more difficult. I think all of us took the closure of beds a bit too far really. It was the rage in the '60s getting people up and home and reducing beds. And I personally think that the asylum

and the long-term hospital has a very real place. They should be nicer, better places, but to get rid of them too rapidly and too drastically is pretty difficult.[46]

My last quoted comment comes from someone who had been thinking deeply about the future of the specialty:

> I don't think there should be any geriatrics in an ideal world. I think it's a necessary evil. If you had really good GPs and really good consultants, then it doesn't matter how old a patient is or how ill they are, they would be looked after properly. But it doesn't work out in practice. Old people, particularly when they are demented and particularly when they are dirty, will always be neglected by the clever doctors. They are neglected by their GPs. They're neglected by the general services, to be fair. So I think you have to have a geriatric service. I think you *had* to have one. I think you *still* must have one.[47]

Notes

1 Interview 105. Oswald Taylor Brown, b. 1916 in Scotland; doctors on his mother's side of the family; studied medicine at Glasgow University; war service; held posts in geriatric medicine in Glasgow and Dundee.
2 A term coined by E.J. Miller and G.V. Gwynne in their study of residential care, *A Life Apart*, 1972, London: Tavistock.
3 Jefferys, M., 'Geriatric medicine: some ethical issues associated with its development', in Grubb, A. (ed.) *Choices and Decisions in Health Care*, 1993, Chichester, John Wiley.
4 I was appointed visiting researcher at Royal Holloway and Bedford New College, London under the sponsorship of Professor Mike Bury, and with the support and collaboration of two experienced, though technically retired, social researchers Anthea Holme and Hazel Houghton-Matthews.
5 All the interviewees agreed to let us tape their interviews and, with few exceptions, they also allowed us to lodge the tapes and transcripts in the National Life Story Collection of the British Library.
6 Interview 106. William Ferguson Anderson, b. 1914; only child; his father was killed in the First World War; educated at Edinburgh; cousin was a doctor; war service; senior lecturer at the Welsh National School; appointed to a chair in geriatric medicine at Glasgow in 1965.
7 Interview 316. Stanley Joseph Firth, b. 1902 in Manchester; mother a nurse and father a schoolmaster; later became master and matron of a workhouse; qualified at Manchester University in 1925; 1932 medical officer in charge at Brighton; appointed consulting physician in geriatric medicine in 1956; retired 1967.

8 Interview 205. John Norman Agate; b. 1919; educated at Cambridge; uncles were doctors; medical student during Second World War; senior registrar, then researcher; after the war took a job at Bradford in a new department of geriatric medicine; later appointed at Ipswich.

9 Interview 226. John Clifford Firth, no d.o.b. recorded; father a chemist; qualified at University College London in 1941; active war service; registrar at St James, Balham; 1952 asked to set up geriatric unit with beds at St Benedicts; 1964 appointed consultant at Hertfordshire Hospital.

10 Interview 205.

11 Interview 206. Maurice Henry Papworth; no d.o.b. recorded; geriatrician in Maidenhead; Harley Street; taught at Liverpool.

12 Interview 306. Ronald Verdun Dent, b. 1916; father a Norfolk farmer; village school, then grammar school, Norfolk; studied medicine at Cambridge; scholar at Charing Cross Hospital; qualified 1940; war service in the navy 1944; appointed to Chase Farm Hospital, Enfield 1947; deputy medical superintendent at Southend, 1952; appointed consultant at Crumpsall Hospital, Manchester until retirement.

13 Interview 213. Robert Glendenning, b. 1918; father a pathologist; educated at Cambridge, then London Hospital; worked at London Hospital, Manchester; registrar at Newcastle; senior registrar at Sunderland; consultant at Bendford.

14 Interview 112. Joseph M. Greenwood, b. 1908; father a draper; stepmother a nursing sister; uncle a GP; Manchester University; appointed to Crumpsall Municipal Hospital; resident medical officer, later deputy medical superintendent at Withington Hospital, Manchester; joined the Ministry of Health during wartime; met Marjory Warren; 1965 first consultant in geriatric medicine in the north of England.

15 Interview 112.

16 Interview 209. John Wedgwood, b. 1919; father involved in family business; mother started first contraceptive clinic in the Potteries during the 1930s; started medical career during Second World War; worked in East Anglia and Middlesex; later Royal Home and Hospital for Incurables at Putney.

17 Interview 306.

18 Interview 205.

19 Interview 105.

20 Interview 106.

21 Interview 214. Wilfred Fone, b. 1915; qualified Guys; house job London; war service; post-war appointment at Liverpool; later chair of geriatric medicine at Liverpool.

22 No biography of Marjory Warren has ever been published and the few accounts which she wrote, though they document her work, focus on the case she was seeking to make for the specialty of geriatric medicine. For a brief and helpful account of her work and of the period in which she, and others, were seeking to make changes in the medical treatment and care of older people, see Evers, H., 'The historical development of geriatric medicine as a speciality', in Johnson, J. & Slater, R. (eds) *Ageing and Later Life*, 1993, London, Sage.

23 Interview 122. Lionel Cosin, b. 1910; father a small shopkeeper, older brother studied medicine; trained at Guys; qualified in 1933; surgeon at Prince of Wales, Tottenham; 1936 FRCS; medical superintendent at an Essex hospital during the war; medical director at Langthorne Hospital, Leytonstone; 1949 moved to Cowley Road, Oxford.

24 Interview 106.

25 Interview 112.

26 Interview 316.

27 Interview 203. Mabel Andrews, b. 1906; qualified in 1928 in Belfast; first house job in Manchester in 1934; husband first consultant physician in Cornwall in 1939; mayor of Truro; started Age Concern in Cornwall; worked part time covering for first geriatric physician, Tom Wilson.

28 Interview 206.

29 Interview 224. Lawrence Nagley, b. 1911; qualified in 1934; worked at Stafford and Dudley Road, Birmingham; first geriatrician appointed in the NHS.

30 Interview 216. M.S. Kataria, b. 1917; attended school in India; father a school inspector, parents died early; qualified as MD; army service; locum for Marjory Warren; says that geriatrics originated from pioneers and Indian doctors, 'locals wouldn't touch it'; English conjoint exam at Guy's; 1947 West Middlesex; registrar at St Francis which amalgamated with Maudsley in 1954.

31 Interview 105.

32 Interview 202. Thomas Scott Wilson, b. 1918; youngest of five boys; parents were teachers in Belfast; trained in Northern Ireland; 1942–1947 RAF; demobbed and took job with London County Council; appointed geriatrician in Cornwall.

33 Interview 201. Eric Vodden Bradshaw, b. 1919; father a civil servant; trained in Scotland; house job and senior registrar in 1946; research for Boots the Chemist; geriatric physician job at Nottingham; consultant at day hospital; ended career working in Cornwall.

34 Interview 205.

35 Interview 207. Hugo Droller, b. 1919 in Germany; left in 1930s; medical career began in Leeds; clinical assistant at Sheffield; interned; then army service, demobbed in 1947; post-war job in Leeds organising provision for older people.

36 Interview 202.

37 Interview 226.

38 Interview 214.

39 Interview 306

40 Interview 303. Thomas N. Rudd, b. 1906; father company secretary and manager; trained at London; war service; afterwards worked in Devon, later Southampton.

41 Interview 106.

42 Interview 316.

43 Interview 301. George Fowler Adams, b. 1916, Yorkshire; brought up in Northern Ireland; war service; then worked in Northern Ireland.

44 Interview 310. Philip Arnold, b. 1920; father a bank official; trained at University College, London; first house job at Chichester; war service; then registrar at University College Hospital; worked with Lord Amulree at St Pancras in a newish geriatric unit; 1953 job in geriatrics in Oxfordshire and Buckinghamshire; consultant geriatrician at Poole, Dorset.
45 Interview 306.
46 Interview 209.
47 Interview 201.

4

THE LAST YEARS OF THE WORKHOUSE, 1930–1965

John Adams

The recent celebrations marking 50 years of the National Health Service revealed much about British attitudes to health and social welfare, as the spotlight remained almost totally focused on the advances in acute medical care taking place in prestigious hospitals. The fact that 1948 also saw the abolition of the Poor Law and sweeping changes in the system of care for many vulnerable groups in society passed almost unnoticed. The end of the Poor Law should also have represented the final curtain for the workhouse, but its sturdy walls ensured a continuing existence in the new world of the welfare state. Like a character in a horror film, it may have been pronounced dead but it refused to die. For several decades the former workhouse buildings were both an essential resource for the new NHS and a constant reminder of the past that had been renounced. As the tide of opinion turned against institutional care and in favour of care in the community, the former workhouses and asylums provided easy targets for reformers. Now that this transition looks much more problematic than once it did, there is a fresh incentive to re-examine policy in terms of the continuities between the old and the new.

In this chapter, based on interviews with the staff who administered the workhouses, an attempt is made to begin this process of re-assessment starting from the passing of the Local Government Act, 1929. This piece of legislation, which came into effect in 1930, transferred the powers of Boards of Guardians for the administration of the Poor Law to the public assistance committees of counties and county boroughs. While the first date in the title has some basis in the legislative framework under which workhouse masters were required to work, the choice of 1965 requires some explanation. After the legislative changes of 1948, it was assumed that some former workhouses would have a brief period as hospitals before being replaced with new buildings, while others would provide temporary residential accommodation for older people, before being replaced by smaller residential homes which could provide a higher standard of care.[1] Workhouse masters would disappear with the demise of the building. The reality was that many of the former workhouses survived well into the 1960s, managed by the same masters who were now restyled 'wardens'. The selection of 1965 was made because that year saw the closure of Luxborough Lodge, the former St Marylebone Workhouse, a landmark in central London. Another date which could have been chosen was 1985, because that year saw the closure of the Camberwell Reception Centre, the final incarnation of the old Gordon Road Workhouse.[2] A case could be made for regarding this venerable if unloved institution as the last workhouse of them all. Finally, it could be argued that as so many former workhouse buildings still survive, and often continue to provide care services for very similar groups such as older people and people admitted for reasons of mental illness or distress as they have always done, the workhouse is still with us, run by masters under the new guise of 'patient services managers'.

This chapter is based on material derived from tape-recorded interviews and informal discussions carried out over the past 12 years with 10 leading members of the former Association of Health and Residential Care Officers. This organisation was founded in 1898 as the National Association of Masters and Matrons of Workhouses. In 1931 the title was changed to the National Association of Administrators of Local Government Establishments in order to reflect the new role of local authorities in administering services. The introduction of the National Health Service and the passing of the National Assistance Act 1948 were followed by a further change of title to the Association of Hospital and Welfare Administrators, and this penultimate version lasted from 1949 to 1970.[3]

The workhouse master in context

The workhouse has proved to be one of the most enduring features of both the English townscape and rural landscape, despite the ambivalence or even open hostility with which it has been regarded throughout its existence. Many of the remaining buildings date at least in part from the years immediately following the passing of the

Poor Law Amendment Act of 1834 which required groups of parishes, known as Unions, to underwrite the heavy cost of construction. Some of these, such as the one at Wellingborough in Northamptonshire, were designed on the 'panopticon' plan. A central circular building with wings radiating from it enabled staff to maintain continuous observation over the inmates. This arrangement had strong similarities to the nineteenth-century prison.[4] In other areas, such as the county of Norfolk, a local tradition of expressing pride of place and patronage through the buildings provided to house the poor resulted in the design of workhouses which resembled the country houses of the gentry.[5] The poor, however, were not impressed by this investment in stone, bricks and mortar which had been made on their behalf. With memories of the French Revolution still fresh in the minds of all, local labourers were not slow in making a connection between the intimidating new buildings which were being erected on the fringes of the towns and the notorious prison of the Bastille.[6]

Those framing the legislation, however, believed that they had created a system which, unlike the prison, provided an ever-present incentive for the inmate to leave. This was the principle of 'less eligibility' which meant that the discipline, labour and restrictions imposed by the workhouse regime should encourage those who could support themselves by their own efforts outside to do so. For those who were genuinely unable to cope outside the institution, the aim was to provide all the necessities of life in a way that made the workhouse 'a place of comparative comfort'.[7] This may have been the intention of the central authorities, but the fragmentation of a system administered by locally elected Boards of Guardians allowed a number of scandals of neglect and abuse to occur in the early years. At Andover workhouse in 1845, the paupers were reduced to such a level of hunger that they began to gnaw the rotting bones that they were required to grind into powder as their labour task.[8] The subsequent Parliamentary Committee of Inquiry, and the campaign for action led by *The Times*, resulted in major organisational changes and also focused attention on the key posts of master and matron. The rapid development of a new national network of institutions which required a wide range of skills and personal qualities to be deployed in often difficult circumstances meant that guardians had no existing occupational group with its own standards and traditions on which they could draw. As a result, appointments were made on the basis of experience which appeared to be relevant to the new occupation. It was the military background of Colin McDougal, who had fought at the battle of Waterloo and been given a discharge as a staff sergeant in 1836 as 'worn out', that led to his appointment as the master of Andover workhouse.[9] After this disastrous episode, the Andover Guardians demonstrated their philosophy of workhouse management once again by appointing to the post of master a former prison officer from Parkhurst gaol. He lasted only three years in the job as the Guardians dismissed him for taking liberties with female paupers.

It is inevitably the worst cases of cruelty and neglect by workhouse masters that drew most attention at the time and provide such compelling material for the modern historian, but it is necessary to balance these accounts with those of efficient and humane masters who gave good service to both guardians and paupers. One such was George Edward Douglas, who was appointed as master of the St Marylebone Workhouse in 1862. It is perhaps significant that, unlike many masters of the time who were recruited from the harsh worlds of the army or the prisons, Douglas had worked his way up through the posts of storekeeper and master's clerk in the institution before this promotion. Any workhouse in the centre of a great city was certain to require firmness and stamina on the part of the master in order to control the often unruly inmates, but Douglas was able to combine this with a sensitive appreciation of the needs of the vulnerable.[10]

In the same way that the scandalous behaviour of some of the early workhouse masters of the 1840s and 1850s has come to be seen as typical for all subsequent holders of the post, so the changing nature of the workhouse itself has often not been fully appreciated. There is a tendency for local histories to dwell in detail on the regime in the middle years of the nineteenth century and then move abruptly to the 'coming of the welfare state' in 1948 as if nothing of significance had occurred in the interim. Yet a century invariably brings change to an institution and the workhouse is no exception. By 1914, the 'mixed' workhouse providing shelter for the able-bodied unemployed, vagrants, the chronic sick, those 'lunatics, idiots and imbeciles' who did not present severe management problems, the aged, expectant mothers and young children still existed in many places, but some unions had built separate infirmaries for the sick or specialised institutions for the aged and 'cottage homes' for children.[11] Even where separate accommodation had not been developed, the character of the workhouse had changed. It had ceased to be the main focus of society's efforts to grapple with unemployment, with all the social tensions and disciplinary problems which that brought, and had become instead a refuge or hospice for those who were unable to cope alone in the society which lay outside its wall. Now more than ever the master of a workhouse needed to have managerial abilities which were coupled with the insight and imagination to ameliorate the worst aspects of institutional routines in order to improve the quality of life for the long-stay inmates. Given the importance of the role which workhouse masters played for more than a century in administering and delivering services at a local level for most of the vulnerable groups within society, it is surprising how little attention they have received from historians. The appeal made by Gutchen well over 10 years ago for historians to move beyond literary stereotypes, such as Dickens' Mr Bumble in *Oliver Twist*, and evaluate the work of real masters based on the documentary evidence remains largely unanswered.[12] The most thorough and balanced account of the role of workhouse masters is that undertaken by Crowther, but her review ends in 1929 with the abolition of the Boards of Guardians.[13]

Having previously reviewed some of the literature on workhouse masters, hospital stewards, superintendents of public assistance institutions and the wardens of local authority residential homes, I was expecting to meet men who were, to use some of Peter Townsend's adjectives, 'blunt', 'hearty' or 'extraordinarily rough-hewn and Micawberish'.[14] To my great surprise, I found myself interviewing articulate professional men who could have been retired hospital consultants, architects or solicitors. My first questions to all of them concerned the reasons for their choice of career. One of the wardens interviewed by Townsend gave the difficulty of finding work during the 1930s slump as the reason why he entered the service. This was also the reason given by all my informants, but clearly the 'accidental' nature of career choice can produce high-calibre officers as well as the unsuitable ones identified by Townsend. Lionel Lewis explained:

> Well, it was just an accident really. I wasn't particularly worried where I went, but I had taken my senior Oxford School Certificate and we were just looking for a job. When I put in for the job as junior clerk at 12/6d a week there were 200 applicants. And I didn't get the job because we had three interviews and we had a general knowledge test, writing test, arithmetic and all kinds of

peculiar things – for a 12/6d a week job! They finally cut down the 200 to twenty, and from eighty to forty, and the final interview was twenty of us. I didn't get the job, but I walked home with a young man who'd got it, and he was two years older than I was and he said, I'm not going to take the job – I'm going into the civil service. So the next day I had a letter from the Town Clerk and he said the job was mine if I liked to have it – and that's how I started.[15]

For one of the officers, a lack of positive commitment to a career in the service was overcome by outside influences:

I joined the Poor Law on 2nd December 1929. I was born in 1913, so I was just sixteen when I joined the service – that was under the Board of Guardians.
Did you have to have an interview?
Yes, with the Board of Guardians. . . . The job was advertised at 30/- a week, but because I was so young they offered me the job at £1 a week. It happened that one of my uncles was a member of the Board of Guardians at the time and also the master of the institution had had a lot of dealings with my elder brother, who he wanted to be his clerk. But my brother didn't want it – he emigrated to Canada – so the next best thing was me. He interviewed me before I went before the Board of Guardians and more or less suggested that they should appoint me.[16]

In the lottery of competition for scarce jobs, a lack of influence with the Board of Guardians could also pay dividends. The post of junior clerk at the Toxteth Park Workhouse in Liverpool came to the attention of one applicant through his membership of the Liverpool Clerks Association, but that organisation could not influence the outcome:

Having interviewed all of us, I was called back in again and was told that there was nothing to choose between any of us. But as I was the only one who hadn't got any connections or been spoken for, they'd decided to appoint me . . . that was on the 12th July 1927 and the next question was, when can you start?
And I said, any time you want – so they said, tomorrow![17]

Having joined a service which had been widely criticised since its establishment, I asked whether they were aware of the stigma which the Poor Law carried. Ray Livesey recalled:

> No worries as a youngster – that didn't apply. It's only in later years that one comes to realise that this kind of stigma did apply. In fact, with the benefit of hindsight, one can look back over the years ... and feel a great sense of sorrow that there was so much, shall we say unhappiness, in the very fact of being housed in these large wards and dayrooms and so on.[18]

Whatever the shortcomings of the workhouse system, junior clerks had no option but to conform to the rigid discipline upon which it was founded. Although all those I interviewed were aware of this tendency, not all of them had experienced it at first hand:

> One of the problems was – these harsh conditions imposed upon staff were the result of the older workhouse masters who graduated, you see, through the Poor Law. And who were still in spite of the transfer to the county councils in 1930, they were still thinking back in terms of the old-style Victorian workhouse discipline and they were imposing this on members of staff. Well I was very lucky that I never came across this type of conduct and behaviour.[19]

The dominant impression was of two distinct cultures of care co-existing in the 1930s: one characterised by traditional workhouse discipline; the other provided role models for a more compassionate and caring interpretation of the role of master and this was to influence these new recruits:

> I suppose there were always bad masters and bad matrons – I've come across a few of them – but generally the masters and matrons were very humane people; tolerant of all the things that happened. And in many ways they were looked upon as the 'head of the family'.[20]

It could be argued that from the decision to interview former office-holders in an occupational association, the views expressed would inevitably be those of an elite group rather than typical of officers as a whole. Yet the recognition that such an elite actually existed helps to correct the general view of Poor Law Officers as an undifferentiated occupational group characterised by low expectations and lower achievements.[21] In my view, it was the consistent failure of both government and campaigners to recognise the positive contributions that this elite group could make to the evolution of policy which led directly to some of the fundamental problems which still afflict residential care. In particular the refusal to recognise and support the officers' attempts to achieve professional status based upon a specific educational programme undermined the status of residential care officers and set the scene for several decades of neglect of their educational and training needs. The subsequent catalogue of scandals both in homes for older people and in children's homes continued to take governments by surprise, but could often be seen as stemming from that calculated neglect. It is necessary to examine the achievements of reforming administrators in the last years of the workhouse since one of the reasons why a professional educational system was ultimately denied them was the belief that such education as had been available had simply resulted in the reinforcement of narrow and complacent determination to continue with the status quo in a system that was plainly in urgent need of reform.

Professional qualifications in the workhouse

The characteristics which distinguish a profession from other occupations have been widely debated by sociologists, but there is no doubt that Poor Law Officers regarded the possession of a specialist body of knowledge confirmed by the gaining of a certificate or diploma as its hallmark. Three groups with whom they had frequent contact – doctors, nurses and lawyers – had all obtained, to a greater or lesser extent, this distinguishing feature by the early years of the twentieth century and so the officers were anxious to follow this route themselves. The first course was intended for relieving officers and was held in 1903, with other groups soon developing specialist courses for their own needs.[22] Once the decision had been taken to develop courses, the question of their content had to be addressed. For the master of a mixed institution such as a workhouse, it proved to be impossible to identify a specialist area of knowledge that was appropriate so a generalist collection of subjects had to suffice. Lionel Lewis described his studies in 1932:

When I was 18 there was such a thing called the Institution
and Hospital Officers Certificate of the Poor Law Examinations Board and unfortunately when I went to take it they
changed it into a two-year syllabus. So that you studied the
Poor Law Acts, Public Assistance Orders, the Casual Poor
Orders, Relief Regulations, Lunacy and Mental Treatment
Acts 1930. You did books and accounts, mercantile law,
English, buildings and construction. I had to know how to
do a specification for building . . . this ward needs redeco-
rating, it's so-and-so and so-and-so, prepare a specification
for any building work and any painting work to be done. I
took my exam in 1936 – we held the highest certificate that
you could get at that particular time, so in effect you had
qualified yourself to run a hospital or an institution.

Despite the growing accretion of academic trappings borrowed
from medical education, such as medals for receiving the highest
marks, there was always the knowledge that gaining this qualification was not regarded as essential by the central authorities for
appointment as a master. The presence of representatives from
the Ministry of Health on the examining board could not conceal
its ambivalent attitude towards courses for officers:

And that year I were sitting the Poor Law Examinations
for the Poor Law Examinations Board – that was in April
1933. And I passed and was top in England and Wales,
for which I got the Mary Hill Memorial Medal . . . well
that sort of helped and consolidated my position [as
clerk/steward of a municipal hospital]. In the Public
Assistance Order 1930, you'll find that to be a senior Poor
Law Officer, you can be one if you have got certain [expe-
rience], but if you've got the master's certificate you *are*
one – so that rather sort of clinched it.[23]

In practice, as officers keen to move in a 'professional' direction were only too well aware, the members of a public assistance
committee was as likely to be swayed by their own judgements of
character as they were by the possession of a certificate when they
came to appoint a master:

I remember somebody saying that someone had got the
job [of master]. They asked him, what are the qualities

of a master? He said, I think he should be a jack-of all-
trades, a good husband and a good father – and he got
the job![24]

By the end of the 1930s the distinction between the roles of
superintendent of a 'mixed' public assistance institution and that
of steward in a local authority infirmary was becoming more
marked and in 1943 stewards established their own section of the
National Association of Administrators of Local Government
Establishments. The administrators of the voluntary hospitals,
using their different system of accounts as a pretext, tried to
prevent entry by the municipal infirmary officers:

> Well I thought having got the Master's certificate I'd
> better get more qualifications and I was debarred from
> studying for the Institute of Hospital Administrators (IHA)
> because you had to have a job in the voluntary hospital
> service. Because I was 'municipal' I couldn't take their
> exams, so I took a secretarial course with the Corporation
> of Certified Secretaries, which in addition to ordinary
> business studies had a separate section for hospitals, with
> no bar, although the examination was based on the volun-
> tary hospital system of their accounts. I took their exams
> over a period of three years so I got that qualification,
> and then it was during the War – I'm not going to the
> Forces, so I'll do something else. So I went to Liverpool
> University for the Diploma in Public Administration.[25]

By the end of the Second World War, the attitude of the IHA
had softened to some extent and a minority of Poor Law masters
now became eligible for associate membership under a special
scheme.[26] The creation of the National Health Service meant that
administrators from the voluntary and municipal sectors had to
compete for the new posts, with the former having the prestige
of their former jobs to assist them, but at least the new career
structure with its recognised professional qualifications was now
in place. One of my interviewees succeeded in obtaining the most
desirable post – Group Secretary – in the new structure, and
became, as he described it, 'lord of all I surveyed'.[27] Three of the
others were successful in becoming a hospital secretary, the next
rung down in the hierarchy but with the opportunity for close
contact with patient care. For the rest, either by choice or because

their institution did not have enough beds to qualify them as hospital officers, the future lay in residential care for older people after 1948.

The early years of the new service

In addition to the formal qualifications decribed above, progression in a career in the public assistance institution required ascent up each rung of the ladder with every promotion usually involving a move to another part of the country. A typical career path would involve appointment as a junior clerk, followed by promotion to senior clerk, storekeeper, and then assistant master. It was possible to gain the top post of master while a single man, but it was more usual to apply for the joint appointment of master and matron as a married couple.[28] While the main change that hospital administrators had to face after 1948 was a new system of accounts, those running the former workhouses which had now become residential homes found that they were faced with a competely new philosophy of care but few of the resources to put it into practice. In particular, their Master's Certificate could provide little help as it was largely concerned with the implementation of Poor Law legislation which was now to be abolished.[29] There were some local authorities which planned in good time for the changes that were coming:

> The Public Assistance Officer [for Monmouthshire] came to see me and said, the new Act is coming out in '48 and we are going to open an old people's home in Cwmbran before the Act actually comes into force. Now will you come along to tell us what you want? So he took me along to a tumble-down old house with black-out curtains still up . . . old carpets on the floor which were made up of sack bags, beds that were collapsing. And I went in and he said, anything you want you just order it – and start the house going.. . . and took out about twenty old men from the workhouse.[30]

The fact that the new local authority residential homes for older people began their existence in many areas in the former workhouse buildings is well known, but what is less widely appreciated is that the tone of life was often set not by new residents moving in from the community but by a hard core of former workhouse inmates. Control over the more challenging elements in this population had been maintained by a system of punishments administered by the master, but under the new system control had to be maintained with no sanctions to fall back on:

> [Prior to 1948] you could stop their privileges – stop them from going out, stop their tobacco, stop the sweets, or whatever it was, so you had certain punishments you could inflict. Because immediately the '48 Acts came in, you had nothing – nothing at all. So that everything was completely taken out of your hands and very often that was one of our complaints. That the 'residents', as we used to call them then, could do exactly what they wanted. I mean they could throw hot cups of tea at attendants – which they did quite often – and hit them with sticks, and there was nothing you could do about it.[31]

Having set up a new system of residential care which aimed to sweep away the old Poor Law attitudes, practices and training schemes, successive governments failed to put new arrangements in place. As a result, the new wardens were left to struggle on as best they could. Many of them felt that the former relationships had much still to recommend them. Lionel Lewis put forward his viewpoint:

> [After 1948] they used to call you 'master' and 'matron' and it was out of respect for your position. In addition to that it was like calling you 'father' and 'mother' really. When I left Faversham in 1970, they were still calling me 'master' because they just couldn't get out of the habit – particularly the older ones.

The issue of whether the new wardens and matrons should still reside in the former workhouses or in newly acquired homes was particularly contentious. Some social workers felt that residential posts accounted for much of the remaining culture of the old workhouse which often clung to the new homes. Many wardens, on the other hand, believed that being residents in the same home as the older people in their charge helped to create the 'family' atmosphere that they prized so highly:

> [In 1961 I fell out with my superior officer] as he made us mobile. He said that officers-in-charge should not

become too familiar with their patients. They should be there to look after patients like a nurse in a hospital – go in and do her eight hours duty and then go home – and *you* should be the same. And I disagreed so I [moved to another County].[32]

The desire to retain a residential service and the joint appointment of a husband and wife to manage it, which subsequently came to be seen as the negation of all that was progressive in the provision of residential care, did not necessarily reflect a lack of knowledge of current government policies and the philosophy which underpinned them:

> We had the White Paper [? Ministry of Health Circular 49/47 *Care of the Aged in Public Assistance Homes and Institutions* 1947] and as I read it I said that we should make up a 'home' for old people. First of all, if you are going to have a home you've got to have a man and a woman and the home is based around those two people. And as you run a home, you run this for old people – as if they are your own mum and dad. Even if you've got twenty or thirty of them you've got to treat them as if you've only got two. You've got to give them the same facilities to come and go as they like, to express their own opinions, to do about the house what they want to do.[33]

By the 1960s there was an increasing realisation that residential care services were in crisis and that the new world envisaged in 1948 had largely failed to materialise. The scene was set by the publication of Townsend's major survey of residential homes for older people, published in 1962.[34] He was able to show that many vast former workhouse buildings were still in use despite the ambitious plans to replace them with small, purpose-built homes. He had many critical things to say about some of the former Poor Law staff he found in charge of them, but his more positive comments about those wardens 'held in respect and affection' did not have the same impact.[35] This concern culminated in the setting up of a committee of inquiry into the staffing of all types of residential homes by the National Council of Social Service, under the chairmanship of Lady Williams.[36] The Williams Committee concluded that the staff shortages which characterised residential care were attributable to the lack of status in the eyes of the general public who fail to appreciate that 'this is a profession that requires specific training'. Parallels were drawn with the nursing profession to suggest that training was the key to public esteem. 'Every profession, as it emerges, is characterised by the training which it prescribes.'[37]

The Williams Committee had thus come to focus on the one aspect which was missing from so many of the plans and campaigns to abolish the Poor Law: staff training and professional recognition. By regarding change largely in terms of new administrative arrangements and new buildings, the reformers had failed to recognise that it would be the same staff who would have to carry these plans out. Official recognition of Poor Law qualifications was grudging before 1948 and very few new courses became available after that date. As a result of this policy of neglect, the Williams Committee found that only 18 per cent of staff in children's homes held a residential Child Care Certificate, while the figure for the specific qualification in residential care for older people was only 2 per cent.[38] Most staff were therefore left with no alternative but to struggle on in the familiar old routines, whether or not they were appropriate to the new era.

The Williams Committee was able to diagnose the national lack of training and relate that to high levels of staff turnover and resultant poor care, but the oral evidence collected in this project is able to show something of the potential that they were arguing could be released from well-educated staff with professional aspirations. Although it is an aspect of the history of care which has received very little attention from historians, the former workhouse officers from this elite sample were often fully involved in contemporary efforts to improve care.

Could workhouse masters be innovators?

Traditional accounts of medical history are dominated by the lone pioneer who singlehandedly overcomes universal hostility and obstruction to establish the efficacy of a new treatment or service innovation. In the case of modern approaches to the care and treatment of older people, sole credit is claimed for a group of doctors rather than an individual practitioner, but the emphasis remains on the solitary nature of their struggle against the all-pervasive forces of resistance. The work of pioneering physicians such as Marjory Warren and Trevor Howell and their influence on the founding of the Medical Society for the Care of the Elderly,

which later became the British Geriatrics Society, is now widely
known and justly celebrated (see Margot Jefferys' chapter in this
volume).[39] What is often missing from these accounts, however, is
any sense of perspective regarding the changing context in which
they were working. This has the effect of writing some lower status
occupational groups, such as workhouse nurses and workhouse
masters, out of the historical narrative altogether. In fact the
struggle to improve conditions for 'deserving' groups in the workhouse is almost as old as the New Poor Law itself. Louisa Twining,
Charles Dickens, Dr Joseph Rogers and Florence Nightingale are
among the eminent Victorians who worked and campaigned to
this end.[40] Respectable older people who came to see out their
days in the workhouse evoked particular sympathy not just from
campaigners but from the wider community outside the iron rail-
ings of the institution. This sympathy found a focus in different
priorities at different times, but by the inter-war years it had come
to take the form of a concern with the need to fill the vacant
hours spent lying in bed or sitting on hard wooden chairs.
Entertainment not only provided enjoyment for the inmates but
also carried the tangible message that they had not been forgotten
by the rest of society, as these former Poor Law Officers recalled:

> When I was at Darnton House [Ashton-under-Lyne], and
> this was pre-1930, you find it hard to believe that every
> day-room, pretty well, had a loud-speaker broadcasting
> the news and radio programmes. And the main set was
> housed in the Master's office and there were lines going
> out to all the day-rooms, so that entertainment was
> provided for the residents.[41]

> [In 1930] we used to have a talking picture show once
> a week and in addition to that we also had visitations
> from all the big stars – because there was such a thing as
> the Newport Empire. They used to contact us and say on
> a particular day – a Sunday when it was their spare day
> – all the stars would come up and give the inmates and
> any of the hospital patients who could come down – a
> show. So you saw all the big stars.[42]

In the years just before the Second World War, the emphasis
shifted from entertainment to the reorganisation of care practices
in order to improve the quality of life of older people and children. At the same time as Dr Marjory Warren was transforming

care in the 'chronic sick' wards at the West Middlesex County Hospital, a reforming master and matron – Don and Doris Ernsting – were improving standards in south Wales. Their careers serve as a case study of the dynamic approach to the process of change which many of this elite group of officers brought to the world of the institution once they had come to hold the key posts:

> We married in September 1939, having been appointed master and matron of the Pembroke Institution. This was an institution of just over 100 beds, with a separate children's home of thirty beds, [of which] we were also superintendent and matron. We found that the diet was poor. The cook was quite unsuitable and in fact we did manage to terminate her services. We found that the laundry had been dismantled about seven months previously . . . arrangements had been made with a commercial laundry for much to be dealt with, but we found that the foul linen from the sick ward had not been boiled for that period. Some which had been dealt with by 'hand laundry' was drying, for instance, in the women's day room. Well, we got this machinery assembled and I had the job of instructing the staff in how to use [it].
>
> We improved conditions all round. My wife greatly improved the nursing services and also the conditions for the children in the Homes. [She spent] a lot of time seeing they had new suitable dresses for the girls and they were very appreciative of this. And also we did arrange for one of the girls to go to a High School – which had never been done before.[43]

With the outbreak of war, the former Infirmary, now renamed Woodbine House Hospital, was designated as an Emergency Medical Services Hospital.[44] As the area had a high concentration of military installations in the vicinity it attracted major bombing raids which made heavy demands upon the staff of the hospital. After administering the hospital during this critical period which provided little opportunity for further reform, the Ernstings moved to Lancashire to take up the joint appointment as master and matron of Fishpool Institution, Bolton. On arrival, matron Ernsting surveyed the capabilities of the largely female population of long-term patients of all kinds. Out of a total of 506 patients, 117 were able to do simple work and of these 86 expressed the wish to undertake diversional therapy. Her husband described her efforts to provide appropriate activities for them:

> It was a constant period of improvements. In 1946/7, we suggested to the [Public Assistance] Committee that we should introduce a ladies' hairdressing salon with chairs, hood driers and mirrors. There was some criticism in the local paper – letters – but the overwhelming opinion in the paper was in favour of what we were doing. This developed when we were taken over by the Bolton District Hospital Management Committee [in 1948] and we gradually developed this into a Group service. We had thirteen hospitals in Bolton and we provided a service for all the long-stay female patients.[45]

New services like this one required both capital and revenue spending. Other improvements, such as the provision of mirrors so that patients in the chronic sick wards who previously had only the wall to look at could now see to the street outside, cost very little. What was required was the insight to realise what modifications would improve the quality of patients' lives and the self-confidence and tenacity to present them to the local politicians. One of the innovations at Bolton attracted ministerial interest:

> 'In about 1946–7 I had taken the view that nothing was being done for patients' eyesight and I thought that people's sight deteriorated so slowly that really one didn't appreciate the sight was so poor. The Committee agreed that I could call in a rota of local opticians and examine the eyesight of all the patients. I think of the 600, about 152 were quite unsuitable for sight aids, but of the remainder 62 per cent required sight aids – even if it meant a magnifying glass . . . This scheme was taken up by our local Member of Parliament who put it to Aneurin Bevan, the Minister at the time. He congratulated the Committee on the scheme and said it was going to be notified to various social welfare departments. It was pointed out however that this scheme would become part of the Consultant Medical Services on 5th July 1948.

Following the Appointed Day, Don Ernsting became Hospital Secretary of the then Townleys Branch in Bolton and in 1949 he also assumed the duties of Deputy Group Secretary of Bolton and District Hospitals. From this new position it was a natural progression to forming alliances with doctors who were equally concerned to develop the services that were being provided:

> At Townleys, we had a keen consultant geriatrician and in the very early 1950s we opened up a geriatric day hospital. I recall that I went down with him to St Pancras Hospital where Lord Amulree – he was extremely interested in geriatrics – [was working]. We also developed a psychiatric day hospital and an industrial unit for the patients, which provided a very useful service.

This partnership between a former master turned NHS administrator and a newly minted consultant geriatrician was in fact a common basis for service development in this period. Writing the administrators out of the historical account may help to bolster professional pride within medicine but cannot reflect the often complex ways in which innovations were actually brought about.

Conclusion

If history is the story of winners and losers then there has been no doubt as to which category is appropriate for the former workhouse masters. As the representatives of a system that was criticised from all sides and finally swept away in 1948, they have been consigned in the popular imagination to a place in the Victorian chamber of horrors. Colin McDougal of Andover workhouse has come to be regarded as typifying masters for the next century of their existence. The central fallacy, however, lies not in mistaking the exceptionally brutal for the average but in imagining that a service as large and complex as the Poor Law and Public Assistance could be replaced overnight with a new and different creation.[46] In practice, the same staff had generally to care for the same residents in the same buildings as before the changeover. This inability to recognise essential continuities in the new system led to a total failure to support progressive and innovative approaches to care demonstrated by the professional organisation representing masters and the collapse of educational initiatives. The Association of Hospital and Welfare Administrators (AHWA), as the organisation was named at this period, recognised that the qualifications which it had struggled so hard to establish would become obsolete in 1948, so it proposed that they should be replaced by new qualifications to be awarded by an 'Incorporated Society of Institutional Administrators' to give professional status to the non-medical lay administrator. This proposal came to nothing and as the government itself had no proposals to put in their place, the result was the almost total lack of appropriate training opportunities for residential staff noted by Lady Williams in her Report nearly 20 years later.[47]

While the Association's lobbying efforts were undoubtedly hampered by its links with a discredited Victorian past, it finally put itself beyond the pale with its campaign launched in 1944 as 'One Code for all the Social Services and one only', later abbreviated to 'One Code for All'.[48] This was directly opposed to the philosophy of the new services which lay in a divide between 'health needs' which were to be met by the NHS and 'social needs' which were to be the responsibility of the National Assistance Board and local social services departments. To supporters of the new plans, this campaign appeared to be an attempt to mould the new arrangements on the all-embracing lines of the Poor Law and so was easily dismissed as reflecting the self-interest of a group of reactionary staff.[49] It highlighted the difficulty, and ultimately the absurdity, of making a distinction between the health and social needs of frail older people.[50] Far from being self-serving and backward-looking, this proposal addresses the issues of service co-ordination and 'cost shunting' which have continued to blight the system up to the present day.[51] By failing to support the professionalising aspirations of an elite grouping of former masters, the reforming post-war government sowed the seeds of continuing structural problems in the health and social services.

Acknowledgements

I am grateful to Laurence Dopson, doyen of writers on health care and its history, without whose assistance and encouragement this research would not have been carried out, and to the members of the former Association of Health and Residential Care Officers who so generously shared their memories with me. The interpretations and opinions expressed here are, of course, my responsibility alone.

This chapter is dedicated to my parents.

Notes

1 R. Means and R. Smith, 'From public assistance institutions to "sunshine hotels": changing state perceptions about residential care for elderly people, 1928–48', in D. Jerrome (ed.), *Ageing in Modern Society: contemporary approaches*, London, Croom Helm, 1983, pp. 199–206.
2 J. Adams, 'Caring for the casual poor', *Oral History*, 1989, vol. 17, no. 1, pp. 29–35.
3 L. Lewis, *Association of Health and Residential Care Officers: a short history (1898–1984)*, Faversham, L. Lewis, (n.d.).
4 M. Foucault, *Discipline and Punish: the birth of the prison*, Harmondsworth, Penguin, 1991.
5 A. Digby, *Pauper Palaces*, London, Routledge & Kegan Paul, 1978, p. 66.
6 N. Land, *Victorian Workhouse: a study of Bromsgrove Union Workhouse 1836–1901*, Studeley, Brewin Books, 1990.
7 M.A. Crowther, *The Workhouse System 1834–1929: the history of an English social institution*, London, Methuen, 1983, p. 41.
8 I. Anstruther, *The Scandal of Andover Workhouse*, Gloucester, Alan Sutton, 1984. S. Webb and B. Webb, *English Poor Law History: Part II: the last hundred years*, vol. 1, London, Frank Cass, 1929 edition, reprinted 1963, pp. 179–82.
9 Anstruther, op. cit., p. 125.
10 A.R. Neate, *The St Marylebone Workhouse and Institution 1730–1965*, London, St Marylebone Society, 1967.
11 M.A. Crowther, 'The later years of the workhouse 1890–1929', in P. Thane (ed.), *The Origins of British Social Policy*, London, Croom Helm, 1978, pp. 36–55.
12 R.M. Gutchen, 'Masters of workhouses under the New Poor Law', *The Local Historian*, 1984, vol. 16, no. 2, pp. 93–9.
13 Crowther, *The Workhouse System*.
14 P. Townsend, *The Last Refuge: a survey of residential institutions and homes for the aged in England and Wales*, London, Routledge & Kegan Paul, 1962, p. 86.
15 Mr Lionel Lewis (born 1914).
16 Mr Clifford Beddis (born 1913).
17 Mr A.D. Malcolm (born 1909).
18 Mr Ray Livesey (born 1911).
19 Mr Livesey.
20 Mr Lewis.
21 Crowther (1983) is one of the few historians of the workhouse to have provided a detailed account of these issues up to 1929.
22 Crowther, *The Workhouse System*, pp. 145–6.
23 Mr John Dawber (born 1925).
24 Mr Frank Hinchliffe (born 1917).
25 Mr Dawber.
26 Information from Mr Edwin Berry (born 1915).
27 Mr Dawber.
28 J. Adams, 'Master and matron: work and marriage in the public assistance institution', *Royal College of Nursing History of Nursing Society Journal*, 1992/3, vol. 4, no. 3, pp. 125–30.

29 National Assistance Act, 1948. Part III of the Act was concerned with the provision of residential accommodation for older people.
30 Mr Beddis.
31 Mr Lewis.
32 Mr Beddis.
33 Mr Beddis.
34 Townsend, op. cit.
35 Ibid., p. 87.
36 G. Williams, *Caring for People: staffing residential homes*, London, George Allen & Unwin, 1967.
37 Williams, op. cit., pp. 143–4.
38 Ibid., p. 164.
39 See also G. Bennett and S. Ebrahim, *The Essentials of Health Care of the Elderly*, London, Edward Arnold, 1992, pp. 57–60; H. Evers, 'The historical development of geriatric medicine as a specialty', in J. Johnson and R. Slater (eds.), *Ageing and Later Life*, London, Sage, 1993, pp. 319–26.
40 Crowther, *The Workhouse System*; R. White, *Social Change and the Development of the Nursing Profession: a study of the Poor Law Nursing Service 1848–1948*, London, Henry Kimpton, 1978.
41 Mr Livesey.
42 Mr Lewis.
43 Mr Don Ernsting (born 1913).
44 C. Hughes, *The 150th Anniversary of Riverside, Pembroke, 1839–1989*, Pembroke, Dyfed County Council, 1989.
45 Mr Ernsting.
46 The full title of the National Assistance Act, 1948, states that its purpose is to 'terminate the existing poor law and to provide in lieu thereof for the assistance of persons in need by the National Assistance Board and by local authorities'.
47 Williams, op. cit.
48 W.E. Morgan, *The Future Institutional Service*, Blackburn, NAALGE, 1944.
49 In fact all utterances by the Association tended to be regarded in this light: see N. Roberts, *Our Future Selves*, London, George Allen & Unwin, 1970.
50 For about 20 years after 1948 there were indeed a number of institutions with both hospital beds, managed by the NHS, and residential beds, managed by the local authority. These so-called 'joint-user' establishments were not successful as there was little incentive for local authorities to make the necessary investment in them since it was always intended that their beds would be re-located in new, purpose-built residential homes for older people. See C.S. Brumpton, *Memorandum on the Possible Effects of Legislation in Connection with the National Assistance Bill and the Repeal of the Poor Law Acts, upon the Administration of Local Authority Welfare Establishments*, Blackburn, NAALGE, 1948; J. Moss, *Hadden's Health and Welfare Services Handbook*, London, Hadden, Best & Co., 1948; Townsend, op. cit., p. 35.
51 J. Bond, 'Living arrangements of elderly people', in J. Bond, P. Coleman and S. Peace (eds.), *Ageing in Society: introduction to social gerontology*, 2nd edition, London, Sage, 1993, pp. 200–25.

5

THE CONTRIBUTION OF PROFESSIONAL EDUCATION AND TRAINING TO BECOMING A MIDWIFE, 1938–1951

Maxine Rhodes

Although the struggle for professional status among midwives has been well documented,[1] there has been little detailed research into other aspects of midwifery, such as the education and training of midwifery pupils, the work of midwives once qualified and their role within the developing maternity services, and their relationship with the women they cared for. Recently, some of these issues have received the attention of researchers, many of whom have found oral history methodology to be vital to their work.[2] However, while much of the emphasis has been on either the working lives of midwives or their relationship with women as mothers, little attention has actually been paid to how a woman became a midwife: that is, to the construction and development of the professional persona and the body of knowledge upon which this was based.

Midwifery knowledge was not based on technical skills alone but was influenced by other issues such as power in the workplace, experiential knowledge and the moral environment in which pupils operated.[3] As a result it is insufficient simply to recount the subject matter of training (made explicit, of course, in the syllabus) as a way of understanding the development of the professional self. Of far greater significance are the meanings attached to the subject matter, the type of knowledge upon which this was based and how these reflected the power and status of midwives. Important messages about what a midwife should be were passed on to pupils through their relationships with other medical health care workers (tutors, qualified midwives and doctors) who disseminated midwifery knowledge in training, and these relationships (which formed the professional 'gaze', to borrow from Foucault[4]) had important consequences for the status of midwives and for the standards of care offered. By exploring the experience of education and training and their contribution to the process of becoming a midwife, it is possible to see how one body of medical knowledge affected power relationships and professional development.[5]

Such elements are subjective and the processes they produced are not well documented. They can therefore be explored only by the use of personal testimony. Documentary evidence provides much useful information about the construction and dissemination of midwifery knowledge, but it tends to give a rather one-dimensional view of its impact, interpretation and practical application; for instance midwifery textbooks, rule books of the Central Midwives Board (the midwives' regulatory body) and lecture notes only identify 'best practice', giving no indication of how this operated in reality. While this is clearly useful in itself as a way to understanding some of the content of midwifery knowledge and what it was deemed necessary for the midwife to know, such sources offer no insight into how both pupils and midwifery educators engaged with this knowledge, how it was utilised in practice and how it contributed to the midwife's own sense of her professional self. It is only through an exploration of the individual experience of education and training (the pupil's first interaction with the essence of midwifery knowledge) that the position of the midwife within the medical hierarchy and her relationship with other midwives, with health professionals and with mothers can be fully understood. Oral history methodology, with its emphasis on legitimising the use of individual experience, is particularly appropriate for exploring the relationship between knowledge, power and professionalisation. By interviewing midwives themselves – in this case a group of women who trained between 1938 and 1951[6] – the complex process of becoming a midwife can therefore be explored in depth.

The development of training

Courses of training, their content and their organisation were essentially controlled by the Central Midwives Board (CMB) which itself had been created by the first Midwives Act of 1902 to regulate the profession and maintain a register of legitimate practitioners. Midwifery education and training programmes had undergone several changes since 1902 which essentially broadened their content and lengthened the period of training for all pupils, while requiring women without nurse training (the direct-entry pupils) to be instructed for a longer period than those who were nurse trained. Further significant alterations were to come in 1938, largely in response to the changes brought about by the 1936 Midwives Act, and training programmes were now in two parts. Part One of the training was based within the maternity hospital setting, with combined theoretical and practical training, and was to be of six months' duration for nurses and 18 months for direct entry pupils. Part Two was primarily practical and could either be entirely based in the community with students attending home births for six months (known as *being on the District*) or could be split, with three months in a hospital and three months on the District.[7] These organisational changes were introduced to counter criticisms levelled at the profession concerning standards of care and were important in helping to define the midwife's role. However, the CMB remained responsible for creating the syllabus and therefore for deciding what the pupil midwife needed to know. While there were many aspects to her training, she was essentially regarded as the 'practitioner with responsibility for normal childbirth',[8] a definition which reinforced her status within the medical hierarchy by ensuring that there was no confusion between her work and the work of doctors.

As a result she was to be instructed in elementary anatomy, physiology, hygiene and sanitation and their relationship to normal pregnancy, childbirth and care of infants.[9] In addition, she needed to be taught to identify any deviation from the norm and therefore her education had to explore subjects such as signs and symptoms of abnormal pregnancy, labour and the puerperium[10] as well as obstetric emergencies and their management.[11] However, such training in abnormal pregnancy and childbirth had to be carefully organised to avoid any confusion in the midwife's mind between her work and the more highly regarded work of doctors. Consequently, references were made in teaching texts to the need for recruits to be alert and independently minded, while at the same time care was being taken to ensure they did not begin to regard themselves as the equals of medics. One way of doing this was constantly to remind midwives of their roles: being responsible for normal childbirth, acting as assistants to doctors and being aware of the rules of their profession. The author of one popular text, commenting on the inclusion of a chapter on 'Obstetric Operations', neatly summarised this approach: 'Although the midwife is never called upon to perform these operations, she ought to know many things regarding them if she is to take an intelligent interest in her work, and if she is to act as a skilled assistant to the medical practitioner.'[12] In this way the subject matter of what was taught to pupils helped reinforce rather than improve her position within the medical team.

What is immediately striking about the organisation of midwifery training is its emphasis upon institutional maternity care and its location within the maternity hospital. Much of the pupils' time was spent in the maternity hospital and while the purpose of such emphasis was arguably to familiarise pupils with procedures and theory and to provide examples of emergencies and abnormalities, the organisation of the training itself provided a distorted image of practice. In reality, the majority of the qualified midwife's work was with normal births (indeed she was forbidden by the CMB rules from attending any 'abnormality'[13]) and took place within the domestic setting – during 1944 only 31 per cent of midwives were practising in hospitals, nursing homes and other institutions.[14] While some acknowledgement was given to the importance of district experience, training within the hospital setting was consistently regarded as superior in that it offered the chance to see 'correct' procedures. The organisation of training, therefore, and the environment in which it took place sent important messages to pupils about their status as qualified practitioners. By emphasising the superiority of the hospital environment, training implied that the work of the domiciliary midwife was somehow of a lower status than that performed within the maternity hospital. In this way, midwifery education actively contributed to maintaining the persistently low status of midwives within the hierarchy of medical health care workers.[15]

Vocation or career?

Examination of the recruitment patterns of this sample, however, reveals that pupils themselves viewed the profession rather differently. Although the women in the sample had come to midwifery via a variety of routes, they fell broadly into two categories. Those who were nurses before becoming midwives spoke of always wanting to nurse and saw midwifery training as the logical next step. For these women, the midwifery qualification was a way of completing their training. The direct-entry midwives had different reasons for taking up midwifery and spoke of this step as a way of improving themselves and their career prospects. Most had been in unfulfilling or low-paid work before taking up the training. One said: 'I wanted to do something with my life,'[16] while another, commenting on the variety of employment, kept telling herself: 'I can do better than this.'[17] These responses were typical among direct-entry midwives who clearly saw midwifery as offering them higher status in the labour force. For these women, midwifery training provided the opportunity of a rewarding and fulfilling career and such attitudes thereby indicate some discrepancy between public and medical perceptions of the status of midwives.

Despite changes to the organisation of training courses and more widely held concerns over the standards of midwifery care, there were few changes to the formal entry requirements for pupils in this period. Nurses were almost guaranteed a place by virtue of their initial qualification while direct-entry pupils had to be over 21 years of age, have a good standard of general education and provide a certificate signed by two responsible people (such as teachers or priests) to show that they were 'trustworthy, sober and of good moral character'.[18] These entry qualifications reflected conflicting concerns felt throughout the profession: how to encourage more women to train without at the same time putting at risk the reputation of the profession. Anxiety at the shortage of practising midwives (an issue that was especially apparent during and after the Second World War) was not going to be eased by raising the educational requirements. On the other hand, standards could not be lowered for fear of risking the accusation of poor moral and mental character among the recruits. Professional memories of the damage done by the untrained handywoman or Mrs Gamp figure were too fresh to allow this. Despite these concerns, there were few incentives offered to women to train and salaries were not commensurate with their duties and responsibilities – about £40 per year for a direct-entry pupil, with nurse trained pupils being slightly better off on £65 per year.[19]

Historically, entry into midwifery was not restricted simply to those women who had undergone nurse training and the persistent presence of the direct-entry pupil contributed to the occupation retaining its independence from nursing and its separate identity as a specialism within medicine. However, direct-entry pupils[20] did not, in this period at least, account for more than a small proportion of the midwifery labour force – in the 1940s only approximately 4 per cent of pupils had no nurse training.[21] Despite being small in number, these 'non-nurse' trained personnel caused tensions within the profession, often being regarded by midwifery tutors and other members of the medical team as inferior to the nurse trained entrant. While this was not a cause of significant internal divisions amongst the pupils, who did not generally regard nurse training as a necessary prerequisite (or conversely a disadvantage) to practice, their superiors sometimes made a distinction between the two groups which may have had some impact on pupils' self-image and the way they viewed their colleagues. The matron of one training school, for instance, commented while praising one of her midwifery pupils: 'Of course you are General Trained and that makes a difference.'[22] The very existence of the direct-entry pupil no doubt contributed to midwifery being regarded as inferior to other branches of medicine but among midwives themselves a strong professional consciousness was formed which tended to unify rather than divide them as a workforce.

This awareness of a common purpose was encouraged by the organisation of the training programme and the individuals' practical experience. All the midwives interviewed followed the same pattern and completed Parts One and Two consecutively as was the norm (except for Nurse E who had not enjoyed her experience of Part One and completed Part Two only after colleagues persuaded her. She then went on to spend the rest of her working life as a district midwife even though she had not originally intended to do so).

Table 5.1 shows the geographical location of the pupils' training which in each case clearly reflects the structural pattern of the training programme implemented from 1938. In this sample, all pupil midwives spent the first part of their training in a maternity hospital as was the norm, and while there was some variation in location of their training, there was great similarity in the interviewees' recollections of their experiences. Training was designed to instil the importance of discipline and the value of hard work and all the women commented upon the arduous nature of their duties, particularly when ward work had to be combined with study and lectures had to be attended even if they occurred in off-duty times. Pupil midwives were vital to the running of maternity hospitals and worked from the very beginning of their training

Table 5.1 Training patterns of the sample

Name	Training	Part One	Part Two
Nurse A	1940–1	Gate Burton Hall[a]	Hull District
Nurse B	1938–9	Hospital Hull	Hull District
Midwife C	1947–9	Hospital Hull	Hull District
Nurse D	1950–1	Hospital Leeds	Hull District
Nurse E	1944 and 1947	Hospital Ilford	Hull District
Midwife F	1946–8	Hospital Hull	Hospital Bridlington/ Withernsea District
Nurse G	1944–5	Hospital Burnley	Hospital Grimsby/ Hull District
Midwife H	1947–9	Hospital Hull	Hospital Sheffield/ Sheffield District

Note [a]During the Second World War the Municipal Maternity Hospital in Hull moved to Gate Burton Hall in Lincolnshire.

at all aspects of the job, both manual (dusting wards and other cleaning jobs) and medical (in the ante-natal and post-natal wards as well as in the delivery room), as well as being required to attend all lectures and produce evidence of competent record keeping. One interviewee listed some of the jobs carried out by pupils on the post-natal ward: 'Duties included bed-making, temperature taking, bed-pan rounds, vulval toilet and care of perineal stitches. . . . Special attention was given to the care of the breasts (and) we supervised mothers feeding their babies.'[23] Once the assessments and examinations needed to complete Part One had been passed, Part Two could be taken and for all trainees this was of six months' duration. This part of the training resulted in increased responsibility as the midwives prepared for practice. In this sample, most completed their training on the District, although three combined this with hospital work. Their reasons for doing so varied, although one initially disapproved of home births, recalling: 'I thought at that time that it was appalling that women should have their babies at home. When I had done my District training I liked it so much I stayed on the District.'[24] Clearly pupils underwent a period of great personal change during training as they were immersed in the values and attitudes of the midwifery profession, but it is only through close examination of individual experiences that the importance of education and training in the transformation from trainee to professional can be revealed.

Knowing your place

Midwifery training was not only concerned with transferring the technical skills and information a pupil would need in practice but was also important in locating midwives within a particular hierarchy and moral landscape. Professional medicine developed an intricate system of rank which placed specialists and general practitioners, for example, above midwives and health visitors. It is worth noting the gender-specific nature of this hierarchy which placed completely female occupations in an inferior position, often regarding them as 'non-medical'. Adherence to this hierarchy had to be instilled into pupils and while there were few overall differences between the testimony of direct-entry and nurse trained midwives, some distinction can be made between the two groups and their attitudes to this structure. The nurse trained midwife generally accepted the strict hierarchy within the hospital and indeed seemed to prefer it; she often cited the present-day lack of an established chain of command (as she knew it) as proof of falling standards: 'When we were doing our training (and) the doctors came on the ward you stood to attention. . . . It's not like it was, the standard has gone down something shocking.'[25] Such attitudes appear to have been a reflection of the content of general nurse training which instilled obedience and loyalty to senior members of staff. This extract from one of the midwives' lecture notes (taken as a pupil nurse during 1936) confirms this and shows how nurse trained pupils came to midwifery with a clear sense of the code of conduct required of them:

> Hospital etiquette . . . consists in showing respect to seniors and those in authority. Always rise when being spoken to. . . . Shut and open the ward doors for doctor and see they have clean hot water. . . . Always keep patients quiet while doctor is on the ward. . . . When taking orders never lounge but stand erect . . . .[26]

Nurses were left in no doubt of their position within the medical team and, given this, the attitude of the nurse trained midwives is perhaps unsurprising.

The direct-entry pupils tended to have a different attitude to the issue of deference and adherence to hospital etiquette and, while broadly respecting the rules under which they worked, seemed to be less committed to the system of rank and their place within it. On the whole, they tended to ridicule the system – although one direct-entry pupil did not like the system at all and commented that she was no different from (and certainly not inferior to) any other member of staff.[27] However, whether they approved or not, hospital etiquette had to be followed. The most complicated routines were reserved for the visit of the Consultant; one direct-entry midwife recalled mockingly how this system worked and commented that the Consultant

> was regarded more or less as God; he was so important
> ... he would walk with his hands behind his back and
> then there would be the doctors in order behind him,
> then the Sister, the nurses and that's how you would
> parade around him.[28]

This, however, was not the only purpose of training; it was also used to instil a moral code which served two functions: firstly, it reinforced the position of midwifery by helping to define the boundaries of the midwives' work; secondly, it helped promote the development of a professional consciousness through pride in the work they did. Pupils were constantly made aware of the rules of the profession which centred around their relationship with the doctor and their responsibilities to the mother. As a result, midwives quickly developed an understanding of their sphere of influence and this tended to remain with them throughout their professional life: 'If you were at all worried, I mean, it was your duty as a midwife to; it was one of the rules ... if a patient hadn't booked a doctor you would call him on a medical aid.'[29]

Consequently, certain issues were regarded as being outside the scope of the midwives' work. Contraception, for example, was not an issue discussed by tutors, principally because of its connotations: most midwives when asked about the issue of birth control simply responded that this was not part of their work but was the preserve of the health visitor (who took over once the midwife had completed her period of observation and care of the mother and baby). These professional boundaries between midwives and other health care workers were part of the professional code and were clearly outlined in training. They were rarely crossed and to do so was to risk creating tensions between individuals.

There were, however, other more cultural reasons why contraception was an awkward topic for midwives. Qualified midwives had, for some time, been trying to disassociate themselves from the image of the handywoman (who was known to help prevent conception as well as to aid birth) and contraception tended to be equated, in the professional consciousness at least, with abortion – which, of course, was illegal. Although most cases of abortion were not catered for within the maternity hospital (or if they were, they were separated from other mothers in isolation wards), some of the midwives recalled how they came into contact with both spontaneous and induced abortions while training. Naturally occurring abortions had to be monitored and midwives often sat with the women for the duration of the process.[30] Women dying of failed or incomplete abortions were often used to reinforce the moral code – particularly if these abortions were suspected of being self-induced – to illustrate the dangers of the practice and to warn pupils against becoming involved: 'We were taken to see this lady. The smell was atrocious. She had gangrene. A knitting needle had been used on her. So I mean we were taken in to see her . . . to learn a lesson.'[31] Sometimes women would confess to midwives if they failed to abort and therefore went to full term, often seeing the pains of childbirth as a punishment: 'One who had been to a chemist . . . she had rather a long, drawn out, difficult labour and she blamed it, you see, on her doing this. She hadn't succeeded, you see, and she said, "Is it because I've done this?"'[32] However, any suggestion that the midwife herself was in any way involved had to be avoided to protect her professional status. Moreover, as midwives represented 'the authorities', it is unlikely that women would have openly approached them about abortion techniques in any case.

Creating a professional persona

Professional unity was also encouraged by their training, as the boundaries of the midwives' work were clearly defined. This resulted in midwives being fiercely proud of their position as 'the practitioner with responsibility for normal childbirth' and jealously guarding their preserve. Most made reference to the importance of independence ('You worked on your own, making your own decisions and coping on your own'[33]) and while they adhered to the rules of their profession by calling for medical assistance in complicated cases, they often bitterly resented any interference by doctors in 'normal' childbirth. One midwife keenly protected her territory, commenting on her later work in the maternity hospital: 'They (the doctors) knew where they stood with me . . . I could be as awkward as them.'[34] Professional parameters were always protected, but other midwives had easier relationships with doctors although they firmly believed that if midwifery skills were correctly applied, the presence of doctors at any normal birth would be unnecessary: 'As long as you know your midwifery rules, what you shouldn't do and what you should do, when you should call in medical aid and when you shouldn't. If you know your midwifery as we all ought to do . . . you shouldn't have no trouble.'[35] Most interviewees made reference to the pride they felt in their work and the special position they occupied: 'We were very privileged . . . I have seen these babies before anyone else. It's a privilege to have done it.' [36] Others focused on their ability to improve a woman's experience by passing on the benefit of their training:

I felt humble always that I could be with a woman (during birth) . . . you learnt all about the things they were going through and advice; you could maybe drop a pearl (of wisdom) or two – nothing was more fulfilling to me than being a midwife.[37]

Once again, training and education ensured midwives knew the limits of their role but at the same time encouraged professional pride and independence.

The moral environment was not solely confined to professional issues, but was also extended to personal character and behaviour. Pupil midwives were closely monitored throughout their training and they were expected to be totally committed to their work. As members of a closed community, all pupils were expected to live in (at least during Part One) as boarders, either in the maternity hospital or at the midwifery centre (when completing Part Two) where their accommodation and meals were provided. Communal life had both benefits and disadvantages but there was no option to this arrangement and even married women (of whom there was one in this sample) had to live at the maternity hospital. In this way, a sense of professional identity, duty and responsibility could be quickly established. Some of the pupils relished living in: 'As everyone was resident . . . there was quite a lot of fun really and (we) shared everybody else's romance or whatever was going on.'[38] Others remarked on the attention given to them by the maids, particularly on days off: 'I can always remember when it used to be my day off – it used to be a real treat. We used to have our breakfast brought into our room by a maid. . . . We liked it. It was lovely: it was a community.' [39] Interviewees also commented on the rigidly hierarchical nature of their community, the strict rules and the way the power structures found on the ward were repeated within the living quarters. One midwife recalled how Matron would not eat in the same dining room as the other staff but usually took meals in her quarters,[40] while another recalled how the ranks did not mix, even at table where pupils sat apart from senior staff: 'You didn't sit with a Staff Nurse or a Sister, you were in your place.'[41] Clearly the body of midwifery knowledge that pupils came into contact with during training incorporated elements reflecting the moral geography of the workplace – including some acknowledgement of the issues of status and rank as well as taking account of the historical issues within the profession. It was defined not only by midwifery tutors but also through a discourse with doctors and specialists (who formed an influential part of the CMB and had their own professional agendas) who were not, of course, primarily interested in improving the status of midwives.

The experience of midwifery training

Nursing and midwifery were, during this period, regarded by the public as suitable occupations for women and ones which occupied an elevated position. They were often perceived as rather glamorous and romantic professions, but this was far from the truth. While on the wards completing Part One of the training course, the pupils were rotated between the different departments and experienced the work of the ante-natal, post-natal and labour wards. Their days were organised in shifts and they were required to carry out any duty demanded of them. They were never allowed to be 'idle' and had a number of jobs to perform, much of which was routine drudgery ranging from making beds and dusting to cleaning instruments:

> In between doing all these other things we were stood on the corridor making cotton wool balls and packing these bags to go to be sterilised. There used to be the pads in those. Same as the syringes, no ready syringes in packets . . . they had to be washed and put in spirit; they were kept in trays with spirit in, so really hard work. Same as the bed pans now that was! I mean, there was no mothers going to the toilet – you had the bed-pans to empty.[42]

From the beginning of training, they watched babies being born and were soon involved in deliveries. One midwife recalled her first birth:

> First baby I saw, my goodness, me eyes nearly fell out me 'ead. I couldn't believe it! Because in those days, I mean like childbirth and all that wasn't talked about. But by, when you think . . . it's marvellous isn't it?[43]

There was also friendly rivalry in racing to be first to attend deliveries: 'The bell used to go and if you were on duty . . . it used to be a toss up between the (other) students and you, you see, so it was who got there first.'[44] Most had little knowledge about the process of reproduction and so training offered a crash course in sex education: 'Before I went there strangely enough, I didn't really know where babies came from hardly. . . . It was all new to me but I thought it was marvellous.'[45]

All pupils were required under the rules of the CMB to be responsible for ten deliveries and the care of at least 20 mothers during the puerperium, and as a result much of their time was spent with women after birth. Mothers stayed in bed for nine days and during this time, their babies were largely cared for by the pupil midwives who bathed them and changed them before bringing them to the mothers for feeding. Much emphasis was placed on the need for breastfeeding (which was either encouraged or established by coercion) and the supervision of breastfeeding was another of the pupils' duties. Women had to breastfeed and if this was not achieved, a form had to be filled in recording the reason why.

The pupils also cared for the mothers during their stay in hospital which was usually for 14 days. Mothers were given liquorice powder on the second night following birth to ensure the bowels were working – all the midwives commented that this was the worst part of their duties as they were responsible for the cleaning of bedpans:

> Now the worst day for bedpans was on the second night. . . . They were all given half a cup of liquorice powder . . . this horrible green liquid and they all had to drink that. Well, you can imagine what the bedpans were like the next day! So that was pretty horrific.[46]

Much of the emphasis during training was placed upon the cleanliness of the mother:

> You were gowned and masked and sat them on a sterile bed pan. When they'd used it, you had to wash them from the umbilicus to the knee with, we called them bottom bowls ... then either you or someone else came round with the swabbing trolley and they were swabbed down.[47]

This reflected the generally held concern about the outbreak and spread of puerperal fever[48] which could result in maternal death. As a consequence, pupil midwives were required to swab the women five times a day, a routine which, it was hoped, would be taken with them into domiciliary practice. Mothers were allowed to get up on the ninth day, and thereafter the pupils' work was more observational; they were now required to monitor the progress of both mothers and infants, as well as giving instruction on bathing the baby.

While not all of the interviewees completed Part Two on the District, those who did so in Hull tended to live at the Midwifery Centre in the city centre and served the local working-class community, usually providing midwifery care to some of the poorest women. Conditions at the Midwifery Centre were not luxurious and the pupils' accommodation was infested with fleas which the interviewees thought they had brought from the clients' homes. One midwife recalled some of the methods used to deal with the problem:

> The places that you delivered babies in were oh, shocking, on Hessle Road and down there. I remember one case particularly, one night when I went back (to the Midwifery Centre), oh I had to have a tablet of soap under me pillow to kill all the fleas ... you used to come back infested.[49]

Many commented, however, that it was simply impossible to eliminate them completely:

> We all used to pick up a lot of fleas because of the houses we went in. One of the first things we did when we finished was to go and have a bath but we used to shake our clothes over the bath to get rid of the fleas and it

didn't matter how we tried that house (the Midwifery Centre) was infested with fleas.[50]

District work also made great demands of the pupils and while it was supposed to be organised in shifts, pupils offered continuity of care and often worked during their time off. To comply with the CMB rules, pupils had to be responsible for 20 labours during this six-month period, of which ten had to be in the mothers' own homes. This, however, was a minimum requirement and in reality, their case load could be considerably greater than this at around ten deliveries per month: 'You could go from one delivery to another in the night and maybe end up with two or three deliveries.'[51]

Pupils were required to provide the associated ante-natal and post-natal care for mothers as well as attending the birth, and there were numerous comments about the arduous nature of Part Two training. One remembered the effects of this: 'We'd been out maybe working all day and all night and all the next day . . . I've gone to sleep momentarily on my bike.'[52] Furthermore, Part Two involved a greater degree of independent practice and many recalled how they were required to take responsibility for their own cases and only to call in the tutor if difficulties arose which they could not tackle alone: 'You went out with a midwife and eventually . . . you were to go by yourself and just called in for a second opinion . . . so you used to get deliveries by yourself.'[53] The experience of Part Two could be particularly hard if all the women for whom a pupil was responsible gave birth in quick succession:

> It was a busy life. . . . We had quite a lot of nights up . . . you were allotted your own patients and you had to look after these and deliver them. If two or three of your patients came together you might have two or three nights up on the trot.[54]

The pupil midwives also often had to work in difficult circumstances as many of their clients lived in poor accommodation, often without water, heat or lighting: 'We used to carry a candle and money for the telephone . . . because it wasn't unusual to find if you wanted a doctor or a 'phone call that they'd no money.'[55] Some were sympathetic to the needs of these mothers while others felt that their situation was often a result of either ignorance or idleness or both. One commented: 'They don't know how to clean, these people. This is what we were told to do, try and educate these people into a better way of life. I did my best. . . . A little bit of praise went a long way.'[56] While all the midwives interviewed recalled adapting their practice to the surroundings in which they found themselves, training tended to instil a certain moral superiority into pupils and this attitude had important implications for the care some women received. Some midwives recognised the efforts mothers made to prepare for birth but often felt that their usual approach to housework was more slovenly:

> They did clean the rooms up nicely for you actually going for the delivery but . . . they didn't do any more cleaning after that. It gradually got worse and worse until it came to the fourteenth day and you couldn't see anything.[57]

The training programme did little to encourage the pupil midwife to understand the individual circumstances of the women she was to care for, but rather was often judgmental of those who did not provide either the 'correct' equipment or environment for birth.

The pupils' work was not finished once they had completed their rounds; as well as being on call at night, they also had to prepare their bags for the next day's work which, before the widespread use of disposable liners and sterile packs, meant a great deal of extra work boiling liners and instruments:

> After tea you went into this big shed to strip your bag and boil your enamel bowls and gloves up, wash your aprons . . . and the place was filled with steam, and if you'd had any deliveries that day your delivery bag had to be . . . boiled and sterilised and your bag repacked for the next day. So sometimes you was in there until ten o'clock at night after you'd done a day's work.[58]

Furthermore, they had to keep a record of the women they attended and this was inspected by the Supervisor on a regular basis and had to be rewritten if deemed 'untidy'. Telephone calls in the middle of the night were not always welcome; indeed, one midwife recalled how she would try to persuade the mothers that they were not really in labour:

> You say 'Are you sure you've started? Are they regular? Oh they aren't very strong yet, are they?', and you know

full well you might as well get out of bed and get on but you don't . . . get yourself on your bike and take yourself off with all happiness. After a few minutes you wake yourself up and get on with your job. [59]

At the end of Part Two there were further examinations to be passed before receiving the Central Midwives Board Certificate and becoming a midwife.

Once qualified, midwives went on to practice and used their experiences to further refine what they had been taught. Obviously, variations occurred but what they learnt in training remained the foundation of their practice. One illustration of this was the issue of maintaining an intact perineum[60] during labour to avoid the need for stitches. Episiotomies[61] were not regarded as part of normal midwifery and it was seen as the height of bad practice to let a woman tear: 'They very rarely tore because it was a crime. Oh you hadn't to let a patient get torn. "How could she afford a doctor?" we were told. "She can't afford to pay a doctor; she just hasn't to get torn."'[62]

Many of the interviewees commented that tears were unnecessary and resulted from the bad management of labour: 'It's if you try to rush it that the trouble starts you see because it doesn't give the perineum time to stretch.'[63] This reflected the attitudes of their tutors and illustrates the enormous impact their education had on practice. Furthermore, even when qualified, midwives were not allowed to perform any suturing and had to call a doctor if this was required. To do so, however, was in essence to admit failure and all the midwives commented that the women they attended rarely tore because they had been taught to manage the birth properly.

Conclusion

Midwifery education and training was vitally important in transforming pupils into professionals, not only by virtue of its structure and content but also through the interpretation of what was taught. Midwifery education reflected attitudes about the status and role of midwives within the maternity services and encouraged pupils to internalise these and conform to certain standards. At the same time, training made enormous demands of pupils both professionally and personally. The body of knowledge presented to pupils therefore not only contained the technical skills needed to support, monitor and treat pregnant and childbearing women but also included a professional code which emphasised (and supported) the moral landscape of the workplace and the power structures which existed within the medical profession. Training encouraged independence and pride among recruits and practitioners (but only within the boundaries of what was regarded as 'normal' childbirth) and at the same time contributed to the maintenance of distinctions between doctors' work and midwives' work. In this way, midwifery education was crucial to the development of the professional persona and had important consequences for practice, while at the same time helping pupils to locate themselves within the culture of childbirth. Only through the use of personal testimony is it possible to explore these issues and fully assess the impact of the experience of training on the individual midwife.

Notes

1 See for example: J. Donnison, *Midwives and Medical Men*, London, Historical Publications, 1988.
2 See for example: J. Allison, *Delivered at Home*, London, Chapman and Hall, 1996, N. Leap and B. Hunter, *The Midwife's Tale*, London, Scarlet Press, 1993, and L. Marks, '"They're magicians": Midwives, Doctors and Hospitals. Women's Experiences of Childbirth in East London and Woolwich in the Inter-War Years', *Oral History*, Volume 23, Number 1, Spring 1995.
3 For a more detailed discussion of how knowledge is formed see M. Foucault, *The Archaeology of Knowledge*, London, Routledge, 1995, p. 182.
4 See M. Foucault, *The Birth of the Clinic: An archaeology of medical perception*, London, Tavistock, 1973.
5 These themes and ideas have recently been of interest to medical historians. See for example: C. Jones and R. Porter (eds.), *Reassessing Foucault. Power, medicine and the body*, London, Routledge, 1994. However, little attention has been paid to those workforces dominated by women such as midwifery.
6 All of the sample of eight retired midwives trained (at some point) and went on to practise in the same place – Kingston upon Hull in East Yorkshire.
7 For further information see: J. Towler and J. Bramall, *Midwives in History and Society*, London, Croom Helm, 1986.
8 Throughout the interviews midwives referred to themselves in this way.
9 Central Midwives Board, *Rules*, London, Spottiswoode, Ballantyne and Co., 1928, pp. 12–13.
10 The period following birth when the reproductive organs return to their pre-pregnant state. The midwife was responsible for the mother in the first 14 days of this process.

11 Central Midwives Board, op. cit., p. 13.
12 J.S. Fairbairn, *A Text-Book for Midwives*, Oxford, Humphrey Milford and Oxford University Press, 1930, p. 305.
13 Rule E20 of the Central Midwives Board stated that 'In all cases of illness of the patient or child, or any abnormality occurring during pregnancy, labour or lying-in, a midwife must forthwith call into her assistance a registered medical practitioner', Central Midwives Board, op. cit., p. 28.
14 Ministry of Health et al., *Report of the Working Party on Midwives*, London, H.M.S.O., 1949, p. 92.
15 The subject matter of midwifery education and the physical space in which training took place form an important part of midwifery knowledge. Such issues are not the prime focus of this chapter but are the subject of other, more detailed research.
16 Interview with Mrs B Tape 7.
17 Interview with Mrs S Tape 4.
18 Central Midwives Board, op. cit., Form 1, p. 47.
19 Ministry of Health, *Report of the Midwives Salaries Committee*, London, H.M.S.O., 1943, p. 8.
20 Prefixed 'midwife' in Table 5.1 as opposed to nurse trained pupils prefixed 'nurse'.
21 Ministry of Health, 1943, op. cit., p. 27.
22 Interview with Mrs SY Tape 8.
23 Letter from midwife who wishes to remain anonymous.
24 Interview with Mrs SW Tape 9.
25 Interview with Mrs F Tape 3
26 Pupil Nurse Lecture Notes 1936, unpublished.
27 Interview with Mrs S Tape 4.
28 Ibid.
29 Interview with Mrs SW Tape 9.
30 Interviews with Mrs SH Tapes 1 and 2 and Mrs SY Tape 8.
31 Interview with Mrs B Tape 7.
32 Interview with Mrs SW Tape 9.
33 Ibid.
34 Interview with Mrs SH Tapes 1 and 2.
35 Interview with Mrs F Tape 3.
36 Interview with Mrs B Tape 7.
37 Interview with Mrs SH Tapes 1 and 2.
38 Interview with Mrs B Tape 7.
39 Interview with Mrs S Tape 4.
40 Ibid.
41 Interview with Mrs B Tape 7.
42 Interview with Mrs S Tape 4.
43 Interview with Mrs F Tape 3.
44 Interview with Miss P Tape 5.
45 Interview with Mrs S Tape 4.
46 Ibid.
47 Interview with Mrs B Tape 7.
48 A rise of temperature brought about by infection.
49 Interview with Mrs F Tape 3.

50 Interview with Mrs S Tape 4.
51 Interview with Mrs SH Tapes 1 and 2.
52 Ibid.
53 Interview with Miss P Tape 5.
54 Interview with a midwife who wishes to remain anonymous.
55 Interview with Mrs B Tape 7.
56 Interview with Mrs SY Tape 8.
57 Interview with Miss P Tape 5.
58 Interview with Mrs S Tape 4.
59 Interview with Mrs SH Tapes 1 and 2.
60 The area extending from the vagina to the anus which can be cut or torn to aid delivery.
61 A deliberate cut to the perineum.
62 Interview with Mrs SW Tape 9.
63 Interview with Mrs F Tape 3.

6

RECOLLECTIONS OF LIFE 'ON THE DISTRICT' IN SCOTLAND, 1940–1970

Rona Ferguson

I remember saying 'Well I would like a country district with a cottage where I could have my parents', then I don't know what made me add it 'I'd like a cottage with roses round the door'. Well I didn't get it in the first instance but I got it eventually – with roses round the door.

> (Name of informant withheld by request)

This was the request of one nurse at the start of her career when asked by the Superintendent of Scotland what type of district she had in mind for her work. As well as being the personal dream of one woman, her idea suggests something of the romantic notion with which district nursing in the first half of the century is remembered.

Origins

The organised nursing care of people in their homes has its origins in nineteenth-century philanthropy when charitable societies employed women to nurse the poor under the supervision of a 'lady'. Having been impressed by a nurse who cared for his sick wife, Quaker shipbuilder William Rathbone then employed the nurse to tend the sick poor within his area with the idea that this would encourage a return to health and to work as against spiralling sickness and descent into further poverty. The need for trained nurses soon became evident and was filled to some extent by Rathbone's offer to build a new training school for the Liverpool Infirmary in return for the nursing staff trained to work in the districts of Liverpool. Over his subsequent years in parliament Rathbone continued his involvement in the growth of district nursing, maintaining contact with Florence Nightingale who worked for the promotion of educated and highly trained nurses and the recognition of nursing as a profession. Under Miss Nightingale's direction, the Metropolitan Nursing Association, founded in 1874, trained nurses for work in the districts and emphasised the need for a respectful approach of the nurse towards the patient in his or her home.

Dingwall, Rafferty and Webster describe early district nurses as 'mission women' working within schemes which reflect 'two principles in the organisation of mid-Victorian philanthropy. . . . One is the co-opting of working-class women to the task of maintaining order and social discipline. The other is the importance of the household as a model for the relationship between women from different social classes.'[1] This class-distinctive model remained the structure of district nursing organisation well into the twentieth century with the professional and higher classes sitting on the Nursing Association committees, overseeing the working nurse. However, these 'mission women' soon gave way to the trained home nurse concerned to exemplify models of health and hygiene but unconcerned with the religious beliefs of the patients. Throughout the early twentieth century this attitude prevailed in the training scheme of the Queen's Nursing Institute (QNI or 'Queen's')[2] set up in 1887, where the nurses were taught to accept the role of 'visitor' in the home of their patient while maintaining the educative role in matters of health and hygiene. The QNI was funded by the Women's Jubilee Offering to Queen Victoria and dedicated to the promotion of the district nursing service in the form of institutionalised training. It operated in England, Scotland and Ireland and was the paramount training institution for district nursing in the period 1940–1970.

While the origin of district nursing and the QNI is documented by several authors,[3] the daily toil of district nurses and the context in which they worked is under-represented in the literature. The papers of the Queen's Nursing Institute are now catalogued and accessible at the Contemporary Medical Archive Centre, Wellcome Institute, London, with those of the QNI, Scottish Branch, held at the Royal College of Nursing archive in Edinburgh. Many records of the local Nursing Associations have not survived but some information on their organisation, financial status and the working conditions of their nurses is collected in Burdett's *Hospitals and Charities Yearbook*. Up to now the availability of sources has facilitated study of the institution and the district nursing service rather than the experience within it.

This chapter is largely based on oral testimonies taken from elderly retired district nurses who had worked in Scotland. Almost exclusively women, the informants were selected from the historical files of the QNI Scotland where details of their age, year of Queen's training, first district and early supervisor's report were held. Matched to the QNI Scotland current files, their present addresses could be found and in many cases there was also a brief report from the Welfare Committee Visitor commenting on their state of health. From these files an initial selection of 150 interviewees was made to allow a spread of informants who had worked in rural, island or city districts, who were fit and able to be interviewed and who now lived within affordable travelling distance. To date 40 interviews have been undertaken with those who worked during the period 1940 to 1970. At the request of the QNI Scotland,[4] priority was given to the most elderly within this selection. Where available, documentary sources have been consulted and have clarified, to some extent, the organisational structure within which district nursing was administered. However, given that many records of district nursing associations have been destroyed, the major source of information remains the testimonies of those involved at the time. This presents inherent problems for the historian as personal perspectives are often rearranged in memory to make sense of present attitudes, to reinforce positive or negative aspects, or simply to justify a life's work.

Although it is the subjective memory which forms the basis of this chapter and thereby largely a positive perspective which is presented, it is important to keep in mind the intrinsic difficulties in the notion of the 'home visitor' to which district nursing owes its history. In various sources these difficulties have been explained in terms of class distinction, moral dogmatism, scientific theorising and political control. District nursing does not escape such criticism although it appears to have maintained a more favourable public image than some other services. Set against the other two major 'home visitors' of this century (the health visitor and the social worker), the district nurse, through the very emergence of the others, has tried to establish an identity as rooted in the commitment to nursing and caring.

While the instructive and advisory role of the health visitor has been judged as intrusive or critical of mothers and family practices, and the intervention of social workers to gain practical solutions to family problems condemned as the heavy hand of the state working to middle-class, theory-laden models, district nursing's concern with the individual's medical health care has continued to see the home nurse as essentially a carer. The district nurse visited only when required to treat (in that the patient would already have disclosed symptoms, usually to the doctor). The relationship with patients may have lacked sympathy or understanding or cultivated in the nurse an air of superiority, but the prime intention, to treat the sick and bring comfort to the dying, has not been questioned with the same critical edge as the others. Such self-criticism is not reported here in the words of those who spent a lifetime in district nursing. In full knowledge of the subjectivity of recollection, this chapter presents some of the features of district nursing *as it is remembered*. Whether legend or truth, it reflects particular and popular perceptions which are neither verified nor refuted by written sources.

Scotland – training and beyond

In Scotland, qualified general nurses could apply for district nursing training either to QNI Scotland headquarters at Castle Terrace, Edinburgh or to the QNI training home in Glasgow where they were trained in the procedures and attitude suitable for nursing in the home. In 1940 district nurses were to be found distributed throughout Scotland with a total of 1,134 nurses employed by all the associations affiliated to the QNI Scotland. Edinburgh City, where the training headquarters was located at Castle Terrace, claimed the largest proportion with 74 nurses (6.5 per cent). Fife County had 64 nurses on its staff while the islands of Shetland and Lewis employed 17 and 19 respectively. However, it was Glasgow City, employing a total of 65 nurses (5 per cent) which recorded the majority of cases attended (12,879 general; 1,862 maternity) and made the most visits (269,336) in the course of that year.[5] The nurses lived in at the training homes where conditions were basic and the regime invariably remembered as strict. Although general training as a ward nurse in a hospital was also laden with hierarchy and rules, several nurses reported a feeling of irritation with the Queen's discipline requiring obedience to rules which even then seemed both petty and outdated:

Things like, if you washed your hair in your own bathroom on the ground floor and you went down to the basement to make a cup of tea at 10 o'clock at night, someone might come to the front door Miss X, and if you were to pass there without your white cap on it would be a great insult to the profession . . . and she [the Supervisor] used to send us on duty to work, and we were given a half roll on each plate in the morning, a half roll, and she sat and picked at her half roll at the head of the table, she dined with us, and we all went out say at half past eight and her maid, at quarter to nine, took her up a full plate of breakfast.

(Name of informant withheld by request)

The example above regarding the possible sighting of a 'capless' Queen's nurse was cited by several nurses. However, such pettiness was offset by a recognition of the high esteem in which Queen's nurses were held by the public and the status the training offered them:

Mind you everybody looked up to the Queen's. If you got into a bus even an old buddy would offer you a seat and I would say, 'no thanks, but if you take my bag', 'oh what a weight', they would say when you put the bag down on their knee.

(Name of informant withheld by request)

This respect for the Queen's nurse was not always echoed by other health service staff. The nurse quoted above decided to go into district nursing when,

One day I was on Child Welfare in the Gorbals and one day I paid a visit to a new baby and mother and when the door opened she said 'Oh I thought it was the Queen's nurse that was comin'. It was some dressing that the baby needed. So I spoke away and got my particulars but you know I couldn't get out that house quick enough because the district nurse was coming in to do something that I wasnae allowed to do. I mean the Queen's nurse, and that put the Peter on it.

(Name of informant withheld by request)

When she told her supervisor that she intended to take her district training the reply came, '"Sister" she said, "going down the ladder instead of up the ladder." "Oh", I said, "I don't think I'm going down the ladder at all doing my district nursing.'"

The financial burden of further training was often keenly felt but the feeling of comradeship which existed among the nurses in training compensated in some way, helped to reinforce a sense of belonging to the Queen's Institute and counterbalanced the rigours of discipline experienced:

> We did get a small salary and . . . of course because we had our uniform and food and lodgings . . . my mother . . . she was quite good, she would give me something perhaps once a month or something . . . I remember there was an occasion there was four of us in a group and it was the day before payday, none of us had any money left and I said 'Oh I'll just go write to my mother I got a letter from her this morning'. Well, inside her letter she had enclosed a ten shilling note so we all went out on the strength of this ten shilling note, you could have got a lot for ten shillings in those days, you know.
>
> (Miss Esther MacLeod)

After the war a number of men who had undertaken nursing duties in the Services looked to nursing as a civilian career. Although the QNI Annual Reports make no mention of accepting males into training for district nursing, several undertook training at Castle Terrace in the post-war years and one remained on the staff there for several years before accepting a post in Orkney. Their numbers appear to have been few but one male informant recalled being well accepted by the female nurses and of particular use on the district where they were often assigned cases involving heavy lifting. Although lodged separately from the female nurses and with an 'unspoken agreement' to leave midwifery cases to the women, male trainee district nurses enjoyed the same feeling of comradeship as their female counterparts.

The first five months at Queen's were spent on general work such as baths, dressings, enemas and so on, and the daily routine at Castle Terrace was described by one nurse as follows:

> We were wakened at 7 o'clock in the morning, downstairs at 7.25 for prayers and then breakfast and then the work, if there was new patients for your district that was given out. Miss, oh what was her name, head at that time, gave

out the districts and we had up 'til I think 9 o'clock or was it quarter to nine, to make our beds and other things just before we went out. And then lunch was usually 1 o'clock and then you went out at 4.30 again and did the return visits.

(Miss Annie Wright)

Early afternoons were devoted to lectures or study:

We got lectures on child welfare, hygiene, all about drains and that kind of thing, social services what there was at that time, and then we went out, when we went out for our night visits you probably had to go to different districts.

(Miss Annie Wright)

You got pulled off the district to do your lectures and they were very very full lectures and you were expected to write these up at night and about once a week these were taken in and they were scrutinised by the supervisors and ticked and marked good, bad or indifferent.

(Mr James Orr)

The local administrative framework

Affiliated to the QNI were local District Nursing Associations which, recognising the need for home nursing care, took on the administration of the service within their own community. Through a system of house-to-house collections, the Associations gathered subscriptions from the public entitling them to free nursing care at the point of delivery with an additional fee of 10/6d due for midwifery services.[6] Before the advent of the National Health Service, employees' insurance covered medical treatment but only applied to the working man in a family and so the subscription scheme operated by the District Nursing Association made health care accessible to women and children.[7] The Association committee, usually comprising the local minister and several 'upstanding' people within the community, was responsible for appointing the district nurse, administering a salary, maintaining the nurse's accommodation and arranging holidays and off-duty time. In return the nurse was 'responsible to the Secretary [District Nursing Association] for the general working of the district and should draw attention to any point that might require discussion, or might need to be brought to the notice of her Committee'.[8] Although the Association managed the funds, non-members or particular cases could be required to make payment directly to the nurse. In such cases, 'all fees and subscriptions collected by the nurse [were] to be handed over with receipt book weekly or monthly to the Secretary or Treasurer as may be arranged'.[9] Testimonies indicate that the exchange of money between nurse and patient was not a regular feature of the work, with many reporting that they never handled money at all. Others recall taking fees, retaining the sums in their own homes and depositing them with the Nursing Association on a weekly or monthly basis.

On balance, the nurses seemed somewhat unconcerned about the administrative system behind their Association. In their recollections, little significance is given to the financial organisation of nursing care; it is the people and the conditions which remain firmly in their memory. Where patients' payments were cited, informants recalled amounts with uncertainty which served to distance them from the financial aspects of their work. This reinforces the idea echoed by many of the nurses that they were concerned only to 'care for people'. Indicative of a particular view of nursing, the lack of clarity with which the cost of the service to the patient is remembered emphasises 'caring' almost to the exclusion of economic exigencies. When set against the current high priority given to cost-effectiveness, two distinct philosophies emerge regarding nursing: as essentially a patient-centred, caring activity or as a service which can only be considered effective if properly accounted for. It is perhaps not surprising that the elderly nurses who made their working time 'on the district' the central basis of their life, feel a certain empathy with the former rather than with the impersonal reductionism implied in the latter:

> Four shillings I think they paid. Would it be four shillings a year? Four shillings a year for the services of the nurse day or night. . . . I was never involved in any payment of any kind. I think my next district, I think there were rules if you were out overnight, not a confinement, there was, I don't know if there was a set amount, I've a feeling there was a set amount the patient was supposed to pay.
> (Mrs Stark)

Although there is an implied equality in the system of a flat-rate subscription covering all required nursing care (exclusive of midwifery), the comment below suggests that the ethos of a private nursing system continued to impact on the local Associations' work:

> An old lady and her husband stayed with her mother, they had the attic flat ... they paid extra and they got first visit. No matter I passed half my district getting there and supposing I had first new visits, I got two new visits about every day ... they were supposed to get first visits your new visits, but I'd have to pass them to come to this ... it was a big surgical dressing she got.
>
> (Mrs Stark)

The Association also provided accommodation for the nurse in the form of paid lodgings or a house gifted by a local family of standing. Basic furniture was generally provided but nurses often bought additional extras to make the place homely. In the case of a Perthshire District in the 1920s where a house was not available, the nurse was initially lodged in a room costing £1 per week plus 2 tons of coal.[10] Linen and household items were provided by the Association and one inventory reads as follows: '2 pairs sheets, 4 pillow slips, towels, bedcover, tablecloth, 3 tablespoons, 4 dessert spoons, 3 large forks, 2 small, 3 large knives, 2 small etc'.[11] In the same district in 1935 the fact that the nurse was accommodated in a house with no bathroom was discussed by the Association Committee as a matter of concern. It was decided that this ought to be remedied and the committee agreed the motion to build a small four room cottage for their nurse. Four hundred pounds of Association funds was dedicated to the building fund, the remainder to be raised by 'special subscriptions'. Complete with garage and at a total cost of £769 5s 7d, the house was ready for occupation in May 1936.

The provision of accommodation was not a negligible factor for those women considering a career in district nursing. Security in this form offered nurses the opportunity to enjoy a lifestyle independent of their families, although in many cases they remained unmarried and the principal carers of elderly parents:

> I liked working in the community ... I decided I could go in for nursing, now that would give security because I would have board, lodgings and so on ... em, then I got a single district where a cottage was provided.
>
> (Miss MacLeod)

Another thing that maybe influenced me ... the four older sisters had all their own lives and were away from the home and I had said to father and mother that I would make a home for them and I saw district nursing, with a cottage, a possibility of having them ... as a chance of making a home for them eventually when I got a district.

(Name of informant withheld by request)

Similarly, transport for the nurse was often donated through the Association with gifts of bicycles and cars in many districts. However, in the early days, particularly in city districts, public transport and walking remained for many years the principal means of getting from one patient to the next.

Duties on the district

It is with great pride and few regrets that the informants in this study remembered their working lives as district nurses. Despite the years of training rewarded with long hours and low pay, those interviewed remained faithful to their choice of career, even over the possibility of marriage and children. For the majority of women who remained unmarried, marriage and district nursing were regarded as incompatible because the demands on time and energy required to fulfil the function of nurse precluded the devotion they might have given to family. Indeed, many perceived the increasing employment of married district nurses as a contributory factor in what they see as change for the worse in the service. Those who did manage to combine marriage and work tended to be settled in city districts where midwifery services were provided separately by the local authority. In this situation, the district nurse undertook only general duties, perhaps with health visiting included, allowing her to structure her day within normal working hours. This was not the case in the 'triple-duty' districts so common to the Scottish service. Exclusive to female nurses, the triple duty included general nursing, health visiting and midwifery and, at a time when the majority of births took place at home, this necessitated unscheduled night work delivering babies. With large numbers of sparsely populated, remote areas throughout Scotland, the 'triple-duty' nurse was the norm outside the cities and large towns. Responsible for the nursing care of those within her district from the newborn through all life's stages to the elderly and the dying, the triple-duty nurse held a central position within her community:

> The triple-duty nurse knew everybody on her district because you're working with the whole lot right up until they die . . . we had more contact with the folk somehow or other . . . folk confide in you and they get to know you and they tell you things you wouldnae breathe to another soul . . . we were invited to all the weddings 'cos we knew the folk.
>
> (Mrs Henderson)

Triple duty also provided a continuity of care within the community:

> That was the beauty of being on a district where you were doing triple duties. The mother called you when she was expecting her baby, you attended her through ante-natal time, through the birth, you saw the child the first five years of life until they went to school, you followed them through school . . . and then perhaps this young one went off and she maybe left the village for a while but she came back and she would come and have her baby that I've delivered many a baby's baby . . . that was fun.
>
> (Name of informant withheld by request)

Working closely with the local GP, the nurse's caseload was made up of those patients whom the GP recommended for visits to give injections, bathing and dressings. Although ultimately responsible to the Nursing Association, the rural district nurse took a daily caseload from the doctor, where in the cities this was commonly distributed through the nurses' training homes. Assessment of the district nurse's work was provided by nursing supervisors who accompanied the district nurse to a small number of cases, generally a couple of times a year. Feelings about the supervisory visits were split between those who valued the visit and those who found it an insulting nuisance:

> You had to look up to your Superintendent, I did anyway.
>
> (Name of informant withheld by request)

> Some of them [supervisors] were very old fashioned in their attitudes . . . this is another thing that used to annoy

me, they used to come out with us for supervisory visits and come out and see whether you were giving an injection properly. Now in these days you were lucky if you had a coal fire and you had to boil up your syringes in an old pan and that used to be devastating cos they would stand and watch over you y'know ... we were highly trained people we didn't really need that type of thing, we didn't need that type of thing.

(Name of informant withheld by request)

The supervisor also checked the nurse's 'book' and sent a report to the local Nursing Association on observed skills and practice. Other than this book, there was nothing in the way of officially documented case records and so the nurse was expected to present the record book to the Association on a monthly basis:

They (the supervisors) looked at your book, they did examine your daily book and ... I don't know what they were looking for, I can't quite remember the books that we had you certainly had all your patients and you also had your daily visits, some that got every day some that got ... one went down in the space ... I suppose we'd add these up at the end of the month and end of the year or whatever, but these were the books, the books were examined.

(Name of informant withheld by request)

Given the infrequency of the supervisory visits and the ambivalent feelings towards them, for many the GP remained the only regular point of contact for discussion of the work. It was therefore important that the district nurse engender a good working relationship with the doctor in the area. This is not to say that the district nurse was entirely directed by the GP for despite the doctor's official authority on both diagnosis and treatment, most nurses reported feeling in control of their own daily schedule with many feeling able to challenge their GP on matters of treatment and some considering variations in nursing care to be their own decisions:

I once healed a varicose ulcer with honey. It was a huge ulcer on this old lady's leg and I had tried absolutely everything and I thought well, I think I'll try honey, and

I spread it onto a dressing and put it onto her leg and I left it for a whole week and each time I went back, there was new skin growing round about and I eventually healed it. It was really amazing. The doctor didn't interfere in this kind of procedure, leaving the dressings to the nurse.

(Miss Porter)

In contrast to the rule-bound discipline prevalent in hospital wards, this self-determination was felt to be a very positive part of district nursing. Coupled with the 'outdoor' aspect necessary in travelling from one patient to another, it provided a freedom from authority and rigidity which many nurses found oppressive in the hospital system.

District nursing also offered an alternative and more holistic approach to patient care:

I felt that rather than just think about a patient and the patient's illness you'd to think about the environment, you had to think about the family, the effect that the patient had on the family and vice versa the effect that the family had on the patient, that's really why it appealed to me rather than being confined to a hospital ward.

(Mr James Orr)

As nurses were instructed during district training, 'when you are in hospital the patient is the visitor but on the district you are the visitor in their homes'. This was the golden rule of home nursing and nurses remember being welcomed very warmly in most homes:

On a very wet day, one of my patients, she was a very old lady, she really was a darling, and when I used to go in she said, 'now, never mind about me. Take off your shoes and stockings and get everything dried in front of the fire before you go out again.'

(Miss Porter)

The nurse in the community

Working 'on the district' provided the nurse with a secure place in a community, in terms both of the role and of accommodation. In taking the nurse out of the confines of the hospital system it allowed a certain freedom from dogmatic authority and placed the nurse at the centre of a community along with the doctor, the minister and the policeman. On the other hand, the nurse, particularly the rural triple-duty nurse, was on call 24 hours a day, often with little holiday relief, salary was comparatively low (increased from £75 to £100 per annum in 1937) and working conditions could be difficult. Called out in all weathers, delivering babies and bringing comfort to the dying, she is often remembered as a popular figure within the community known and loved by all, and approachable at all times to fathers, mothers and children alike. As suggested above, there is a tendency to paint a romantic picture of the strong but gentle, usually female, rural district nurse working out of her country cottage 'with roses round the door'. This is an image conjured up not only by those of the public who remain grateful for district nursing services but by the nurses themselves who had experienced the attendant difficulties of working 'on the district'. It is an image which gains greater credence when set against the similarly popular view that present-day district nursing is ineffectively organised or at least confused, rendering today's nurse 'on the district' almost invisible. The difficulties of a past era, though remembered, are in retrospect portrayed as sacrifices to the essential task, that of dedication to the care of the patient regardless of prevailing conditions and with little attention to the cost:

> When I first went to Huntly we had an awful lot of the hawker folks. They stayed in huts when I first went there and then they got in tae what wus known as the old houses and they got in there but then that was taken over for buildin and again they got put out an out into camps in the Market B( ), and there was a visiting lot there one turn and there was a baby appeared. I was called out to the confinement and all that a had tae see, it was gettin dark, was a little lamp with a jam jar and the bottom docked off the top o' it for a light – mother and baby got on fine . . . now by that time there was a social service, the – what did they call them at that time? I went to him and got clothes for the baby, but they were away witbin a few days.
> (Miss Annie Wright)

Taken as a whole, the testimonies offer a positive perspective of what it was like to be a district nurse before the 1970s which may stem from this particular view of nursing as a uniquely caring activity.

The anecdotal evidence indicates conditions and procedures experienced by past district nurses which would be considered almost unworkable today. For example, the lack of modern equipment made the routine treatments such as dressings a time-consuming task:

> If we were doing a dressing we had to get a tin and line it with a white hankie, make up all our swabs, bake them in the oven, and it was alright, but for instruments we had to boil them in a saucepan and once I was having a supervision and I said to the old man, 'now whatever you do, don't use my pot for anything tomorrow morning', so when I went he had cooked the porridge in it. We had little kidney dishes in our bags so I boiled my instruments in the kidney dish. And we had no gloves. What dangers we were in. For the dressing that we took off we had to make a little paper poke with newspaper and I remember being shown in Castle Terrace how to make it and I'm not normally stupid at making things but I couldn't get it into my head and eventually I mastered the art . . . I could still do it I think. In those days of course we were lucky because there were coal fires but latterly everything had to go into the bins.
>
> (Miss Porter)

Such basics as sterile equipment were considered to be an immense improvement,

> being able to have sterile dressings and sterile syringes. You know we used to boil a syringe between each house and use a needle over and over again, boil it between each house, and the needles used to be sent away to be sharpened. You collected a few and took them in to Castle Terrace and they were sent away. And they were really steel needles you know. And for colostomies, they didn't have any of these little bags that they have now, they used sphagnum moss bags. Little bags made of sphagnum moss, that was put on the colostomy with a many-tailed bandage round . . . and there were quite a lot on the district.
>
> (Miss Porter)

Medical and nursing techniques required different skills and new drug therapies have now reduced the need for traditional nursing skills:

> In training days there was not even M&B, you've maybe heard of the sulphonamide drugs, we didn't even have that for treating the like of pneumonia. Our treatment for pneumonia in these days was four-hourly poulticing and it was usually linseed poulticing and four-hourly sponging and aspirin. After the war we got the antibiotics and that made a great difference. I can remember one young fellow, a married lad but he had pneumonia and I was attending him very regularly and remember meeting doctor at his bedside one evening and doctor said, 'I'm afraid nurse', I said 'look if there's anything within my power we're going to keep Alistair here'. And he was by then onto antibiotics because doctor had been in the army during the war and was able to get antibiotics although they perhaps weren't very common on district at that time. And we pulled him through.
>
> (Name of informant withheld by request)

The growth of other services and the expansion of community-based care teams have lessened the non-nursing tasks which reinforced good relationships among the nurse and her patients and which were taken on so readily in the past:

> You were a Jenny-a'-thing. And the people needed you and the help that they needed was very often not entirely all nursing. I mean they wouldn't have any breakfast, they wouldn't have had a cup of tea, their fire wouldn't have been put on. Now of course that's changed.
>
> (Name of informant withheld by request)

> Now we used to very often, when people were on their own, you would go in and they maybe hadn't had any breakfast. You used to light their fire, give them breakfast, give them something. We used to do that, we all did that at the time. You're not allowed to do anything like that nowadays.
>
> (Name of informant withheld by request)

Phrases such as, 'in my day' and 'they don't do that now' are ubiquitous in the retelling of anecdotes, further distancing what is the remembered reality of the informants from the exigencies of current community nursing.

Conclusion

The informants here report a clear identification of their role, both as professional colleagues and nurses to their patients. This may be due in some measure to an apparently simple structure of working relationships compared to that of district nurses today. Prior to the NHS Act coming into force in 1948, nurses were accountable to the local Associations as their employer, liaised with GPs regarding cases, were inspected by Superintendents and provided with refresher training courses by the QNI. Career prospects could be enhanced by further training in midwifery or as a health visitor, giving the opportunity for sideways movement and, while some aspired to becoming supervisors, many wished only to remain on the district, working closely with their patients. Patient care may have been shared with health visitors and midwives but in many cases, particularly in rural or triple-duty areas, the district nurse took on that role also.

After 1948, local authorities took on the administration of district nursing services including training but many continued to use the existing expertise of the otherwise redundant Associations. This organisational structure pre-dated the teamwork era prevalent since the 1970s and it afforded the early district nurses independence in their work which can be described either as isolating or autonomous. Furthermore, almost all informants suggested a distinct lack of confidence in the system of community nursing, incorporating district nursing, in operation today. This raises the question as to whether there is a definition of 'district nursing' which is both valid and appropriate to the service of the past and that practised today or whether the present interpretation of their function is unrecognisable in light of experiences recalled from the past. Is the early experience of district nursing prone to mythologisation by the selective memory and can this memory be challenged? In an attempt to answer such questions and in adopting a less subjective view, one might look at key events which affected the working practice of the district nurse: the introduction of the National Health Service; the development of new drugs and technologies; the growing dominance of the hospital and the obstetrician in maternity care resulting in a dramatic drop in home births; the acceptance of married women into the profession requiring structured working hours; the increase in social services and development of community health policies and the reorganisation of the service within an increasingly unwieldy welfare state.

Before the NHS, nurses attended patients who could not afford to call the doctor first and doctors sometimes refused to call until the 'money was on the table'. The exchange of money was an integral part of health care, yet informants placed little emphasis on this as though it were an insignificant issue. Extant documentary sources indicate meticulous accounting of Nursing Association funds but the nurses themselves had little memory of financial matters.[12] Several informants conceded that the cost of home nursing was a hardship in some cases and it is reasonable to assume that in districts where extreme poverty prevailed this was more common but nurses often took the collection of payment to be a matter of their own discretion and so the official policy of the system was not always implemented nor were these omissions recorded. In theory everyone paid an affordable sum, in practice the nurse exercised a personal judgement and the level of discretionary decisions remains subject to the memory of the nurses involved. This difference between what is disclosed in recall and what is recorded in documentary evidence serves to reinforce a notion of district nursing which is comfortable rather than an 'accurate' statement of conditions. Similarly, statistical evidence indicates with a certain accuracy the decreasing number of births which took place in the home requiring the services of a district nurse as midwife but the effect of this shift on district nursing is more fully realised when recalled by the nurses themselves. Many welcomed the increasing regularity of their working hours with the drop in home confinements giving them a greater freedom in their social life while others felt the move to hospitals to be an implicit criticism of their work.

Before the 1960s in relation to social care of their patients, little professional help was available beyond the hospital almoner and so it was not uncommon for the district nurse to act as counsellor, acquiring clothing for the needy, preparing food or seeking housing advice on someone's behalf, none of which were incumbent upon her other than in a moral sense. One would expect, then, the growth of the social services to have produced a welcome co-operation between the services which produced a reduction of the nurses' tasks, allowing more time for actual nursing. In reality, the nurses report an uneasy relationship between district nurse and social worker coupled with a scepticism towards the social services as a whole. With a tradition of involvement in people's familial and social circumstances and a belief in this as integral to the understanding of their health, the district nurse found the separation of health and social problems into two different spheres extremely difficult to accept. In areas where the district nurse was also health visitor, more typically in small communities, the roles merged harmoniously. In cities, where the post of health visitor was frequently separate, a high level of co-operation tended to prevail as, unlike social workers, the health visitor was regarded as a fellow 'health' worker albeit with a much reduced nursing remit. As with the other changes discussed, the introduction of the 'professional' social worker with a specialist knowledge of matters hitherto dealt with by the nurse informally, but yet having no nursing experience, may have been perceived as an erosion of the traditional role of the district nurse as a central figure in health care with the freedom to exercise discretion and having a unique knowledge of her patient community.

As progress in medical treatment and expertise has advanced, eradicating many of the ills which necessitated prolonged nursing care, so too the diversion of health care responsibility among a much-expanded health and social care team has altered the intimate relationship between district nurse and patient. It is this relationship which was so keenly remembered by the informants in this study, a relationship which defined their working lives but which is untold in the documentary sources. Perhaps, then, to ignore the impressionistic or anecdotal evidence would be to misconstrue the nature of district nursing in the period before 1970. The question as to whether or not the district nurse of the past is the subject of myth is perhaps not a logical one when the most compelling evidence we have is held by the subject itself.

> It was like a story, not like real life, just being on the district.
>
> (Miss Helen Edwards)

Notes

1 R. Dingwall, M.A. Rafferty and C. Webster, *An Introduction to the Social History of Nursing*, London, Routledge, 1988, p. 175.
2 Originally The Queen Victoria Jubilee Institute for Nurses, it later became The Queen's Institute for District Nurses and is now the Queen's Nursing Institute.
3 See Dingwall et al., op. cit.; M. Stocks, *A Hundred Years of District*

Nursing, London, George Allen & Unwin, 1960; M. Baly, B. Robottom and J. M. Clark, *District Nursing*, 2nd edition, Oxford, Heinemann Nursing, 1990; M. Baly, *Florence Nightingale and the Nursing Legacy*, London, Croom Helm, 1986.
4 The QNI Scotland financed an oral history pilot project in 1996–7. This work is now continuing for a further two years funded by The Wellcome Trust, London.
5 Fifty-second Annual Report 1940, Queen's Institute of District Nursing, Scottish Branch, QNI Scotland, Edinburgh, QNI/D.2.
6 Comrie and District Minute Book 1920–1948, RCN Archive, Edinburgh.
7 There were three Schemes for Nursing Services available in 1943: The Home Nursing Contributory Scheme involving an annual payment of 4s 4d at the place of employment to cover the employee and all non-wage earning dependants; The Membership Scheme where the annual payment was 6s and was collected regularly from the member's home; and The Subscribing Donor Scheme which entitled domestic staff to free nursing care along with the employer on payment by the employer of 10s per annum. See *Annual Report 1943*, Queen's Institute of District Nursing, Scottish Branch, QNI Scotland, Edinburgh.
8 'The Duties and Powers of the Hon. Secretaries' *The Queen's Nursing Institute, Scotland Newsletter*, May 1997, pp. 2–3.
9 Ibid.
10 Comrie and District Minute Book 1920–1948, RCN Archive, Edinburgh, QNI/D.2.
11 Ibid.
12 Comrie and District Cash Book, RCN Archive, Edinburgh, QNI/D.2.

7

INSTITUTIONAL ABUSE

Memories of a 'special' school for visually impaired girls – a personal account

Sally French with John Swain

At seven precisely a loud hand bell rings.
We strip off our beds and collect our wash things;
Then queue up in silence is what we must do,
First for a basin, again for the loo.
Then get dressed in haste; we must each make our bed
Before seven-thirty when prayers will be said.
We solemnly kneel at the sound of the bell
And silently pray for release from this hell.
(An extract from a poem by Susan Nicholls,
an ex-pupil of Barclay School[1])

This chapter is based upon in-depth interviews with eight visually impaired women who spent all or most of their school days in a particular residential school for visually impaired girls in the 1950s and 1960s. The chapter is also based upon my own memories of the school which I attended as a pupil for four years between the ages of nine and thirteen. Although the interviews were wide-ranging, all of the women spoke at length about the continual physical, psychological and emotional abuse perpetrated by the care staff who were in charge of them outside school hours.

The history of disabled people in Britain is centrally one of segregation and isolation. This was crystallised in a statement by Vic Finkelstein, a major figure in the disabled people's movement, to John Swain. In the late 1970s, on the way to a seminar entitled 'The Problems of Integration', referring to the integration of disabled children in mainstream schools, John Swain suggested to Vic

Finkelstein that, 'this sounds as if it will be interesting'. His response was, 'Not at all. Integration is the problem for non-disabled people and professionals. Segregation is the problem for disabled people.'

Sifting through the literature for examples of oral histories reflecting the lived experiences of disabled people in segregated institutions, including special schools, is frustrating; there is precious little. There are a few exceptional biographies and auto-biographies documenting individual experiences,[2] and there is a substantial oral history of disabled people by Humphries and Gordon.[3] This lack of history from the perspectives of disabled people themselves is no simple oversight. History is owned and documented by those in power, and invisibility and silence are cornerstones of oppression.

The past 20 years or so, however, have seen the rise of the disabled people's movement in Britain, with the emergence of organisations controlled by disabled people themselves. At the heart of the movement is a social model in which disability is understood as the denial of basic human and civil rights. The individual and collective empowerment of disabled people has increasingly led to histories being written from this viewpoint, including an oral history of the growth of the disabled people's movement.[4]

There are histories of segregated special schools in the literature. For the most part, they are the official histories of non-disabled people and professionals, documenting such things as changing numbers and types of schools, and numbers of pupils for whom they provide. These histories also document the official rationales for changing policies and the dominant humanistic ideology justifying segregated education. A history written by a headteacher of a special school[5] is an example. There are, too, though much rarer, very different sociological histories, of which Tomlinson[6] is a landmark. She traces the origins and growth of segregated education to particular vested interests, including those of medical, psychological and educational personnel, and political ruling groups. Rarer still are studies of the views of recipients of special education, with Wade and Moore[7] being a notable example, though these could not be said to be well-developed oral histories.

The present chapter contributes to the growing literature on the history of disabled people written from the experiences of disabled people. In the context of this particular book, the history of health and welfare is manifest in what was primarily an educational provision. The particular institution which is the context of the experiences related in this research was not an anomaly. It was a segregated provision, and like many other such institutions provided many services. Indeed, the rationale of many arguments for segregation is founded on supposed economic or organisational imperatives of housing multiple services under one roof.

The research reported here is, in a number of respects, unique in terms of the existing literature. It documents the history of life in the Barclay School for Partially Sighted Girls, a residential special school from the viewpoint of women placed in this particular type of segregated provision. Furthermore, the researcher herself attended the school and thus writes from the viewpoint of personal experience as well as reporting the experiences of others. In the following section of this chapter we outline the context of the research from three viewpoints: the general history of residential special schools; the history of this particular school; and the nature of the research. The next section is an analysis of experiences of abuse in a residential school ostensibly providing care and education for visually impaired girls. We conclude by discussing the significance of the research both for those personally involved and in relation to current education policy.

The context

Segregated schooling

At this point we shall provide a broader context for the oral history with a brief account of special education in the 1950s and 1960s, particularly in relation to the provision of residential schools for 'partially sighted' children (to use the official jargon of the time).

It was with the 1944 Education Act and the special school regulations that followed that segregated schools for partially sighted children, separated from blind children, became one of 11 categories of special schools provided for 11 categories of disabled children by local education authorities. In terms of the official history, the 1950s and 1960s could be said to be the heyday of the growth of special schools, in terms of both the rate of increase of numbers of young people segregated from the mainstream and the dominance of the segregationist ideology. The provision of residential schools was justified in terms of the use of effective resources in the face of the small and widely scattered school-age population of partially sighted children.[8] It was a time, too, of the building up of the National Health Service and the school health service, with increased provision for medical treatment, spectacles and other aids.[9]

The Barclay School

I, and the women I interviewed, attended Barclay School for Partially Sighted Girls before its closure in 1969. Like many of the special schools at that time, however, the origins of Barclay School lay in an earlier era. As an institution it was opened in 1893 and was set up for blind and partially blind young women, not originally as a school, but through commercial interests for trade and vocational training. It was originally intended to be a home for young women between 16 and 21 years of age, but over the years came to cater only for children. As I found when I investigated documents relating to this institution, little was expected of the children.[10] The 1935 *Annual Report* stated:

> The aim is that a normal girl, leaving the Barclay Home at sixteen should be able, if required, to cut out and make a simple frock or child's garment, cook and serve a simple dinner nicely, be able to keep a house clean and orderly and, in addition, to employ her spare moments in making a basket or jumper.[11]

In 1941, during the Second World War, the school was evacuated to a Queen Anne mansion (the former house of the Churchill family) in the Berkshire countryside where it remained until its closure and it is within this setting that the school is recalled in this chapter. Following the 1944 Education Act the school provided board and education for partially sighted girls.

Methodology

The eight women who were interviewed were all traced through a school reunion which took place in 1990. An attempt was made to find women who had spent all or most of their school-days at the school; such women were in a minority. All of the women were known to me although, prior to the reunion, no contact had been made with them for more than 20 years. The women, who were all in their forties, were interviewed individually using a semi-

structured format. The interviews were tape-recorded and transcribed and a thematic analysis was undertaken. The participants
were all given pseudonyms and for the purpose of this chapter they
are: Ruth and Celia who are sisters, Joy and Gwen also sisters,
Andrea, Harriet, Stella and Eve.

There were just eight women interviewed who had attended
one particular school so it is not possible automatically to gener-
alise their experiences to visually impaired people in other schools
at this time. Nevertheless, the accounts given by the women tallied
strongly with each other as well as with my own memories of the
school and those of other accounts written by ex-pupils.[12] It could
be argued that my own involvement with the women and the
topic being researched would render me biased and lacking in
objectivity. The question of how close the researcher should be
to the research participants is, of course, a major one within social
research. The nature of 'objectivity' within research has undergone critical scrutiny by feminists[13] and disabled people themselves[14] who regard a detached stance on the part of the researcher
as an abuse of power. Banister et al. ask:

> What does it mean for the process and product if the
> researcher feels disengaged from the topic or process of
> study? While this is the affective state usually assumed
> within research processes, it itself speaks of the power
> of the researcher and the ways in which the project of
> producing knowledge and truth suppresses the labour and
> positions of the persons producing it.[15]

Having spent four formative years of my childhood with these
women within this institution, it felt inappropriate and was, indeed,
impossible for me to detach myself from them. For these reasons
I have chosen to interweave my memories with those of the women
throughout this account. As an 'insider' I believe that the women
trusted me with their stories and that, like Mitchell, my insider
status 'lent clarity rather than confusion to my work'.[16]

The interviews and my experiences were analysed in terms of
the main recurring themes relating to forms of abuse. It is recognised in the literature that physical, psychological and emotional
abuse cannot be disentangled. In this chapter we will concentrate
on psychological and emotional abuse which all the women found
more damaging than physical abuse both at the time and in their
subsequent lives. O'Hagan defines emotional abuse as:

The sustained, repetitive, inappropriate emotional response to the child's expression of emotion and its accompanying expressive behaviour.[17]

And psychological abuse as:

The sustained, inappropriate behaviour which damages, or substantially reduces, the creative and developmental potential of critically important mental processes of a child.[18]

Emotional abuse can damage self-esteem and impede a child's ability to express and respond to feelings adequately and appropriately. Psychological abuse can retard intelligence, language, attention, perception, memory and moral development.[19]

Growing up in a special school

The following is an analysis of my own experiences and those of the women I interviewed: our memories of a 'special' school for visually impaired girls. It shows that the emotional and psychological abuse we experienced focused on many aspects of our lives including our bodies, our opportunities for social, emotional and psychological development, our identities and our relationships with our families. On occasions the abuse even degenerated into psychological terrorism.

The body

Our bodies and bodily functions were under constant scrutiny and control. There were, for example, set times for going to the toilet which were insufficiently frequent. We all had to queue outside one toilet, even though there were many others in the house. If we took more than a few seconds the care staff would hammer on the door or barge in telling us to get a move on. Frequently they would send the back half of the queue away saying they were tired of seeing us jiggling around, that we had 'toilets on the brain' and that it was time we grew up and thought about something else for a change. Ruth recalled:

There was a total lack of privacy, you were all together in these big rooms, all got dressed together, all in the bathrooms together. Even the toilets had no locks on the

door, you had to sit there and yell 'Somebody's in' right
up until you were sixteen.

Behaviour such as bed-wetting and nail biting was punished and
made public. Young children were smacked (often with rulers) and
were made to wash their sheets by hand. Andrea could remember
being stood in the corner with her wet sheets tied around her
neck. Older girls were made to indicate on a calendar which days
they were 'wet' and which days they were 'dry'. This was discussed
and analysed in front of us all. Nail biting was punished by stopping us from swimming, one of the rare treats we had.

Minor illnesses and ailments were not acknowledged or believed
or, if they were, the girl concerned was made to feel responsible
for being ill. Joy recalled:

> I wasn't ill much, but I took measles back with me once.
> Four or five days after returning I wasn't feeling very well
> and then an epidemic spread throughout the school so I
> wasn't very popular. I was made to feel I had done it on
> purpose.

This treatment made us afraid to report illness or injuries which
were sometimes only discovered when they had become quite
severe. Harriet recalled:

> Even if I felt really wretched I didn't tell them because
> they would say there was nothing wrong with you, that
> you were putting it on. One half term I felt really wretched
> the whole time but I didn't dare tell them because they
> would have blamed me and said 'It's only because you
> haven't gone home for half term.' If there was nothing
> visible they didn't care. When I was younger I wouldn't
> have known where to find them in the night, I didn't
> know where any of them slept, and even if I had known
> I would have been too scared to go to them.

Girls with ongoing medical conditions, such as asthma, were
given no help, kindness or sympathy. They were publicly shamed
and treated as though they were inventing their illnesses. None of
the institutional routines were modified for them. The care staff
frequently cajoled us into bullying behaviour too and we felt great
pressure to comply with their wishes.

Identity

The daily life of the school was characterised by bullying and berating of us by the care staff. Our first names were rarely used. There was an atmosphere of rejection and a refusal to acknowledge our needs or our worth. Harriet explained:

> They gave you the impression you were at that school because you were some kind of delinquent. I was told that when I left school all I would be fit for was scrubbing out public lavatories, that was the kind of encouragement you had.

We were often said to behave like animals. When, for example, a button came off we were accused of biting it off, or when a hole appeared in an ancient glove we were accused of picking the hole. Despite the harshness of our lives we were constantly told we were 'privileged'; privileged to have good food, privileged to be living in a splendid house with beautiful grounds, privileged that people were spending their precious time on us, privileged that we were only partially sighted and not blind.

Our identities consist of all the characteristics that make us who we are, yet the development of identity was denied the girls of Barclay School. This attack on our identities was severe and prolonged and achieved in overt and covert ways. As Harriet said, 'You weren't your own person you were what they said you were ... I used to feel, "I'm nobody, I'm nothing, I can't do it".' The following account focuses on the reduction of family ties and the attack on the identity of the girls as disabled people and as developing women.

Reduction of family ties

There was a marked lack of contact with our families. We were all required to board and visiting times were restricted to two days a term. Many of the girls lived too far away for visitors. The school was situated near Ascot and Stella, one of the women interviewed, came from Darlington. She was taken to and fro by an escort and her mother never saw the school. Stella remembered that on one occasion she screamed and struggled so much on Darlington station that, not only did she miss the train, but her mother had to buy her some new clothes. She recalled:

166

The last few days of the holiday were ruined. We had to go for a medical before we went back to school and I hated it. Once I'd had that medical my holiday was spoilt because I knew I was going back. I didn't mind so much once I was with the other children, but when I left my parents on the station at home to go with the escort I used to break my heart. It was so terrible, I never wanted to go back. But I did look forward to seeing my little friends again.

No telephone calls were allowed and outgoing letters were strictly censored; we were not permitted to say we were unhappy or even that we had been to the doctor or dentist. For those girls who did have visitors the day could be marred by the sadness of parting. Joy explained:

Visiting days were very hard, it was really bad parting with parents. I remember Mum and Dad coming down to see us and when Dad drove off he would always wave a white handkerchief out of the window so we could see it. That was really hard. We used to like them coming down on a Sunday because the Saturday was gone, if they came on a Sunday you still had it to look forward to, I know it's silly.

Andrea recalled the difficulty of visiting days, not only for herself, but for her parents too:

My Dad used to come and see me when I first went to school but he couldn't cope with it. They knew I wasn't happy because I used to cry and carry on, and I wouldn't let them go, but we never used to discuss it. I was so pleased to be with them when they came, it was only one day a month.

Parents were not invited into the house or made to feel welcome in any way. No matter how far they had travelled they were not offered refreshments but had to turn around and go away immediately. My mother still talks about the time when she was forced to stand in the pouring rain because she had come to collect me 15 minutes early.

The care staff never talked to us about our families except to make scathing remarks. As soon as we came back to school we had a bath and our heads were inspected for lice. At the start of one summer term they discovered I had lice in my hair. There was no sympathy at all, they said that they could see great big ones jumping about and asked me all sorts of questions such as 'Does your mother clean the house?' and 'How many times did you have a bath?'. Derogatory remarks about parents were made without any evidence. They were accused of feeding us on tinned food, allowing us to stay up all night and run around the streets, and letting us eat out of newspapers. Harriet recalled:

> I had very long hair and when it came to hair washing days I always got told off because it took so much washing and drying. They used to say 'Your parents ought to have more sense than to let you have long hair like this.' It was their way of telling you that your parents weren't good enough.

Most of us did not tell our parents about the abuses we experienced at the school. There are many explanations for this. Some of the women did not know that the treatment they were receiving was abusive. As Eve said, 'I think I just accepted it as normal. . . . I thought all people were treated like that, I didn't know any different.'

Some of the women recalled that they did not want to cause their parents upset or worry. As Joy said, 'They knew I didn't like it but I didn't go into great detail because it would only make them unhappy. . . . I knew if I told them things it would make everything worse.' There was a feeling too that nothing could be done. Even when they were very young the girls seemed to understand that their parents had little control over the situation. Their experiences at the school also led them to believe that voicing complaints to parents would be ineffective. Eve said, 'I suppose I thought that they wouldn't take any notice because if you reported anything at school nobody bothered, they'd just tell you to go away or say "Serves you right".'

Some of the women expressed fear of telling their parents because of the repercussions for themselves if their parents complained about the school. Others were not believed by their parents when they did complain. Stella said, 'I told my parents what was going on but my Mum used to say, "Well you must have been naughty to deserve the punishment". She wouldn't take it seriously at all.' Nearly all of us came from working-class homes and our parents trusted authority figures and were in awe and afraid of them. We received subtle messages not to complain about the school from our parents as well, perhaps to maintain their own peace of mind. My mother, for example, would tell people, in front of me, that I liked the school and was happy there.

Denial of disability

Although the purpose of the school was (officially at least) to counteract some of the problems of being visually impaired, it was not uncommon for girls to be ridiculed or punished because of lack of sight. Stella explained why she was stopped from attending the Christmas party, 'The thing I did to deserve it was knocking the plants over in the playroom when I was running around. I just didn't see them, but that wouldn't have been accepted. I was thought to be careless and naughty.' I can remember being mocked and asked, 'Can't you read at your age?' when I could not make out the faded and blotchy name tapes on some towels.

The girls who suffered the most, however, were those who were almost blind and those with additional physical or learning disabilities. There were about 10 such girls at the school. Susan, who was eventually transferred to a school for blind children, was harassed and ridiculed when she could not find the twigs she was supposed to be gathering from the lawn. Her only solution was to break them off the trees but this led to jeering from the care staff who said 'Look at Susan Tanner, she's talking to the trees, she's mad, she's crazy!', inciting us all to join in. Several of us could remember Susan saying how she 'wished the grass was white and the twigs were black'.

Physically disabled girls were made to go on the long crocodile walks which were imposed upon us every Saturday and Sunday afternoon. A particular girl, Glenda, stays in our minds and leaves us all with a deep sense of anger and regret. She was hearing impaired as well as visually impaired and, in addition, had a heart condition, one lung and a spinal deformity. She was pushed and shoved by the care staff on these walks and we were encouraged, indeed sometimes forced, to join in. On many occasions she sat, exhausted, in the road and was dragged to her feet. Glenda was an isolated girl, she had no friends and seemed less than human to us. A year after leaving school she died.

Another girl had cerebral palsy which made her walking slow and difficult. She received the same kind of physical and verbal abuse as Glenda. Her surname was Sparrow and the care staff would say 'I'm sorry girls but we can't go to the Totem Pole (in Windsor Great Park) today because we have the old bird with us.' I also recall a girl being beaten with a ruler on her paralysed arm where she was completely unable to defend herself.

There were huge attempts to make us appear more sighted. Visual aids and contact lenses were being developed at this time and we were the experimental subjects. Ruth, talking of contact lenses, explained, 'I had to sit there with them hurting and my eyes would be really blurry but there was no way I could take them out, nobody seemed at all sympathetic, the attitude was that you were lucky to be chosen.' We were constantly reminded of the high cost of visual aids and that we were not deserving of them.

Suppression of gendered identity

We were not allowed to enhance our physical appearance or femininity in any way. The clothes we wore were old and covered in patches and darns. Stella recalled:

> They frowned upon make-up and I never remember wearing tights or stockings at school. We used to wear awful grey socks and black outdoor shoes even with our own dresses right up until we were sixteen. They didn't like us having fancy hair styles, it was always commented on. They wanted us to look very plain. Everything was passed down, you were lucky to get anything new. The shoes were awful, only once do I remember getting a new pair and I thought I was the bee's knees in them.

The sheets, towels and pyjamas were also old and patched and the blankets very thin and worn. Everything we had was unattractive and second hand. I was slightly plump and on one 'fitting up' day I was given a huge blouse with a size 38 chest being told that I would 'grow into it if not out of it before the term was through'. Every third week I was compelled to wear the blouse with its short sleeves flapping well below my elbows.

Psychological terrorism

Occasionally this psychologically abusive atmosphere degenerated into psychological terrorism. We could all remember that on rare occasions a girl would be confined to a small attic room on the top floor where she would spend all of her time. Her meals and her school work were taken to her. As well as the isolation, this experience was likely to be particularly frightening. The house was, even under normal circumstances, rather eerie as there were no night lights, the floorboards creaked and the trees rustled and made strange patterns on the walls. We constantly excited and frightened ourselves with stories of ghosts.

On one occasion two small girls tried to abscond but were apprehended. The women remembered that as part of their punishment they were forced to walk to the gate late one night when it was dark. Here a man jumped out at them from the bushes and grabbed them. The older girls were convinced that the episode was staged and that the man was merely the gardener.

Repression of emotion

We were expected to be passive and obedient all the time. The expression of emotion – anger, sadness, high spirits – was constantly suppressed. There were frequent complaints about noise and we were often 'on silence' for long periods of time. It was not uncommon to spend whole evenings standing to attention in silence, or standing on the landing late into the night as a punishment for talking in bed. The expression of emotion was punished by segregation and public ridicule. Several of the women could remember a small girl being publicly ridiculed for crying when she learned in a letter of her grandmother's death. She was told 'I could understand you crying if it was your mother, but you don't carry on like that when an old person dies.' No comfort or understanding was ever offered. Expressing emotion was regarded as highly shameful and was rarely witnessed at the school. The suppression of emotion also became a mechanism of resistance whereby we would not allow the care staff to feel they had 'won'.

This emotional repression was also encouraged by our parents as a way of easing their own guilt and pain. One of the women could remember being bribed with toys and new dresses by her parents if she did not cry when returning to school.

Lack of opportunities for development

Everything about the school prevented the girls from developing their potential intellectually, cognitively, emotionally and socially. There were no substitute parents even for children as young as five and the rigid, punitive routine left little time for creativity or play. When very young, the women remembered receiving some comfort and care from older girls although this was strongly discouraged. Stella said:

> We used to help bath the little ones and put them to bed, we were on a rota, it was one of the duties. We knew how to look after them but we weren't allowed to mother them, the matrons didn't like to see us getting friendly with them, they discouraged it.

The women recalled how their time was totally organised and consisted of cleaning and working in the garden. Saturday and Sunday afternoons were spent on a crocodile walk and Sunday morning was spent letter writing and going to church. There were more pleasant activities, like swimming and Brownies, but there was never any choice. The anger of the care staff and the general atmosphere within the school made it difficult to enjoy anything.

Understanding the behaviour of the care staff

We did, of course, live in a closed institution but there were adults in our lives who did not abuse us. The teachers, who came in from outside every weekday, were ineffective (the education was very poor) but not unkind. The Guide and Brownie leaders were regular visitors as were the optician, the doctor and the ophthalmologist. Yet none of these adults offered any help or tried to improve our situation. We did sometimes have kind care staff but they rarely stayed for long. Celia recalled:

> There was one matron who left when I was about ten, she was an old lady and she retired – she wasn't married and we were all her little girls. I found it really hard when she left because she was nice and the person who replaced her was not the same. We did have the odd nice one.

The 'maids' tried to be kind to us by, for example, getting rid of unwanted food, and bringing us 'treats' to eat in bed, but they lacked the power to bring about change. There was a board of governors whose members met quite regularly but they appeared to be friends of the Principal; the school was not under local authority control although it was approved by the Department of Education and underwent inspections.

As children we made no attempt to analyse or understand the behaviour of the care staff; they were simply labelled as 'horrid old women'. As adults, however, we have spent much time speculating on their behaviour and the likely reasons behind it and have concluded that, while having ultimate power over us, they were relatively powerless in a hierarchy of disempowerment. Our analysis fits very closely with that of Wardhaugh and Wilding[20] who believe that corruption is the product of particular kinds of social systems. Drawing on examples of abusive regimes, they conclude that abuse is most likely to occur in 'enclosed' organisations where there is a failure of management, lack of contact with the outside world, low accountability and powerlessness both of the clients and the front-line workers.

The Principal, who managed Barclay School, was a distant figure who occupied the finest rooms of the house and was attended by a personal maid. She seemed to have ultimate power. As children we thought she owned the house but when it closed in 1969 she went to live in a flat. She appeared to enjoy living in grand surroundings and regarded us, we felt, as an inconvenience and a nuisance. She complained a great deal about noise and the care staff were noticeably terrified of her. She sacked people readily and gave very strict instructions about how the school must be run.

There were 90 girls in the school but only four care staff. There were often times when only two were on duty and there were never more than three. They had, therefore, very little opportunity to relate to us as individuals and any disruption to the routine was likely to cause problems. As children we perceived them as excessively cross but as adults their behaviour can be interpreted as resulting from severe stress. One woman described them as 'bundles of nerves'.

Some of their punitive actions and behaviour were probably designed to reduce their own anxiety. On the crocodile walks, for example, one adult was responsible for up to 90 children. In order to keep control they would not allow us to walk with our friends and they became very tense if gaps in the line appeared. A solitary member of staff supervised us swimming in an isolated part of the grounds. In this situation they were extremely tense and would not let even the strong swimmers go out of their depth. A very common punishment was stopping people from swimming and this may have been a tactic to reduce the numbers. They worked very long hours for limited pay and many had no qualifications in child care. Wardhaugh and Wilding state:

> While staff have near-absolute power over many clients, they are in many other respects powerless. They are taken for granted by the organisation, seldom regarded as its heroes, given little support, not consulted about the organisation of their work.[21]

It is possible that the people who looked after us were personally inadequate in some way. They certainly seemed very uneasy outside the institution, unable to cope with parents or other 'outsiders' and generally fearful. This may imply a measure of institutionalisation but may have been entirely due to lack of training and the situation they found themselves in.

The way we were treated in this school can be viewed as a reflection on society which fails to recognise the worth of disabled children. The existence of institutions and the abuse of disabled children is part of a much broader process of oppression and devaluation of disabled people. As Marchant and Cross state:

> Institutional abuse of disabled children cannot be viewed in isolation from the rest of society. Changes are needed at all levels in the value assigned to children with disabilities and therefore the status of services for those children.[22]

Effects on the women of their treatment at the school

All of the women reported a severe lack of confidence when leaving the school and a profound sense of inadequacy and shyness which took many years to reduce or resolve. Harriet said:

> The most damaging thing was the way they destroyed your self-confidence. The way they said that you couldn't do things because you were 'such and such' a person or because of your background. They really put you down.

Many of the women spoke about the difficulties they still experience in making decisions and thinking for themselves. Gwen said:

> You lack confidence because you have never been allowed
> to think for yourself and then suddenly you have to and
> it's hard. I didn't form opinions, I didn't really need to.
> . . . It's hard when you leave school because you are
> waiting all the time to be told what to do.

Some of the women have had spells of severe depression. They
related this to their childhood experiences. People with unstable
families, for example those who had been fostered several times,
seemed to be most vulnerable to the effects of the school. Stella
said that although she would have loved children of her own she
was unable to trust anyone enough to enter into an intimate relationship or marriage and that making physical contact, even a
simple hug, was very difficult. All of the women felt that their
education had been very poor and that this had adversely affected
their employment prospects and their relationships.

Very few strategies of survival were available to the women in
the school. As Wardhaugh and Wilding state:

> Most of those who have been the victims of the corrup-
> tion of care have suffered from powerlessness. . . . They
> have very little power or influence, little knowledge of how
> the organisation works, little awareness of how to assert
> their rights or how to call to account those on whom they
> often depend for the basic elements of living.[23]

We could all remember instances of defiance – answering back,
refusing to do things, temper tantrums, absconding, refusing to
show emotion – but, rather than helping, it invariably led people
into deeper trouble.

The women believed that the most important factor in surviving
the institution was their friendships with each other. Many of these
friendships have proved exceptionally robust, lasting and deep –
often far more so than family ties. Stella explained:

> There was never any affection or mothering not even
> when you were five. . . . Friendships became very impor-
> tant, we leaned on each other a bit, but we should have
> been able to approach the adults more. It was impossible,
> you couldn't go and confide in them, you couldn't
> tell them your little secrets or your little worries because
> it was frowned upon, they didn't want to be close to

you, they were very Victorian in their attitudes towards children.

Attempts were sometimes made at the school to separate friends. This was the most devastating of punishments but never really succeeded as there were insufficient staff to enforce it and we were crowded together in age-specific groups. However, as Celia points out, support from friends was less relevant to very young children:

> When I got older I looked forward to seeing my friends from school again, but for any five-year-old going back to school and thinking 'I won't see Mummy . . .' it's very hard. We had to say goodbye on the station which was ever so difficult, but the escort was very nice. We often went from Christmas to Easter without seeing our parents or getting home.

A further survival strategy adopted by many of the women was 'keeping a low profile' or even attempting to ingratiate themselves with the care staff. Harriet recalled:

> As I got older I found devious ways of sorting my life out so that it would be more pleasant. I used to volunteer for everything, then they would leave me alone, they weren't on my back all the time. . . . But because I used to do this, the other girls thought I was a creep and they used to make life very difficult. I started being hated by the kids, but I could cope with that and I knew I couldn't have it both ways.

Another factor which helped us to survive was our families. We knew we did not 'belong' to the school, that there was another life outside. This did not work very well for very young children, however, or for those who came from difficult or abusive families. The teachers (though ineffective) were not abusive, so we were able to escape into a kinder environment during our lessons.

Although the women can all be described as survivors, none of them believed that they would ever completely recover from their experiences at the school. Stella said:

> I don't think you ever get over something like that 100 per cent. But having said that as long as you can earn

your own living, have a nice home and be independent then your life is not a failure, but there's a cloud hanging over you because you can remember a lot of bad things.

The abuse we experienced at Barclay School did not have as devastating an effect on me as it had on the women I interviewed. This is, I believe, due to the fact that I was nine (rather than five or six) when I went to the school. Even at that young age I had had sufficient experience of life to know that the way we were treated was not at all usual or normal. This positive knowledge of the outside world served to protect me psychologically as I simply did not believe what the care staff said about us. I left Barclay School at the age of 13 and spent my early teenage years in a far more liberal special school where we were less restricted and much better treated.

Conclusion

A considerable amount has been written about visually impaired people from a medical and philanthropic angle but little has been written about them from their own perspective. There is a growing acknowledgement of the importance of listening to the experiences and voices of disabled people and it is hoped that this account, of a few girls in one particular institution, will help to fill this gap in our social history. This account provides an important and vivid contrast with official information[24] which paints a glowing picture of life at the school. As Humphries and Gordon state:

> The experience of physical disability during the first half of the century is almost completely undocumented. We have little idea how it felt to be officially classified as blind, deaf and crippled and be brought up in the harsh Dickensian institutions and special schools where so many children were sent.[25]

As well as the importance of helping to provide an overall understanding of life for disabled people at that time, accounts such as this can be of value to disabled people themselves including the research participants. A chapter already written from these interviews[26] has stimulated one woman to enter counselling and other women have used the chapter as a means of communication. One woman, for example, gave the chapter to her doctor to read and others said that for the first time their childhood experiences were really believed by family and friends, though most would not show it to their parents for fear of upsetting them. Another woman who went to the school said she felt 'great relief' that it was out in the open and 'enormous pride' that we had all survived. In Atkinson and Williams' words:

> Autobiographies and life histories create the opportunity for experiences to be shared, for common interests to be fostered, for common understandings to be forged and for consciousness to be raised. In this way they help to shift the burden of problems from the individual who suffers them and on to the society that imposes them.[27]

Concluding their book, Humphries and Gordon[28] suspected that research into the experiences of disabled people since 1950 would 'discover striking parallels' with the experiences that they documented earlier in the century. Parallels in experiences of psychological and emotional abuse are clearly evident in the experiences of these visually impaired women, and we believe further parallels would be found in more recent experiences of disabled people. The recent policy moves have been towards greater inclusion.[29] However, there has been talk of inclusion since the years when segregated provision was first introduced. What was missing then, and is missing now, are the voices of disabled people themselves to ensure that inclusion involves the recognition and incorporation of disability culture, and not the subsuming of disabled people within the dominant non-disabled culture. The voices of many disabled people will be informed by their experiences in segregated settings, and the lessons from segregation speak to the establishment of inclusive education on disabled people's terms.

Notes

1   S. Nicholls, 'A Day in the Life of . . .', *The New Beacon*, 1989, 73, 868, pp. 304–305.
2   M. Baker, *With All Hopes Dashed in the Human Zoo*, 1990, Warminster, Danny Howell Books; V. Mehta, *Vedi*, 1992, London, Pan Books.
3   S. Humphries and P. Gordon, *Out of Sight: The experience of disability 1900–1950*, 1992, Plymouth, Northcote House.
4   J. Campbel and M. Oliver, *Disability Politics: Understanding our past, changing our future*, 1996, London, Routledge.

5 T. Cole, *Apart or A Part?: Integration and the growth of British special education*, 1989, Milton Keynes, Open University Press.

6 S. Tomlinson, *A Sociology of Special Education*, 1982, London, Routledge & Kegan Paul.

7 B. Wade and M. Moore, *Experiencing Special Education: What young people with special educational needs can tell us*, 1993, Buckingham, Open University Press.

8 E. K. Chapman, *Visually Handicapped Children and Young People*, 1976, London, Routledge & Kegan Paul.

9 G. Corley, D. Robinson and S. Lockett, *Partially Sighted Children*, 1989, London, National Foundation for Educational Research and Nelson.

10 S. French, 'Out of Sight, Out of Mind: the experience and effects of a "special" residential school', in J. Morris (ed.), *Encounters with Strangers: feminism and disability*, 1996, London, The Women's Press.

11 Barclay Home for Blind and Partially Blind Girls, *Annual Report*, 1935, Brighton, Barclay School.

12 J. Monkhouse, *Sight in the Dark*, 1984, Sevenoaks, Hodder and Stoughton; S. Nicholls, 1989, op. cit.

13 P. Banister, E. Burman, I. Parker, M. Taylor and C. Tindall, *Qualitative Methods in Psychology: A research guide*, 1994, Buckingham, Open University Press.

14 C. Barnes and G. Mercer (eds), *Doing Disability Research*, 1997, Leeds, The Disability Press.

15 P. Banister et al., 1994, op. cit., p. 132.

16 H. Mitchell, 'The Insider Researcher', in M. Allott and M. Robb (eds), *Understanding Health and Social Care: An introductory reader*, 1998, London, Sage, p. 35.

17 K. O'Hagan, *Emotional and Psychological Abuse of Children*, 1993, Buckingham, Open University Press, p. 28.

18 Ibid., p. 33.

19 Ibid.

20 J. Wardhaugh and P. Wilding, 'Towards an Explanation of the Corruption of Care', in M. Allott and M. Robb, 1998, op. cit.

21 Ibid., pp. 216–7.

22 R. Marchant and M. Cross, 'Places of Safety? Institutions, disabled children and abuse', in The National Deaf Children's Society, *Abuse and Children Who Are Disabled*, 1993, NSPCC, London, Chailey Heritage, p. 57.

23 J. Wardhaugh and P. Wilding, 1998, op. cit., p. 210.

24 S. French, 1996, op. cit.

25 S. Humphries and P. Gordon, 1992, op. cit., p. 9.

26 S. French, 1996, op. cit.

27 D. Atkinson and F. Williams (eds.), *Know Me As I Am: an anthology of prose, poetry and art by people with learning difficulties*, 1990, London, Hodder and Stoughton.

28 S. Humphries and P. Gordon, 1992, op. cit.

29 DfEE, *Excellence for All Children: Meeting special educational needs*, 1997, London, Stationery Office.

8

ORAL HISTORY AND THE HISTORY OF LEARNING DISABILITY

Jan Walmsley and Dorothy Atkinson

This chapter will examine the place of oral history in the history of learning disability. The chapter is in three parts. The first consists of a review of the way the history of learning disability has been written to date. Its argument is that the main traditions of writing the history of learning disability fail to do justice to the experiences and perspectives of those most centrally involved, people with learning disabilities, their families, and staff. The second part shows how oral history can illuminate the experiences of staff working in learning disability services in the past. It is based on an oral history interview with a Mental Welfare Officer, who recalls the development of learning disability services in one county, Bedfordshire, since the Second World War. The third part shows the contribution people with learning disabilities can make to revealing the history. It is taken from Dorothy Atkinson's *Past Times* project, a two-year oral history project with a group of older people with learning disabilities, also based in Bedfordshire. Through juxtaposing accounts from two different perspectives, we hope to show the importance of collecting a range of oral history accounts in order to appreciate the complexities of writing a history of this much neglected area. To borrow ideas developed by Frisch,[1] we contend that oral history can be both 'more history', adding to the stock of knowledge about historical events, and 'anti-history', challenging conventional perceptions.

Background: a literature review

The history of learning disability has only recently come into vogue as a topic worthy of study in its own right. For many years it has been treated as a subsidiary topic in other histories, such as the history of psychiatry,[2] the history of social hygiene and eugenics,[3] the history of special education,[4] or the history of administrative change.[5] A similar situation prevails in sociology and social policy. Goffman's ideas on institutions,[6] for example, have been highly influential, yet Goffman based none of his work in learning disability hospitals or hostels. Similarly, Michel Foucault, a great inspiration for late twentieth-century social historians, refers far more to practices around people with mental illness or criminal tendencies than to learning disability.

That is not to say there is no history of learning disability. We review below some of the most recent scholarship on the subject, and we also discuss theories, such as labelling theory and normalisation, and movements, such as self-advocacy and the disabled people's movement, which have shaped modern-day understandings of learning disability based on interpretations of the past. What is striking, however, in these approaches is the apparent lack of recognition that there are many players whose lives have been touched and often shaped by their contact with learning disability, and that their voices and experiences have a contribution to make to an understanding of the history.

While recent historiography of learning disability has at last abandoned the 'great male reformer' view which characterised so many of the histories of the past,[7] and has seen the celebratory histories of individual institutions such as those by Monica Diplock on Leavesden Hospital,[8] and Randall Bingley on South Ockendon[9] questioned, there has been little use of oral history by historians. Thomson,[10] for example, in what is otherwise a masterly and pioneering study of the 'problem' of mental deficiency in the inter-war years, did not attempt to access oral accounts. Using secondary sources he is careful to consider and present the views of politicians, administrators and families but seems not to have considered that 'defectives' themselves may have had a point of view. Of course, it would be difficult to incorporate the views of people with learning disabilities based on written sources alone, as many of those who are so labelled have poor levels of literacy, so the inevitable result of not using oral history is that those most centrally affected appear as passive subjects of the decisions others made about them.

This is also true of the recent scholarly volume *From Idiocy to Mental Deficiency*,[11] which has several chapters on the twentieth century, but no place for the viewpoints of those so labelled. Historians seem to be unaware of developments in related disciplines which focus on the rights of people with learning disabilities to be heard[12] and the ways in which their voices can be recorded.[13] As Ann Borsay[14] points out, in a review of three recent American books on the history of disability and mental deficiency, the books' authors are uninformed by current debates in the disability literature. This is reflected in the extent to which titles are chosen which would be quite offensive to anyone with learning disabilities; *Feeble Minded in Our Midst*[15] is a good example.

There is a sense in which latter-day historians are simply carrying forward the long accepted wisdom of practitioners and other experts from the learning disability field. It is they who have spoken for, and against, people with learning disabilities, and who have laid claim to a particular account of history. This is the 'practitioner-pragmatist' view of history[16] as exemplified by the classic account written by Kathleen Jones in the early 1970s. Jones[17] views the history of learning disability up to that point as demonstrating the need for an informed, knowledgeable and trained workforce; professional personnel such as social workers, for example, who could intervene effectively in the lives of people with learning disabilities. The latter were seen as being in need of care, protection and control because they were vulnerable to mistreatment and exploitation, and could easily be led astray. This view of history is 'pragmatic' in the sense that it is less concerned with the rights and wrongs of institutional versus community care, for example, than with the relative effectiveness of the different approaches in relation to the disposal of people who needed 'care' of some sort. In keeping with the climate of the times, the views of the people most centrally involved – professionals, family members and people with learning disabilities – were not directly represented in this historical account.

'Normalisation', a philosophy which asserts that people with learning disabilities should have a right to the patterns of daily life that most people take for granted, became influential in the period following the publication of Jones's book. Writers, researchers and practitioners in the normalisation tradition have taken a particular view of history. This is the 'vicious circle' view, which has portrayed people with learning difficulties as the victims of a pervasive system of 'labelling'. Irving Goffman's *Asylums*[18] was very influential, constructing asylum inmates as the passive victims of labelling and institutionalisation. However, Goffman's ideas about the impact of institutionalisation on the inmates owe more to his observations and theorisation than to personal testimonies.

The labelling process was seen to have both personal and social consequences: on the one hand, a stigmatised identity and, on the other, segregated and poor-quality services and discriminatory practices. The history of learning disability came to be seen as the history of devaluation.[19] Normalisation emerged as a means to change that history; it would transform the vicious circle into a virtuous circle, and re-value hitherto devalued people.

Normalisation – as a means of changing the course of history – found widespread favour, particularly in professional circles in the early 1970s, at a time when institutional care was being widely discredited. The past, and indeed the present, were seen by the exponents of normalisation to be about labelling, exclusion and incarceration; the oppression of a whole class of victims.[20] The task of professionals, now and in the future, was to reverse those trends and to enable people with learning disabilities to take their place in the community. The voices of the 'victims' were not included in these accounts. Rather, normalisation was based on the voices of its proponents, including professionals. As such it served to legitimate professional roles in the community as large hospitals closed and services fragmented into smaller units.[21]

However, the history that normalisation tells, and acts on, is essentially a victim account of history. The argument was no longer about the need for the care and control of people with learning disabilities, but about their need to belong to and be accepted by the community. Acceptance comes at a price: it means fitting in, adopting 'appropriate' dress and behaviour, taking on 'valued social roles' and spending time with 'valued' (non learning disabled) people. The voices of people with learning disabilities are heard neither in this history nor in its antidote. In history they were seen as the victims of an oppressive system. Now normalisation began to dictate that they should lead 'ordinary lives' as defined by (more powerful) others.[22] Normalisation thus became a form of advocacy where professionals represented – as they saw and defined them – the wishes and needs of people with learning disabilities.[23] There was a danger that normalisation might represent a lifestyle valued by its proponents rather than by people with learning disabilities themselves.[24]

Supporters of normalisation have used historical generalisations about devaluation in the past to make a case for better services in the present and future. Authors in this tradition have taken an advocacy position, arguing on behalf of people with learning disabilities by quoting secondhand descriptions of past practices.[25] Ann Chappell[26] has argued that these and other authors are selective in their choice of illustrative material, ignoring, for example, evidence that people with learning disabilities may prefer the company of others with similar experiences to the integration and inclusion which the normalisation dogma dictates. The case for actually listening to people to discover what their often complex, and sometimes contradictory, experiences are and were, seems to be a strong one if any lessons are to be learnt from history.

Just as there was no place for the voices of people with learning disabilities in this advocacy oriented history, there was equally no place for the stories of professionals who were caught up in the discredited policies and practices of the institutional era. From that perspective, paid staff were the deluded tools of an oppressive system. The people who did get a hearing were those who had seen the light, and recognised that they too had become institutionalised, such as Frank Thomas whose graphic diary extracts were a powerful dimension of Joanna Ryan's *The Politics of Mental Handicap*.[27]

Another perspective on history comes from the disabled people's movement. The debates about a social model of disability replacing the medical model which has been seen to hold hegemonic sway in understandings and treatment of disabled people are not essentially historical. Nevertheless, they have a historical dimension, drawing on examples of the way the 'medical model' operated in past practices, such as those of the Leonard Cheshire Homes, founded in the post-war era.[28] The voices of disabled people are central to the construction of the history of the disabled people's movement, and Campbell and Oliver's book is largely written around the memories of disability activists. A claim has been made by disabled writers for including learning disability in the understandings of the past being developed in the wider disability movement. Although Campbell and Oliver[29] make a passing reference to learning disability, they have only one contributor with learning disabilities (out of a total of 29). This is not untypical of the marginalisation of learning disability in the writings of disabled activists. In fact, the particular experiences of people with learning disabilities are in danger of getting lost in the broad politics of disability. Chappell[30] detects a linguistic bias in the writings of disability activists towards an equation of disability with bodily impairment. Despite the rhetoric of inclusion, the voices of people with learning disabilities are largely excluded from the construction of histories of disability. Whether this is the result of prejudice, or simply that the means to access the ideas of people with learning disabilities are lacking is not for us to say. Meanwhile, families and those staff who work with disabled people are inevitably cast as oppressive disciples of the medical model who, *ipso facto*, are undeserving of being heard in their own right.

There is, however, another parallel development whose history is so recent as to be relatively unrecorded. This is the history of learning disability as seen, and recounted, by people with learning disabilities themselves. It is a history which privileges the voices of people with learning disabilities. Its development has its roots in the participation workshops run by CMH (the Campaign for People with Mental Handicaps; now called VIA, or Values Into Action) in the 1970s, in which people with learning disabilities spoke publicly about their past lives and experiences. The 1980s saw the formation of self-advocacy groups, People First organisations and groups/committees in day and residential services.[31] These developments were given a further boost with the 1990 National Health Service and Community Care Act, which emphasised user participation and involvement. Self-advocacy has encouraged people to 'speak up' about their experiences not as 'cases' or 'victims' but as people in their own right. In an anthology of their life stories, for example, people with learning disabilities represented a wide range of personal, and different, experiences based on gender, class and race as well as learning disability.[32] Self-advocacy has meant that many people with learning disabilities have begun to speak for themselves.

The historical manifestations of the self-advocacy movement have been a steady stream of *autobiographies* by people with learning disabilities.[33] They represent the clearest and most direct means by which people can account for their own lives and form the ultimate means of self-representation. In a sense the autobiographical voice is the voice of the self-advocacy movement, where the person who 'speaks up' goes on to become the person who 'writes up'.[34] The single autobiography has the capacity to influence its readers, and a collection of life stories has the potential to become both a political document and an important source of history 'from below'. Some examples of this genre can be found in the anthology edited by Atkinson and Williams, *Know Me As I*

Am.[35] Ultimately, however, autobiographies tell the stories of individuals. They do not tell the stories of groups of people or communities, or collect together the shared memories of times gone by. This is where oral history comes in. Approaches developed by oral historians allow the individual to speak but to do so within a social and historical context, and alongside the voices of others. The oral history approach to recording the history of a mental handicap institution from the point of view of the inmates is well represented by Potts and Fido in *A Fit Person to be Removed*.[36]

However, self-advocacy, like normalisation and the disabled people's movement, is essentially advocacy orientated. Its purpose is to redress injustices, change practices, and further the interests of people with learning disabilities. History is used, but the motivation is not primarily historical. This means that there is a place for the testimonies of people with learning disabilities, but no place for the perspectives of others involved – staff, supporters, families, administrators. Indeed, in self-advocacy terms advisors or supporters are expected to be self-effacing, to be the equivalent of a wheelchair for someone with impaired mobility, a sign language interpreter for the deaf, or a guide dog for a blind person. They are there to facilitate the other person's speaking up, not to speak up for themselves. So although self-advocacy has made an important contribution to promoting the voices of people with learning disabilities, it is not a forum where the voices of all can be heard and recorded. The history developed in self-advocacy circles is a one-sided history.

This chapter will draw on oral history work undertaken by its two authors to show what oral history with different protagonists in the learning disability field can contribute to our knowledge of the past. The material is drawn from two sources. One is Jan Walmsley's thesis, 'Gender, Caring and Learning Disability' which used oral history informants to supplement knowledge about the historical context drawn from written sources.[37] The second source is Dorothy Atkinson's Past Times project, an oral history group with a membership of older people with learning disabilities.[38] These were separate projects but conducted in the same geographical area, Bedfordshire, and with reference to many of the same settings and institutions. We were each collecting oral material but found that we could make little sense of it until we knew more about the events which were the backdrop to people's lives. Passing references were made to people, places and incidents which had little meaning for us. Thus our second strand

of enquiry was to reconstruct the local history of learning disability from other sources: from documents and secondary printed
sources as well as from oral history interviews with key players.
Because this history had never been pieced together, it became
an absorbing and challenging task. But how did the two oral
history sources fit into this picture? They certainly did not tell the
same story.

Cecil: the professional's perspective

Our first example of how oral history can contribute to knowledge
of the twentieth-century history of learning disability is the professional's viewpoint. Cecil French was sought out as an interviewee
in Jan Walmsley's thesis research for two reasons: firstly, as the
only surviving person who had been a Mental Welfare Officer
(MWO) in the county since 1946 when the Bedfordshire Mental
Health Department was set up; secondly, as the author of a booklet
*A History of the Development of the Mental Health Services in Bedfordshire
1948–1970*, published in 1971,[39] and who was therefore knowledgeable about the policy and practices of the period.

Cecil began his working life as a clerk with the Electricity
Company, but by a series of fortuitous accidents he became the
Poor Law Relieving Officer for South Bedfordshire in 1937. In
1948 he and his fellow relieving officers were offered two choices:
to join the newly created Mental Health Department, or to join
what became the DHSS. Cecil chose to join the Mental Health
Department, and became a Mental Welfare Officer, responsible
with one colleague for everyone with a mental illness or learning
disability in South Bedfordshire, except for those in long-stay
hospitals.

At the time the Mental Health Department was set up, community provision in Bedfordshire for people with learning disabilities
was virtually non-existent. There had been one Mental Deficiency
Officer, but despite pre-war pressure from the Board of Control,
the central body responsible for Mental Deficiency Services, no
day or occupation centres existed until a 12-place facility opened
in 1946. During Cecil French's time as an MWO, there were no
residential facilities in the county, other than hospitals. The first
hostel opened in the mid-1970s.

His description of the early years in his post is one of a battle
to provide community services for more people than the resources
permitted:

As far as subnormals[40] were concerned, we had between us 350/400 so they were very very fortunate if they got two visits a year. We always used to aim at that, we used to aim at one a quarter but that didn't ever come off, we didn't have the time.

Providing a degree of support, making available such services as there were which were extremely sketchy in those days. At Bedford there was this little place at Turvey, at Dunstable we started up this Centre at Kirby Road, maximum of 30 places. By and large it was a question of seeing people knew what was available, if anything, and of course the difficulty was that as soon as you provided something it became oversubscribed. And in a county like Bedford which has two conurbations, Bedford and Luton, it's an area where if you said half the population is in a third of the geographical area, you'd be about right. Luton was growing like old boots then.

One was continuously fighting this battle of trying to get extra money every year, and when you'd got the extra £10,000 you thought you'd done really well, but as fast as you provided, it was filled up. We'd cater for twice the number we knew of, and before we finished we'd have to be building an extension.[41]

He explained the fact that many people with learning disabilities (he called them 'subnormals') were unknown to his Department for one of two reasons. The first explanation was lack of facilities, which meant there was no incentive to come forward:

There was nothing for them, you see. Unless things got really desperate and the family at home couldn't cope any more, then they came to us of necessity to get into Bromham (Hospital). Until there was something there wasn't any point in coming forward because we had nothing to offer. But at least it gave ammunition to beat the powers that be saying, well, there's that many. We must have so and so.

The second reason he gave for the difficulty in estimating numbers was stigma:

Our biggest difficulty was getting parents to actually accept the level of handicap that was present. I noticed one of your parents there receiving the letter from the Department of Education which said 'ineducable'. Well, it had to be you see because that was what the Act said. And unless they had been formally found to be ineducable it couldn't come over to the Health Department which was then responsible for providing care and attention, whatever we could get out of the powers that be. Nobody liked that word, but there it was in the Act and it had to be used. The definition of defectives into idiots, imbecile and feeble minded was still in operation.[42] That was a medical thing, you see, they came to us labelled already.

There was a sort of social stigma about it, people were ashamed. In the early days, the presence of a mentally handicapped child was hidden. You didn't know the child existed. There were quite a lot of people who were, as it were, kept quiet, kept in a back room, and it was not at all uncommon for, if something happened to the elderly father and mother all of a sudden, somebody came out of the woodwork, kept in an upstairs room. I've personally had that experience where an elderly father and mother, one dropped dead, the other died shortly afterwards, and lo and behold there was this pale face coming out of the staircase.

The Mental Welfare Officers were responsible for the community side of provision. In the absence of adequate provision, as Cecil was at great pains to point out, the hospitals were a significant resource.

We were the gateway to the hospital. Most of our children went to Bromham. So called 'difficult' cases went to Leavesden (Hertfordshire). I would suggest we had no alternative, when families couldn't cope, or mother and father died, there was nothing else for it, but the hospital. They might well have been capable had accommodation been available, and suitable employment or day care; it could well have been possible for those people to live in a hostel and go out to a workshop or whatever, I'm quite sure of that.

Although Cecil French acknowledged that with the right sort of provision a large number of people would not need to have gone into hospital, the picture painted of Bromham, the local hospital, was quite benign.

> I mean, after all Bromham when I first went there had its own herds. Patients used to work on the farm. They grew cereals, they had their own herds, they had their own pigs, it was completely self-contained. The idea was out of sight, out of mind by and large, and life was as comfortable as you could possibly make it. You see, Bromham Hospital had to employ a lot more staff once they lost their youngsters who were able to work in the laundry, or whatever.

Finding places in hospital for people who needed them was a significant part of the job. Not everyone could go to Bromham, because it was full, or unsuitable:

> It was just a question if we had to find a place for a mentally handicapped person where could you find it. It was a case of finding somewhere, we had Beds people as far away as Devon, that was the only place we could find at the time. There was no question of catchment areas. You went round the country trying to find space. The real problem was if they were placed out of county you had to pay for them, oh yes, a financial disincentive, but you had to, it was a case of needs must.

Cecil French was in general pessimistic about the prospects for community care, seeing the past as a cycle of pious ideas without the money to back them.

> Following the Act of 1959 (Mental Health Act) there were recommendations that there should be day centres for juniors, day centres for adults, residential care for the mentally handicapped to allow them to come out of hospital, but the final part said these would require extra money. It never became available. Never. It never has been, whatever the complexion of the Government, right, left or centre. And I don't honestly know what we do with them nowadays. It's all very well to say there's a hostel but chances are that it's full and there's a waiting list. By and large I think the greatest worry for parents was, still is, 'What will happen to Johnny when I'm gone?'

I'm only too pleased to be out of it, and all my generation would say the same.

We can read Cecil French's account as the product of a similar
sort of thinking to that of Kathleen Jones, described above, the
'practitioner-pragmatist' view of history. His book was published in
1971, around the same time as Jones's *A History of the Mental Health
Services*, and in the microcosm of Bedfordshire, both book and interview account reflect similar preoccupations. His assumption is that
more services meant a better life for the people who needed care,
and relief for their families, and that the authorities were essentially
benign, if under-resourced. The 'handicapped' or subnormals do
not people his account. They were numbers, administrative problems associated with lack of hospital or community places.

The preoccupations of the Past Times group, featured next,
were very different.

Margaret: the patient's perspective

In this part of the chapter the historical events and changing
policies described by Cecil French will be seen through the eyes
and experiences of Margaret, a member of the Past Times group.
This was a group of nine older people with learning disabilities
who met with Dorothy Atkinson over a period of two years. (The
individual and shared memories of the group were published
privately, and a full account of the project is also available.)[43]
Margaret was 'put away', a phrase she uses herself to chilling
effect. Margaret's biography, reconstructed from the transcribed
accounts in the group's publication, *Past Times* (1993), will help
bring together the policies and practices of the past. She saw,
witnessed and experienced the everyday workings of the regimes
established and maintained by the mental deficiency legislation
and its framework of inspection and control.

Margaret was born in 1921, in Sundon, a village in Bedfordshire
'between Luton and Toddington'. She was the second eldest of
five children. Family life had its difficulties as the following extract
indicates:

My mum was terrible. She used to put my dad in punishment. She used to flirt with another man. He found out. He
come home one day and she was shouting around, and he
come in and asked what was going on, asked her why she

was shouting. She threw the dinner at him! Then he hit her! He hit her and then he walked out, went up the pub. Mum went up the pub then to see where he was. They had another argument up there and she come home. They patched it up, they made it up. He come home six hours after.

Sometimes she wouldn't talk to him. Sometimes she wouldn't talk to any of us! We couldn't do anything, we just put up with it. She might do it all day, sometimes several days. She was thoughtless.

Margaret used one incident to give a flavour of the tensions between her parents. Sometimes these led to arguments, sometimes to days of silence. In looking back on her life, and reflecting on it, Margaret uses the later language of the hospital regime to describe what happened to her father when her mother was angry with him: 'She used to put my dad in punishment'. These were ordinary memories, perhaps, but they have come to be couched in the language of later, less ordinary, times in her life. In addition to her memories of her family in the 1920s, Margaret also recalled aspects of home and village life in the years prior to the start of her hospital career. Some of these memories are captured in the following scenes from her rural childhood:

My mum used to make her own butter when we lived in Sundon, where I was born. I used to help, I used to turn the handle. We used to have a tin bath, used to sit in front of the fire. We sat in the bath, in front of the fire. We used our tin bath for washing clothes out. Mum used to do it, I used to help her.

We used to have a grocer's shop and a butcher's shop in Sundon. I used to go to the butcher's. I used to know the fella' and I used to get meat cheap. I used to go to the grocer's shop an' all, and get some potatoes, cabbage and carrots. There was a picture house down our street. That was in Gas Street, it was on the other side of the road. The Picture Palace it was called. We used to get in for tuppence! I used to like old pictures, Laurel and Hardy, old films. I used to go with my two sisters. We used to have a fair on the village green. There'd be roundabouts and swings.

Margaret's childhood – and her life – changed forever following a severe knee injury when she was only seven years old:

I was up in the garden, on the swing, when a boy come along and hit me on the knee. He hit me with a pram axle, an old thing with rods all the way round it. I fell off the swing with my leg under me, and I broke all the bones in my knee. I was in hospital, Leagrave Hospital, for two years. I was in hospital for a long time with my leg. I was only seven. Mum and dad come and see me. We had a party on my birthday, on the ward. I was there till I was ten.

I was at school in the village till I was 14. I was glad to leave. We had a high and mighty teacher who asked me why I couldn't read and write. I told her I just couldn't do it. We also had a School Inspector come round.

It seems, from Margaret's account, that no allowance was made for the loss of schooling for a crucial two years, and no remedial help offered. Instead a 'high and mighty' teacher berated her for not being able to read and write. She was duly deemed to be 'backward' and, in her own words, was 'put away' in Cell Barnes, a mental deficiency institution. This was in 1936 when she was 14 years old:

When I was a little girl I was put away. I was 14 and a half. I went to Cell Barnes to live because they said I was backward. My dad refused to sign the papers for me to go, but the police came and said he would have to go to prison if he didn't. I cried when I had to go with the welfare officer.

Although Margaret remembers how she cried when the welfare officer took her away, Cell Barnes was, in retrospect, a relative haven compared with what was to come later. Margaret was there for two years. Her first impression was a good one, as she recalls:

At Cell Barnes, when I first got there, the sister spoke to me and said I would be all right. She was kind and gave me a cup of tea. The babies' ward was downstairs, the girls were upstairs and the boys were on the other side.

Margaret's description of the layout of the institution – 'the boys were on the other side' – makes clear that the strict segregation of the sexes, reported by people in institutions elsewhere, was fully

operational in Cell Barnes in the 1930s.[44] Documentary sources
also confirm the physical separation of boys and girls, men and
women, in mental deficiency institutions.[45] School lessons were, it
seemed, already a thing of the past, because on the very next day
Margaret was set to work:

> I was 14 and a half. I started work the next morning,
> sewing buttons on shirts and trousers, and repairing
> clothes till 4 o'clock. Then we went back to the ward and
> had a sit down. In the evenings we used to go to the Girl
> Guides and play games and have singsongs, which I
> enjoyed. We also played netball and had dances on
> Saturday nights when we wore our best clothes. We went
> to church on Sundays.

Again these details of everyday institutional life in the inter-war
years are confirmed by reports from elsewhere. Institutions were
meant to be as self-sufficient as possible, and clothes were made
and repaired on site mostly by inmates. Sports, particularly team
games, were characteristic of the time, as were troops of Boy
Scouts and Girl Guides in mental deficiency institutions in the
1930s.[46] The Saturday night dances, and church on Sundays,
seemed to be regular features of institutional life according to
oral accounts from hospitals elsewhere.[47] Margaret's life changed
again when, aged 16, she was moved to Bromham House in
Bedfordshire:

> I left there when I was 16, and then I went to Bromham
> Hospital near Bedford. I thought how big it was, and
> they were building a lot of new wards. I was on F1 and
> then I moved to F2. I ran away from there. The sister
> on the ward didn't like me and I didn't like her. I was
> there 20 years and I was always scrubbing. After 20 years
> we changed over. I went to F4 the children's ward, the
> babies' ward. We had a sister down there who I used to
> get on with.
> Sister Smith was on F2. When I was in the stores one
> day, there was a lot of mats and Smith said I had to clean
> 'em all. So I threw 'em at her! And she fell over! She put
> me in punishment there. I ran away from F2. We hid in
> a haystack and got frost-bitten feet. I ran away with
> another girl and caught yellow jaundice.

The sister would keep on at me, saying my work wasn't done properly. She was being horrible. I'd scrubbed the ward and she said I had to do it over again. I said, 'Well I aren't going to do it over again!' I told the doctor. He come round and he wanted to know what I was doing on the stairs again. I said, 'I've been told to do it again, it wasn't done properly.'

I planned it with the other girl, we planned it together. She was fed up. She was doing the dayroom and dining room, cleaning and polishing. Then I was put on it, as well as scrubbing. We planned to get into Bedford, walk across the fields.

Margaret's first impression of Bromham was 'how big it was', and how they seemed to be building a lot of new wards. This was 1938 and, it was true, Bromham was going through a period of rapid expansion. There were no Girl Guides, netball team or singsongs mentioned in this account. The emphasis was on work and punishment. As well as recalling particular incidents such as throwing the mats at Sister Smith (not her real name), re-scrubbing an already well-scrubbed ward and talking to the doctor on the stairs, Margaret's story ranges over many years of misery. This was not just an odd unhappy week in her life, this *was* her life. She was at Bromham for 36 years in all, but spent 20 of them on a ward where she, and the seemingly all-powerful Sister Smith, did not get on. Margaret spent 20 years of her life scrubbing floors, a job which she hated. Each act of defiance on her part led to her being 'put in punishment', which meant yet more scrubbing.

Margaret's account reflects the first-hand experiences of people in other institutions where a strict regime of work operated, and where punishments, such as extra scrubbing duties, solitary confinement and loss of privileges were everyday occurrences.[48] The emphasis on work, and the drive towards the self-sufficiency and cost-effectiveness of colonies, is also confirmed in accounts based on documentary sources.[49]

It was not surprising that Margaret ran away. Nor was she alone in her attempt to escape. A contemporary of hers, George Mustard, recalled in later life how he and others had run away from Prudhoe Hospital in Northumberland: 'Lots of us used to always run away'.[50] People ran away from the awfulness of their fate. In reality, though, escape was rarely possible and life was even worse following an enforced return, because running away was a punishable offence. Margaret suffered frost bite, a spell in the 'low grade' ward and a return to the dreaded F2 and Sister Smith. Similarly, Mabel Cooper recalled how, in St Lawrence's Hospital in Caterham in the 1950s, people ran away and, when they were caught and returned, were locked up in G3, the punishment ward: 'They used to make you wear your bed slippers and then you couldn't run away'.[51]

Margaret tried to run away from the day-to-day unhappiness of her life. In the end there was no escape, but it was worth a try. The regime in the 1930s and 1940s was unremittingly grim, as she recalled with much sadness:

> I lived on a miserable ward. It wasn't much fun, especially F2. There was always rows on there, rows with the staff. And the staff shouting around telling the patients to shut up. I didn't get shouted at 'cos I used to keep quiet. I was on F2 a long time, about 20 years.

There was much personal animosity between Margaret and Sister Smith, a point she returned to several times in the group by way of explaining the depth of her misery. She was all too easy a target for someone else's cruelty, and there was little she could do. She was virtually powerless: defiance brought punishment, speaking out invited denial and disbelief and the likelihood of yet more trouble behind closed doors. The vindictiveness on Sister Smith's part meant that Margaret spent much of her life scrubbing: 'One of 'em didn't like me, so I used to do a lot of scrubbing. I was on scrubbing at Bromham.'

There were other consequences of this vendetta for Margaret. She was very fond of her father. When she talked about her parents, she tended to be critical of her mother but spoke warmly about her father, and with some understanding of his dilemma. She recalled how he had initially refused to sign the papers which sent her to Cell Barnes, and had only done so when threatened with prison. He died while she was in Bromham. Margaret was then aged 25, and his death was a terrible blow. Not only that, but she was refused permission to go to his funeral by Sister Smith. There was nothing she could do about it:

> Dad went in 1944. He died in 1944. He was 53. They didn't tell me why he died. My brother, Peter, wouldn't tell me either. He come to Bromham, he was in the army

then. He told me dad had died. I cried, upset myself, I
couldn't eat no food for a couple of weeks. They wouldn't
let me go to the funeral, 'cos I was in the wrong. I was
on F2 and the Irish nurse, sister, wouldn't let me go.

This was a very real loss for Margaret, but it was also a symbolic
loss. The one person in the world who might have fought to get
her out of the institution was now gone. The rest of the family
kept in touch and Margaret talked about their occasional visits to
see her. When her mother died, many years later, she chose not
to go to her funeral. At the time of the *Past Times* project all family
contact had ceased:

Freda, my sister, come to see me once, one August, in
Peter's sidecar. He had his motorbike then. And then he
had a job getting her out because she wasn't well. So she
stayed in the sidecar and I had to go out and see her.
She died.
    Mum died in 1968, she was about 85. Peter told me.
He come and see me. I didn't go to the funeral, I didn't
want to. She used to come and see me in Bromham. She
came on the bus once, then Peter used to bring her in his
car. Peter's got a car now, my brother. He used to come
and see me in Bromham, but now he don't come at all.

Just as Margaret remembers the date she first arrived at Bromham
('That was in May, 1938, the 11th of May'), so she remembers the
date she left: 'I left Bromham in 1974, November 19th, that's when
I left. The staff come and told me, the sister of the ward. I went to
live in the hostel.' The swing away from institutional care towards
care in the community had finally touched Margaret's life. A hostel
had opened in Dunstable and, 38 years after she had first left the
community, Margaret returned there to live.

Discussion

In the literature review, our argument was that the different
approaches to understanding and interpreting the history of learning disability did not attempt to present the picture from the point
of view of different protagonists. Those historians who have turned
their attention to the subject have not recognised the political
importance, or the value, of trying to access the perspectives of

people with learning disabilities. Pragmatist-practitioner accounts operate within a set of assumptions which assert that better services mean better lives. Normalisation theorists also start with assumptions, that people with learning disabilities are victims of an oppressive cycle of labelling and stigmatisation, and select from history to prove their ideas correct, while both the disability movement and the self-advocacy movement privilege the accounts of disabled people, and omit the perspectives of other actors who also had roles in the drama.

In the main body of the chapter we have presented oral history accounts by two individuals, one a paid professional, the other a woman with learning disabilities. Both respondents are talking about one county, Bedfordshire, and the periods they describe overlap substantially. Both furnish details which corroborate and are corroborated by accounts from other sources. Yet the tales they tell are very different, with few points of overlap, save the common interest in Bromham Hospital. Cecil French was interested in services. The information he supplied is valuable factually, to flesh out the written record in his own book and other sources. It is also of interest because his words reveal the ethos of the time when he was at work. In his world view services were needed because 'families couldn't cope'. This gives no insight into the sort of domestic dramas Margaret described in her own home. For Cecil French, people like Margaret and the other members of the *Past Times* group were not individuals, but a group to be provided for with Fabian zeal. Dealing with mental handicap was his job, not his life.

Margaret's life in many senses mirrors policy changes: entry into institutions as they were developing in size in the 1930s; incarceration there during the middle years of the century; and resettlement in 'the community' as the deinstitutionalisation movement got under way. But hers is more than a story of changing policy and practice, it is a whole life with commonalities to others of her generation, as well as differences imposed by her label.

Cecil and Margaret tell very different stories, using different language, and drawing on dramatically different discourses. Cecil is very much in the Kathleen Jones tradition, equating an increase in services with better lives. Margaret is a victim, consonant with normalisation ideas, but she is equally an actor, someone who does not passively accept her fate, but challenges it, by running away, by fighting back and by putting her own side of the story.

In considering what these accounts add to information derived from written sources, it becomes apparent that these are both 'more history' and 'anti-history'. Cecil's voice is consonant with the account in Jones's 1972 book. Indeed, as the author of many of the documents available to historians in the form of minutes, reports and the like, and the author of the authoritative account of the Bedfordshire Mental Health Services, this is unsurprising. His oral account supplements and personalises the written word, but there are few dramatic divergences. The main respect in which his own voice tells a different story is his profound pessimism about community care. He views the swings in policy he has seen during his lifetime cynically, as so many pious hopes and empty promises backed up by inadequate resources. In writing, Margaret's account is more in the 'anti-history' vein. We have deliberately cross-referenced to other sources, mainly derived from oral history, to show that the practices she describes are not fabrications, but common to other inmates in other institutions. But Margaret's account does challenge forcefully the rather benign picture painted by Jones, by French, and by others who have charted the histories of large residential hospitals, such as those by Diplock and Bingley.[52] Such accounts are an important reminder that policies and practices which are apparently intended to be in the best interests of those they are designed to benefit can feel very different to people on the receiving end.

Frisch[53] reminds us that oral history is not just a matter of telling it like it really was, the raw voice of the past calling through the years, but a complex interplay of memory and social interaction with the interviewer. It is not a case of Margaret's or Cecil's accounts being 'better' or more authentic than accounts drawn from the traditional historian's sources. But it is an additional resource, to add into the debates over history and how it is to be constructed, and by whom.

Conclusion

In this chapter we have dwelt on accounts from two perspectives. There are others: the parents' voice is not here, nor is the voice of direct care staff, either in hospitals or in community settings. But the accounts featured here at least begin to show the unique contribution oral history can make to the history of learning disability in bringing past practices to life; in uncovering a range of perspectives; and in reminding us that people with learning disabilities and the staff who worked with them are people as well as labelled objects.

Notes

1 M. Frisch, 'Oral History and *Hard Times:* A Review Essay' (1979) reprinted in Perks, R. and Thomson, A. (eds), *The Oral History Reader*, London, Routledge 1997.
2 M. Thomson, *The 'Problem' of Mental Deficiency in England and Wales*, Oxford, unpublished PhD thesis 1992.
3 G. Jones, *Social Hygiene in 20th Century Britain*, London, Croom Helm 1986.
4 J. Hurt, *Outside the Mainstream*, London, Batsford 1989.
5 K. Jones, *A History of the Mental Health Services*, London, Routledge & Kegan Paul 1972.
6 I. Goffman, *Asylums*, Harmondsworth, Penguin 1961.
7 See for example T. Kanner, *History of the Care and Study of the Mentally Retarded*, Springfield, Illinois, CC Thomas 1964.
8 M. Diplock, *The History of Leavesden Hospital*, private publication, undated.
9 R. Bingley, *South Ockendon: Echoes from an Essex Hospital*, private publication 1994.
10 Thomson, op. cit.
11 D. Wright and A. Digby (eds), *From Idiocy to Mental Deficiency: Historical Perspectives on People with Learning Disabilities*, London, Routledge 1996.
12 P. Ramcharan, G. Roberts, G. Grant and J. Borland (eds), *Empowerment in Everyday Life: Learning Disability*, London, Jessica Kingsley 1996.
13 Open University, *Learning Disability: Working as Equal People*, Milton Keynes 1996 and D. Atkinson, M. Jackson and J. Walmsley (eds), *Forgotten Lives: Exploring the History of Learning Disability*, Kidderminster, BILD 1997.
14 A. Borsay, 'Language and Context: Issues in the historiography of mental impairments in America, *c.* 1800–1970', *Disability and Society*, 1997, Vol. 12, No. 1, pp. 133–141.
15 S. Noll, *Feeble Minded in our Midst: Institutions for the Mentally Retarded in the South 1900–1940*, Chapel Hill and London, University of North Carolina Press 1995.
16 F. Williams and J. Walmsley, *Transitions and Change (Workbook 3 of Learning Disability: Changing Perspectives)*, Milton Keynes, Open University 1990.
17 K. Jones, *A History of the Mental Health Services*, London, Routledge & Kegan Paul 1972.
18 Goffman, op. cit.
19 W. Wolfensberger, *The Principle of Normalisation in Human Services*, Toronto, 1972 and w. Wolfensberger and S. Tullman, 'A Brief Outline of the Principle of Normalisation', *Rehabilitation Psychology*, 1982, Vol. 27, No. 2, pp. 131–145; W. Wolfensberger, 'Social Role Valorisation: A Proposed New Term for the Principle of Normalisation', *Mental Retardation*, 1983, Vol. 21, No. 6, pp. 234–239 and P. Williams, 'The Nature and Foundation of the Concept of Normalisation', in Karas, E. (ed), *Current Issues in Clinical Psychology*, 2, New York, Plenum Press 1985.

20 Wolfensberger, op. cit. and Williams, op. cit.
21 A. Chappell, 'From Normalisation to Where?', in Barton, L. and Oliver, M. (eds), *Disability Studies: Past, Present and Future*, Leeds, Disability Press 1997.
22 B. Perrin and B. Nirje, 'Setting the Records Straight: a critique of some frequent misconceptions of the normalisation principle', in Brechin, A. and Walmsley, J. (eds), *Making Connections*, London, Hodder and Stoughton 1989, and H. Brown and H. Smith, 'Whose Ordinary Life is it Anyway?', *Disability, Handicap and Society*, 1987, Vol. 4, No. 2, pp. 105–119.
23 S. Whitehead, 'The Social Origins of Normalisation', in Brown, H. and Smith, H. (eds), *Normalisation: A Reader for the Nineties*, London, Routledge 1992.
24 M. Bayley, 'Normalisation or Social Role Valorisation: an adequate philosophy?', in Baldwin, S. and Hattersley, J. (eds), *Mental Handicap: Social Science Perspectives*, London, Tavistock/Routledge 1991.
25 D. Felce and S. Toogood, *Close to Home*, Kidderminster, BIMH 1987.
26 A. Chappell, 'Towards a Sociological Critique of the Normalisation Principle', *Disability, Handicap and Society*, 1992, Vol. 7, No. 1, pp. 35–51.
27 J. Ryan and F. Thomas, *The Politics of Mental Handicap*, London, Free Association Books 1990.
28 J. Campbell and M. Oliver, *Disability Politics: Understanding Our Past, Changing Our Future*, London, Routledge 1996.
29 Campbell and Oliver, op. cit.
30 Chappell, op. cit.
31 B. Crawley, *The Growing Voice: A Survey of Self Advocacy Groups in Adult Training Centres and Hospital in Great Britain*, London, Campaign for Mentally Handicapped People 1988.
32 D. Atkinson and F. Williams (eds), *Know Me As I Am: An Anthology of Prose, Poetry and Art by People with Learning Difficulties*, London, Hodder and Stoughton 1990.
33 N. Hunt, *The World of Nigel Hunt*, Beaconsfield, Darwen Finlayson 1967; J. Deacon, *Tongue Tied*, London, National Society for Mentally Handicapped Children 1974; M. Burnside, *My Life Story*, Halifax, Pecket Well College 1991; M. Cooper, 'Mabel Cooper's Life Story', in Atkinson, D., Jackson, M. and Walmsley, J. (eds), *Forgotten Lives: Exploring the History of Learning Disability*, Kidderminster, BILD 1997.
34 D. Atkinson, *An Autobiographical Approach to Learning Disability Research*, Aldershot, Avebury 1997.
35 Atkinson and Williams, op. cit.
36 M. Potts and R. Fido, *A Fit Person to be Removed*, Plymouth, Northcote House 1991.
37 J. Walmsley, *Gender, Caring and Learning Disability*, unpublished PhD thesis, Open University, Milton Keynes 1994.
38 D. Atkinson, *Past Times*, Milton Keynes, private publication 1993.
39 C. French, *A History of the Development of the Mental Health Services in Bedfordshire 1948–1970*, Bedford, Bedfordshire County Council 1971.
40 The term 'subnormal' was introduced in the 1959 Mental Health Act, to replace the term 'mental defective' used in the previous legislation dating from 1913.

41 The statutory minimum for 'certified defectives' was quarterly visits. Cecil did not directly acknowledge that the Bedfordshire MWOs were failing in their statutory duties.
42 These were the terms used in the 1913 Mental Deficiency Act, repealed in 1959.
43 Atkinson, op. cit.
44 Examples are to be found in Potts and Fido, op. cit., and in Cooper, op. cit.
45 Examples are found in A. Stevens, 'Recording the History of an Institution: The Royal Eastern Counties Institution at Colchester', and M. Jackson, 'Images from the Past: Using Photographs', both in D. Atkinson, M. Jackson and J. Walmsley (eds), *Forgotten Lives*, Kidderminster, BILD 1997; see also D. Atkinson and J. Walmsley, 'Using Autobiographical Approaches with People with Learning Difficulties', *Disability and Society*, in press.
46 A. Stevens, 'Changing Attitudes to Disabled People in the Scout Association in Britain (1908–62); a contribution to the history of disability', *Disability and Society*, 1995, Vol. 10, No. 3, pp. 281–294.
47 Potts and Fido, op. cit.
48 See Potts and Fido, op. cit.; Atkinson and Williams, op. cit.; Cooper, op. cit.
49 See Thomson, op. cit.; Atkinson and Walmsley, op. cit.; Jackson, op. cit.; Stevens, op. cit.
50 Atkinson and Williams, op. cit.
51 Cooper, op. cit.
52 Diplock, op. cit.; Bingley, op. cit.
53 Frisch, op. cit.

9

THE RECIPIENTS' VIEW OF WELFARE

Elizabeth Roberts

Introduction

For the purposes of this chapter, the term 'recipient' has been interpreted as any member of the working class in the period 1890–1940 in receipt of assistance from various governmental and other agencies. The recipients were manual workers and their families, wage rather than salary earners who lived in three northern towns, and each of these towns had a rather different economic base. Preston had a heavy dependence on the textile industry – a dependence which was somewhat diminished in the inter-war period partly because of the decline in the cotton trade and partly because of the growth of various engineering concerns. Barrow-in-Furness was predominantly a town of heavy industries such as ship-building, engineering and the production of iron and steel. Lancaster had a more mixed economy, with a particular emphasis on the manufacture of linoleum and oil-cloth and many service industries.

As the chapter is a discussion of the views of the recipients of welfare it has been imperative to draw upon working class testimony. This was collected in oral form at various times in the period 1972–81, in the course of nearly 500 interviews in depth, with about 170 respondents.[1] The interviews covered many aspects of working-class familial, social and working life and were not specifically about 'welfare'. This chapter is an analysis and interpretation of the respondents' views, although included are several examples of them speaking for themselves. As one looks at the oral evidence, it quickly becomes apparent that the recipients' view of welfare is complex, ambiguous, but ultimately intelligible. It is clear that the word 'welfare' is in fact rarely used, except, perhaps predictably, in connection with the Welfare State in the period after the Second World War. A few people spoke of welfare clinics in the inter-war period but these were usually simply called ' clinics', and there appears to be no other reference to the word. It is equally clear that the great majority of working-class families had need of help of some kind at some time during the period. The principal periods of need arose from low pay, unemployment, sickness, old age and bereavement. The chapter concentrates on help for members of the working class in times of specific need, whether chronic or acute. It may be asked why there is no mention of either the provision of education for working-class children or their and their families' attitude towards it. This subject is omitted partly because it is a substantial topic by itself, but mostly because working-class people did not regard 'schooling' as help in time of need: education was not seen as a welfare provision. Some valued it and saw it as an insurance against future need; rather more tolerated it; while some regarded it as a nuisance which prevented children from earning much-needed wages.[2]

Self-help: the moral framework

It is impossible to understand working-class attitudes towards times of need or the help available at these times, without accepting how powerful were the *mores* governing many aspects of working-class life. It is not my purpose to explore the origins of the work ethic (sometimes called Victorian, sometimes Protestant, but one which extended well beyond Victoria's reign and covered Catholics, atheists and agnostics as well as Protestants). Men and women worked not only because of severe economic pressures but also because of a perceived duty to make their contribution. Coupled with the work ethic was a strong belief in the virtue of self-help and a dislike of charity from official bodies. Samuel Smiles is sometimes quoted as the populariser of the ideals of self-help: his book was first published in 1859.[3] While its popularity and influence should not be underrated, it is probably significant that aphorisms about the virtue of self-help first appear in the writings of Aesop in the fifth century BC and were subsequently regularly repeated (Aesop wrote, for example, 'The gods help those that help themselves'[4]); and thus we can assume that these values are very deeply rooted in our culture. Much of the complex attitude to self-help can be seen in this small piece of evidence from

Mrs Mitchell, a Preston woman who was born in 1913 and who was an active member of the Labour Party and a trade union. She discussed the particular problem her own family had had during the depression in the cotton industry in the late 1920s and early 1930s. Despite her brother's experiences of the humiliation of visits to the workhouse and the poverty of living on food-tickets which she deplored, she continued her interview like this, displaying a familiar, ambiguous attitude to the unemployed and the need for self-help:

> In those days men did work, there was no shamming like they do today. They had to work to keep their families. The men in those days, of course you got the odd ones, they took their family responsibilities seriously. You didn't see a lot of ragged children. You would see them in their clogs and they would have everything patched but they were neatly patched and darned socks and that. They were self-conscious. In those days if you got money on the cheap like they do today, well you lived on charity and the neighbours would let you know it, you know – 'they're living on charity, living on the town'. These days they take it for granted that they are entitled to it but they don't think it is coming out of someone else. Those days they worked for their families and they did work hard.
>
> *People gossiped in those days about the people that didn't?*
>
> Well, the ones that didn't work in those days, they were really lazy people. They were always gambling and backing horses. They were always in the public houses, coming home drunk. They were vile and they would have bad language and all that.[5]

It might seem that Mrs Mitchell, influenced by current events, is concerned with comparing, unfavourably, working people of today with those of the past, but a more accurate interpretation of her comments might be that laziness and an inability to support one's family is wrong now and was definitely condemned in her youth, while helping oneself and one's family was to be commended. These attitudes are very common and certainly prevailed in the working class (and beyond) throughout the period 1890–1940. And yet Mrs Mitchell, like so many others, had great sympathy for those in trouble and in need. She herself, as a widow in her twenties and the mother of a handicapped child, was the recipient of many forms of welfare. She may be said to represent an old and continuing view that there were the deserving and the undeserving poor.

The problem of what was the recipients' view of welfare becomes more difficult and paradoxical with the increasing amount of government help for those in need as the century progressed. As will be seen, neither the government nor its representatives, nor the recipients themselves, were able before 1940 to develop a coherent, logical, unambiguous view of welfare which synthesised the elements of self-help, the work ethic, and state help for those in need. However, before state help is examined in any detail, it should be emphasised that throughout the period, much welfare provision was not provided officially but was unofficial, informal and private. This form of help was of paramount importance before the beginnings of state welfare provision under the Liberal government of 1906–14, and continued to be very significant after that date. It is important first to look at the ways in which working-class people were helped in times of need, secondly to assess which help was acceptable and which was less so, and thirdly, to attempt explanations of their attitudes. The various forms of help are described in the recipients' own general order of preference, the least desirable forms of assistance coming last.

Because of the strength of the self-help *mores*, each family did try to help itself in times of trouble. If the chief wage-earner's money was inadequate for the family's needs, stringent economies would be made and possibly a second job might be undertaken. More probably, his wife and/or older children would earn some money in a variety of occupations. Various ways of 'living off the land' were adopted (most notably, keeping an allotment and fishing). Less desirably, credit would be sought from local traders, and even more distasteful were visits to the pawnbroker.[6]

Mutual aid

Almost as strong as the 'self-help' *mores* was the ideal of mutual aid, of cooperation as well as of individualism. The extended family was seen as an essential provider of help and services; it could and did act as an unofficial employment agency, older members putting in a word for young relations; it could provide both goods and money (although more likely the former) in times of sickness and unemployment; it was the principal support of widows and orphans and provided help for the sick, dying and bereaved. Much has been written about the motives for kin helping kin. I have long rejected Michael Anderson's thesis, suggesting, in *Family Structure in Nineteenth Century Lancashire* (1971), that kin were interacting with kin with an 'instrumental calculative attitude'. Kin have not been discovered helping kin for what they could get in return; help was often given at considerable cost, in time, money and effort to the donor.[7] Much less has been said about the attitude of those who received the help. The witnesses themselves are surprisingly silent on the subject: occasionally gratitude is expressed but the deafening silence on this subject and the totally matter-of-fact way such help is remembered tend to lead to the conclusion that it was help which was expected, regarded as completely within the natural order of life, a part of one's normal expectation and entitlement.

The neighbourhood acted in a way not too dissimilar from that of the extended family. Neighbours were not likely to offer *long-term* help – for example, the care of orphans and the aged, but could provide short-term emergency services; for example, loans (usually of goods), gifts (especially of food), child-minding services as and when needed, and help for the sick and their families (usually with food and with services such as washing).[8] Curiously it is much easier to find among the oral evidence examples of neighbours providing help rather than of receiving it. Possibly the survivors are the ones who were always slightly better off; possibly too, people wish to remember being the provider of charity rather than the recipient. But there is, nevertheless, a good deal of evidence from the recipients and their attitude tends again to be grateful but quite matter-of-fact, as an accepted part of the *mores* of a working-class neighbourhood. One woman spoke of her husband's death in the late 1950s when those *mores* were already changing. Her sense of bitterness and betrayal because of the *absence* of neighbourly help and support was still very obvious. It is also apparent that neighbours lived to some extent in the spirit of reciprocity, but not the kind written of by Anderson. Help was not *offered* in the expectation of any return, but help was *accepted* by the recipient who comforted him- or herself with the thought that he or she would be able to pay back the good turn either directly to the donor or to another neighbour 'in lieu'. Mrs Morrison remembers the neighbourliness in one of the poorest areas of Preston in the 1920s:

So how much did your husband get when he was on the dole?

When there was four of us he had 24s. When he was out of work ill we had 14s. because he had missed a stamp and he had a shilling off every week for his shilling stamp. I was paying 5s. a week for rent. If we hadn't had good parents and good neighbours? I had a wonderful neighbour there who had a family of children but her husband was in good work and she would send me a shilling every Friday tea-time, when her husband got his wage, to buy something. She said, 'Treat yourself to something for your tea'! She did that for long enough. Her family are all dead now but she was a wonderful person. Neighbours are wonderful!

How else would they help?

One took the washing in when I was in bed confined, another one took all the children's washing. One would bring me my dinner and another would bring my tea and all this sort of thing. I had a lady across the road who had her leg off and was confined to bed and I would run across and give her a cup of tea when the girls were at work, when she had nobody to attend to her.[9]

Notice how easily Mrs Morrison moves from describing being a recipient of help to being a donor.

Professional help

Family and neighbourhood support would not cover all emergencies; for example, however good women were at diagnosing illness, prescribing for it and generally nursing the patient, there was need for the doctor on occasions of serious illness. The working class at the turn of the century had no expectation of having a doctor's services without paying for them in some way. (The provision of health care for the working classes is a subject worthy of a paper of its own, for it is full of ambiguities and complexities.)[10] The very poor were, of course, entitled to call upon the services of the Poor Law doctor. There are, in fact, only two examples of this provision in the sample. Mrs Burns, remembering her life as an orphan with her grandmother in the 1890s, said:

If you wanted a doctor you went for a recommend, you'd take the recommend to the infirmary and then they would send a doctor down . . .

Would this have been the Guardians?
It must have been. ... I'd go in ... 'Please, I want a recommend for m'grandma. 'What's the matter with your grandma?' 'Don't know, she's ill.'
Did you have to pay for the doctor?
No, I don't think so. It would be recommended because we hadn't money to pay.[11]

Mr Logan, in the 1920s, as the unemployed father of six children, had to apply to the Relieving Officer for a free doctor too:

You went to the Relieving Officer and you got a chit to go to the doctor's, . . . the Relief people would pay.[12]

These two respondents spoke in a matter-of-fact way about this use of the Poor Law doctor, and obviously, to them, there was no disgrace. However, it is obvious that the very great majority of the respondents did expect to pay the doctor; some very poor patients did not actually pay their bill because the doctor, in his charity, did not send one, but equally poor people struggled to pay – and dreaded the weekly arrival of the doctor's debt collector. The obvious self-help solution to the problems of medical costs was the one long advocated by middle-class observers of working-class life. In 1817 the Vicar of Harrow wrote: 'It is the great benefit of Friendly Societies that they teach a man to avert his eye from the workhouse to work, to the blessing of God, on his own endeavour to get his bread by the sweat of his brow.'[13] While supporting the ideal of self-help, many working-class people could not belong to Friendly Societies: obviously with low incomes, weekly contributions of even a few pence could prove to be prohibitive. Less obviously, doctors refused, rather like some examples of modern insurance companies, to enrol in the Societies those judged to be in poor physical shape, and so the most needy could be doubly handicapped. Mr Bowker, for example, in Barrow, belonged to a large family who were all members of the Oddfellows, but he was not admitted, the doctor telling his sister who took him to be examined: 'You can take him back and tell your mother she should have drowned him when he was young, and I'm not going to do it [i.e. admit him].' Mr Bowker was eventually allowed to join the Rechabites.[14] About one-sixth of Barrow's population belonged to a Friendly Society at the beginning of the century.[15] As well as the recognised societies there were many 'unofficial' sick clubs, especially in Preston. These tended to be centred on pubs and were administered by an unofficial committee who decided when and if members were entitled to benefit.[16]

Those who did not belong, for whatever reason, to any form of sick insurance scheme were, however, likely to be acquainted with the principles of insurance. It is ironic that those who could not afford to belong to a Friendly Society to safeguard the health of the living, almost inevitably managed to afford to pay for death/funeral insurance. Perhaps the two important facts we should remember about this period are that the working class were well accustomed to the idea of *paying* for welfare (in the form of the doctor) and to the principle of insurance, which was seen as a form of saving for benefits to which one was entitled by one's payments. Regret is expressed that insurance was not more widely available and that so many were excluded either because they were bad insurance risks or because they could not afford the payments.

Charitable help

Many of the working class were very poor before 1914; for example, no labourer in the area earned as much as Rowntree's suggested poverty line of 21s. 8d.[17] In times of acute hardship help had to be sought from charitable organisations. These were many and various, including soup kitchens, some of which functioned on a regular basis and others which opened only in times of special need. Churches and church missions in the poorer areas tended to provide regular meals for poor children. In Preston, Mrs Pearce remembered going to St John's one night a week, and to Shepherd Street Mission on another night, in order to receive her free soup. This was obviously given out with no questions asked about the children's religious or economic standing. She admitted that she wondered if she was entitled to this help from Protestant churches, since she was both a Catholic and well-fed! She was once asked at the Mission what she had had for breakfast and she had replied truthfully 'boiled ham'. The woman had replied 'My word! You're not doing so bad', but there was no question of stopping her soup. She continued to go because her friends (who *were* hungry) went, and because she liked food.[18] Her parents had no objection to her going, and no-one using these private soup kitchens mentions any sense of shame at so doing. It is impossible to know, even approximately, how many people these charities fed; their existence is not even identifiable through the local press. For emergency soup kitchens there are more precise records, however. The Barrow Iron and Steel works, for example, was closed for 20 months in the years 1908–09 and the 'temporary soup kitchen in the area served 2 million meals during that period'.[19]

Apart from providing food, there were charities which supplied other forms of help. The Lancaster police force had a clog fund which 'shoed' many a needy child; while Preston seemed to specialise in Christmas charities for poor children. There were several of these: one of them was called 'Uncle Sam's breakfast' and is remembered with affection by many respondents, as is Shepherd Street Mission. The *Preston Guardian* recorded in 1895 that Uncle Sam's provided gifts for 2,000 children, while Shepherd Street dealt with 750.[20] The children received a bag containing food and a small present. While it is true that the majority of respondents did not have recourse to these charities, those who did again treated them in a very matter-of-fact way. Mr Thomas went regularly in the 1890s:

> *Did you ever go to Uncle Sam's breakfast?*
> I've been to Uncle Sam's breakfast at half past eight. I've been to Shepherd Street Mission round the corner here at nine o'clock and I've been to some other organisations for my breakfast at ten o'clock. I've taken as many as four breakfasts home on Christmas morning. As I've gone into the places for them and we brought them out in a paper bag, always brought them out in a paper bag – I've had my mother meeting me and taken them home while I've gone to next place and then when I came out of the next place she met me and took them home until I've got as many as four on Christmas morning. Not only me but scores of kiddies used to do the same thing.
> *When you went to the soup kitchen or to the Uncle Sam thing, did they check on who you were?*
> No. They would just give you what you wanted. They never bothered you at all. But when you went for your Christmas breakfast, you had to have a ticket.[21]

One of the most important things Mr Thomas said was, perhaps, the comment on the paper bag. It obviously added a touch of dignity, of seemliness to the whole encounter. Another interesting comment is one he made on the soup kitchen: 'They never bothered you at all.' Even the necessary ticket for the Christmas breakfast was widely and freely available, apparently without question. The respondent was aware, as were other local people, that the money for such charities as Uncle Sam's breakfast was raised by and from other local people. Mr Lawson, whose family was as poor as that of Mr Thomas, recalled how he collected around the area for Uncle Sam's breakfast for about six weeks before Christmas. The event was organised from the Temperance Hall, but he was warned not to visit the middle-class area: 'You don't need to go round Fulwood, because there's moneyed people there and they'll not give you anything, it's a waste of time.'[22] The generosity of the poor in giving these donations was well known to the recipients of these charities (and it can be verified from the donations lists published in the local newspapers).

It may have been that the recipients were happy to believe that this charity was an extension of neighbourhood help which they could repay in some form, at some time. Certainly it is important to stress that charity was accepted and acceptable if it was offered in a dignified way and if it involved no investigation of the recipients' means. This rejection of the intrusiveness of the 'do-gooder' and the demand that charity had 'no strings attached' ran, of course, contrary to every practice urged by the Charity Organisation Society, with its emphasis on 'friendly' visiting and its condemnation of indiscriminate charity: 'Indiscriminate charity only made things worse, it demoralised.'[23]

The Poor Law

Finally, there was the help offered by the Poor Law Guardians. This was, as presumably it was intended to be, the most infrequently sought and the most disliked form of charity. There were various elements in this attitude: the fear of the workhouse, the cross-examination about means, and the humiliating way recipients were treated. Mrs Nixon remembered an incident after her father deserted the family (before the First World War): 'My mother once sent my sister to a Miss Dixon who used to give charity money; [she explained later that this woman worked for the Guardians] . . . she said to my sister "How many of you are there?" I think there was about seven of us. She said "I can give you a ticket for the workhouse." My sister said "We don't want to go to the workhouse." She got a ticket for 5 shillings for some groceries.'[24] But the family was terrified of the threat of the workhouse and did not approach the Guardians again. One explanation for the almost complete commitment of the working class to funeral insurance was undoubtedly the fear and disgrace of having a pauper funeral. Mrs Askew of Barrow spoke for many when she made this remark about the workhouse and indoor relief:

> *I get the impression that a lot of old people were looked after by their families?*
> More often than sent to the workhouse. Oh, to be sent to the workhouse was dreadful. I mean nowadays young people tend to say that their parents should go into a home but they didn't say so much that their parents should go into the workhouse. I think families tended to stick together more. We only had a little bit but we would share it and I think that happened.[25]

This was not a pious platitude. Mrs Askew's grandmother lived with the family for many years, and she was a person who liked her drink and had the annoying habit of pawning the family's possessions to pay for it. On occasions, she also sold the pawn ticket and so the goods were lost for ever. In the sample only two grandmothers are remembered as having been in the workhouse. One went because the family were too poor to keep her, and the other because she too had the habit of pawning the furniture to pay for drink.

It would seem that this pattern of families caring for their elderly was in no way unusual. Edith Sellers in the early years of the century investigated 12 workhouses, some in London and some in rural areas. She estimated that only 16 per cent of the inmates had any relatives with whom they might have lived.[26] In 1906 it was estimated that just under 6 per cent of its elderly population were residing in Poor Law institutions.[27] The workhouse was, therefore, the place of last resort. It was all stated quite clearly in 1909 in the Minority Report on the Poor Law and Relief of Distress:

> We have to report that there exists, in all parts of the kingdom, among all classes, the greatest dislike and distrust of this typical Poor Law institution. The respectable poor, we are told, have a horror of it and they will not go into the House at all unless they are compelled. The whole institution, reports our Medical Investigator 'is abhorred. . . . The workhouse and everything within its walls is anathema

except to the very dregs of the population. It is . . . the
supreme dread of the poor.[28]

Attitudes to the welfare reforms of 1906–1914

Respondents are almost invariably proud of their families
'managing' and include the concept of survival alongside accounts
of more acute hard times. There is little complacency, however,
about the adequacy of these welfare provisions at the beginning
of the century. There was keen and lasting regret at the large
number of premature deaths, especially among children, and
sadness because of the many lives wasted by poverty and disease.
Improved health care and help for the sick was a widely supported
cause, but the ambivalences remained about what the justification
could be for help to those who were merely unemployed without
at the same time suffering other kinds of need. The reforms of
the Liberal government between 1906 and 1914 were a turning
point in the provision of welfare for working-class people. There
were, however, different attitudes to the different measures of
reform. The discretionary Education (Provision of Meals) Act 1906
made little difference to local parents and children because many
local authorities chose not to implement it until after the First
World War. This seems to have been the usual practice outside
London. In 1912–13, there were nearly 100,000 children being
fed by the schools authorities in London, but only 258,000 in the
rest of the country.[29] The Schools Medical Inspection Services
tended to be regarded as another somewhat unpleasant aspect of
school and were not regarded as being important to the well-being
of the working-class children: in some cases the inspections were
rather perfunctory; in others, when defects were discovered, the
family was still left with the problem of paying for the medical
treatment.[30] Old age pensions were welcomed; although they were
income-related, they did not appear to invoke any thorough investigation into working-class financial affairs. In general they were
regarded as a right and as deferred wages rather than as a
charitable hand-out.

The measure which had by far the most significance for the
respondents was the 1911 Insurance Act, which is consistently
recalled as a landmark. Respondents do not usually remember
dates (apart from personal ones) but if asked about national insurance, sometimes reply 'Oh, Lloyd George, 1911' or sometimes
'1912'. Mr Thomas made the following observations:

Did any of your family ever have to go to hospital when you were little?

Never. I can never remember anyone going to hospital from our house. Even the mothers had their babies at home and they never thought about hospital at all. It was all home work. It is only since the National Health Insurance came about, about 1912 if I remember right? I think I paid my first contribution about 1912 and that was when we got our free doctor and that made all the difference in the world to this nation. The Lloyd George Movement was one of the finest this country ever had.[31]

It was welcomed as an extension of the previously limited insurance schemes. No-one regarded it as getting something for nothing, since the sickness and unemployment benefits were paid for and were therefore, obviously, a worker's right. The Insurance Act did much to increase working-class expectations of less cruel times financially when the chief wage earner in the family was sick or unemployed. These expectations were further increased by the speeches made by certain politicians during the First World War.

The inter-war period: continuities and changes

The inter-war period, for the recipients of welfare, was in many ways different to the period before the First World War, but it is important to remember that there were also continuities. There was a continuing ambivalence towards the idea of state help for those in need, resulting from the familiar complex mixture of sympathy for those in trouble, alongside continuing support for the idea of self-help and, on the part of the recipients, a continuing dislike of any official investigation into their financial affairs: this was counterbalanced by the attitude of those *not* in receipt of state help who had a recurring fear of anyone getting something for nothing from official funds. Another feature from an earlier time was the continuing mutual support system in most extended families and most neighbourhoods. More formalised mutual help schemes also continued to flourish. The role of the Friendly Societies after the passing of the National Insurance Act is well known. Rather less well known is the continuing role, in Preston at least, of Catholic guilds. Mr Sharples, growing up in the

ELIZABETH ROBERTS

inter-war period, remembered them very clearly, probably because
his father worked voluntarily for the one in their parish: 'These
guilds were religious organisations . . . the major religious confra-
ternities, but they were also welfare societies. . . . All the members
paid a weekly contribution, . . . in return for this you were entitled
to considerable benefits when you were sick, unemployed, and
when you died. . . . They flourished.'[32]

Private charities continued in existence, although one is left with
the perhaps subjective impression from the respondents that their
role had changed from that before the First World War. When
asked about soup kitchens, older respondents remember their existence in their youth before 1914; no respondents remember them
in the inter-war period in Barrow, although Mr Mulholland
recounted stories of the unemployed having communal meals with
donated food but these were organised by the men themselves
and were not like the old soup kitchens.[33] The responsibility for
the regular feeding of hungry children was taken over by the
Education authorities, and in really bad times this amounted to
more than school dinners. Thus we find that in 1925 a resolution
was passed by the local branch of the National Union of Teachers
asking to be relieved of the job of serving school meals. At the
height of the Depression (1922) they had been providing 2,400
meals a day (this figure had fallen to 330 by 1925). The meals
were: breakfast of tea, bread and butter and jam at 8 a.m., and
a dinner of pie, or stew, or shepherd's pie or hot-pot, with a
steamed pudding to follow.[34] These meals were, however, only
served in certain centres. The Missions and churches which had
played an important part in feeding the poor before the war also
adopted a different role in the inter-war period. Many tried to
provide social activities for the very poor, both for the unemployed
men and for their wives. Mr Boothroyd, for example, who was
unemployed for a long time in an industrial village in central
Lancashire, remembered the young unemployed men in the village
using the church club (with the vicar's support) as a social centre
for cards, bowls and dominoes – although gambling for money
was, naturally, not encouraged.[35] Some of the special children's
charities were, however, as popular as ever. At Christmas 1932,
2,000 children had their treat at the Shepherd Street Mission,
while Uncle Sam's breakfast catered for 1,000.[36]

There are many clear differences in the inter-war period
compared with that before 1914, covering both attitudes and
circumstances. Firstly, as has been mentioned, the Liberal reforms,

216

and especially the 1911 Insurance Act, encouraged working-class people to look to the state for more help in times of sickness and unemployment; moreover, they believed they were entitled to this help because it was paid for. Secondly, the war experiences of many families, coupled with generally increasing real wages, tended to result in rising expectations. Men and women expected – indeed, felt entitled to, and sometimes even demanded – more prosperity, and better food and houses, and many examples of this show up in the oral evidence. The third change of significance was the quite unforeseen change in employment patterns. People before the First World War had known of work being scarce, but none had experienced the mass, prolonged unemployment of the inter-war period. As Table 9.1 shows, the amount of unemployment in Lancashire varied from town to town and from year to year, but it was obviously a serious problem. This was particularly acute in Barrow in the years immediately after the war, with the abrupt ending of the demand for armaments and warships. Thousands of men became unemployed together, often for a period of years, and the social fabric of many working-class areas was adversely affected. Other Lancashire towns also suffered serious difficulties through widespread unemployment. The combination of changed attitudes and circumstances meant that although the old welfare methods of helping those in need generally continued, they were inadequate in the face of long-term

Table 9.1 Percentages of insured workers unemployed in Lancashire, 1922–37

	1922	1923	1929	1931	1932	1937
Barrow	49	24	13	27	34	7
Birkenhead	26	18	17	36	36	23
Blackburn	15	16	14	47	33	21
Bolton	10	15	16	33	27	13
Burnley	11	18	11	37	25	16
Liverpool	13	11	18	30	29	21
Manchester &	13	10	11	24	21	10
Salford						
Oldham	10	21	13	39	30	13
Preston	17	15	14	27	22	11
Rochdale	11	15	8	34	26	9
Wigan	7	5	23	35	32	22

Sources: *Manchester Guardian*, 7 August 1923 (for figures for 1922 and 1923), M.P. Fogarty, *Prospects of the Industrial Areas of Great Britain* (1945), p. 33 (for figures for 1929, 1931, 1932 and 1936).

unemployment and consequently long-term need, especially when those who suffered were also expecting a higher standard of living than before, or at the very least, no deterioration in that standard. The Cabinet was well aware of the particular problem of the skilled unemployed who were used neither to unemployment nor to acute poverty (the typical victims of the Depression in Barrow). They are well described in this report by the Committee on Unemployment to the Cabinet in October 1921:

> A very large proportion of the unemployed today are not the usual type of unskilled or work-shy men but are very largely people who all their lives have been used to good wages and many of whom are still making every effort to avoid having to apply to the Poor Law Guardians for relief. A very large percentage of these men have fought in the War and they are not prepared to see their families endure misery and want without a serious struggle and even disorder.[37]

Although the government well recognised the problem, and even its potential danger, it could not solve it. The problems facing the inter-war governments have been well rehearsed. It rapidly became apparent that the actuarial calculations on which the 1911 Act was based had not taken into account the possibility of high, long-term levels of unemployment. The ideal of a self-financing insurance scheme covering workers in times of sickness and unemployment became impossible. Those whose entitlement to insurance payments ran out had to resort to the Guardians. Thus, the new state insurance system and the old system of poor relief became hopelessly intertwined and confused.

The confusion among some respondents is clear. Mr Logan, when asked about the wages of married women replied thus:

> You had to be very careful because you could lose your dole.
> *This was the Guardians, the Poor Law?*
> They would help you. It was the dole, the unemployment – they would stop it all if they caught you earning a copper or two.[38]

Mr Logan was wrong, as help from the Guardians was, at least in North Lancashire, always means-tested, but unemployment pay, if covered by covenanted benefits, was not. Acute problems regarding state relief existed for the long-term unemployed who either 'ran out' of covenanted benefits or, indeed, were not entitled to them. Only for two short periods in 1924 and 1930[39] were uncovenanted benefits (later called transitional benefits and then transitional payments) *not* means-tested. It is therefore clear why the long-term unemployed saw the whole inter-war period as over-shadowed by the Means Test; it is also clear from the mass of confusing and often contradictory legislation why so many of them had an imprecise understanding of their benefits.[40] The abolition of the system of Poor Law in 1929, destroyed by the problem it had been created in 1834 to solve – the problem of how to relieve the able-bodied unemployed – did not directly improve the lot of the unemployed because under the new Public Assistance Committees, grants were subjected to the Means Test for the long-term unemployed whose insurance entitlement had ended.

The attitudes of the recipients of state welfare funds varied considerably; those who were unemployed for only a short period received their unemployment insurance and felt that the scheme was fine. The majority of the respondents who were also claimants, however, were long-term unemployed. They suffered not only in their pride and dignity but in their pockets too. The unemployed were expected to survive on very low levels of benefits (see Table 9.2). These benefits, if unsupplemented, guaranteed that the unemployed and their families lived in poverty. The problems of establishing poverty lines are well known, but the ones suggested in the inter-war years do, at the very least, indicate some of the contemporary views of what constituted poverty. Bowley and Hogg in work published in 1925 suggested that for a bare standard of physical efficiency to be maintained, a family of five had to have an income of 37s. 6d.[41] The same standard was adopted by the authors of *The Social Survey of Merseyside*, published in 1930.[42] But B.S. Rowntree in his second survey of York argued that 53s. a week was essential for a family of five to receive the necessities of a healthy life.[43] It is clear from Table 9.2 that families where the wage-earner was unemployed did not reach any of these targets. Their poverty was an important influence upon their attitude to state help. The more politically conscious came to view both the Guardians and the Public Assistance Officers as their class enemies (whatever the class or political views of the officials concerned). In Barrow, where unemployment very suddenly and catastrophically reached 49 per cent in 1922, there was a continual

Table 9.2 Rates of Unemployment Benefit

(a) Unemployment Benefit Rates

Date	Single Adult Man	Adult Man, Wife + Two Children	Single Adult Woman
8.1.1913	7s	7s	7s
25.12.1919	11s	11s	11s
8.11.1920	15s	15s	12s
3.3.1921	£1	£1	16s
30.6.1921	15s	15s	12s
10.11.1921	15s	22s	12s
14.8.1924	18s	27s	15s
19.4.1928	17s	28s	15s
13.3.1930	17s	30s	15s
8.10.1931	15s 3d	27s 3d	13s 6d
Unemployment Act 1934	17s	30s	15s
Increase of Benefit Act 1935	17s	32s	15s
Additional Benefits Order 1938	17s	33s	15s

(b) Benefit in Respect of Dependants

Date	Wife	Each Child
10.11.1921	5s	1s
14.8.1924	5s	2s
19.4.1928	7s	2s
13.3.1930	9s	2s
8.10.1931	8s	2s
1934	9s	2s
1935	9s	3s
1938	10s	3s

Sources: Report of Royal Commission on Unemployment Insurance, 1932, p. 20; Rex Pope, Unemployment in N.E. Lancashire (unpublished M. Litt. thesis, Lancaster 1971).

battle (both physical and psychological) between an organised group of unemployed workers and the Guardians (as had been foreseen in the report to the Cabinet). Sometimes they argued on behalf of other less articulate friends when they came to be means-tested and frequently found themselves thrown out of benefit. Mr Mulholland told (at some length) how a group of men entered the Guardians' office (known locally as the 'Wailing Wall') and wedged all the doors shut and then forced the Guardians to promise to act more leniently towards their clients. Mr Mulholland was well informed and knew in fact that the promise was more symbolic than substantial. He added: 'They promised to be fairer, but they couldn't. As a matter of fact, they were bankrupt.'[44]

Certainly the Barrow Guardians dispensed more money in grants or loans than their better-known colleagues in Poplar.[45]

At the other extreme were the very poor who had no inclination for confrontations with the Guardians or the Assistance Board. Some accepted their interference in almost every aspect of their lives, such as the official who burst in one New Year's Day and accused an unemployed man of wasting his money by giving his parents a cup of tea; or the woman who suffered the distraint of her furniture to repay her Poor Law grant; or the others who tolerated the prying into their cupboards and ovens to see how the money was being spent. Their dignity and self-respect were continually being assaulted, and it is not surprising to find few who remember these incidents without anger and bitterness. Others who were entitled to Poor Relief and Public Assistance refused to claim it because of the interference and humiliations they knew such an application would involve. Mrs Dawson, in Barrow, was reported for going out cleaning for a neighbour, and her husband was summonsed and lost six weeks' payments. Mrs Dawson was so upset by the disgrace and the talk of possible prison sentences that she took the family entirely out of the system and worked like a slave for the rest of her life to support her daughter and invalid husband.[46]

Mrs Dawson's problems were those of many others and reflect the insoluble dilemma of government, its officials, and the recipients of welfare in reconciling the old traditions of self-help and the economic policy of cutting state benefits to the minimum. Expressed rather simplistically, the government supported the idea of self-help but saw this as an *alternative* to state benefit (hence the Means Test). The recipients also were in favour of self-help but saw it as a way of *supplementing* state grants which were very low. This dilemma was never solved, and one of its saddest results was the unpleasantness which developed between neighbours in some areas, notably those where there were serious problems of long-term unemployment; ironically, those who believed in self-help and not living on charity reported those who they felt were cheating the providers of relief and assistance. The ones who were reported were inevitably practising their own version of self-help – selling the produce of their allotment or of their fishing expedition, or augmenting the family's income with the wife's part-time wages. Some gave in and abandoned their traditional ways of ensuring survival in times of need. Others, probably for the first time, found themselves acting illegally, simply by carrying on long-established traditions, and only the very well informed found a way through the minefield, but their success did not endear them to their neighbours.

Mrs Wilkinson's husband was unemployed for five years in Barrow. This is part of her account:

> *I know if you did a job on the dole it was knocked off?*
> It was knocked off, yes, it was. So, he started doing this, but he didn't do many chimney-sweepings while he was working, and came on the dole and reported the fact that he did a bit of chimney-sweeping. He knew the man personally that was in the office and they used to know each other before that man got in the office. He was a shop-assistant, that chap, and Wilf knew him before he was in the Labour Exchange and it was him who put Wilf wise what to do. He said: 'Get a little job while you're working and then when you come on the dole, report it and they'll investigate but you're allowed to keep it.' If he earned more than one pound a week he got no dole but he was allowed to earn a pound a week. Audrey was always wanting extra stuff. She couldn't live on stuff we did and she was living far better than we were. She needed it she was so delicate, so when he came on the dole he'd do a few chimneys which helped out. People did report him because this young fellow told him: 'I've had another report about you again.'
> *Weren't people nasty?*
> Hm. They'd never say who. About five times he said: 'You know, you've been reported again, Wilf.'
> *It must have caused a lot of bad feeling?*
> Well no, but it makes you feel a bit small to think folk are checking on you like that.
> *Did it make you a bit less open with the neighbours?*
> I'd to be very careful what I said.[47]

Here is a classic case of the Means Test forcing 'distancing' and 'privatisation' on the working-class family.

It should be emphasised that in areas such as Lancaster and Preston, where chronic and prolonged unemployment was not the serious problem that it was in Barrow, the old self-help and mutual support systems provided by family and neighbours continued to exist, unaffected by the cancer of the fear of anyone getting 'something for nothing' from the state.

Conclusion

There are discernible changes in attitudes to welfare provision over the period under discussion. Whereas at the beginning of the period there seemed to have been little expectation of state help, except from the dreaded Poor Law, by the Second World War it is possible to see an attitude of expecting, as of right, subsidised state help and support, especially for the well-being of mothers and children. This co-existed with the ideals of self-help and paying for benefits through state insurance. It is perhaps significant that this is the only area in which the word 'welfare' is used in the inter-war period. It was also in this sphere that working-class expectations and aspirations had most altered from those pertaining before 1914. Working-class parents no longer accepted as inevitable the dreadful toll of infant death, and working-class women expected more help and more pain relief in their confinements, and believed (possibly inaccurately) that they would be better cared for in hospital.[48] The health of mothers and children was becoming of paramount concern. The recipients were not receiving something for nothing: they were, in fact, seeking welfare provision at a subsidised rate – cheap infant food and free advice at the clinics, and subsidised rates for the poor in maternity wards (at the matron's discretion). The women (still a minority) who used these maternity and infant welfare services incurred no disgrace and certainly felt no shame. They were in one way the harbingers of the post-Second World War society when the great majority came to believe that everyone was entitled to a free medical service as of right, regardless of income. No such easy consensus, however, was to be found for the problems of the long-term unemployed, even in this latter period.

Notes

1 The material was collected in two projects. The first was 'The Quality of Life in Two Lancashire Towns, 1890–1930', and was supported by a Nuffield small grant in 1972–74 and by the S.S.R.C. in 1974–76. The second project was 'Working-class Family and Social Life in Preston, 1890–1940' which was financed by the S.S.R.C. in 1978–81. The work was carried out under the aegis of the Centre for North-West Regional Studies in the University of Lancaster. I should like to express my thanks to my colleagues in the Centre for their help, and most particularly to Mrs Marion McClintock. The interviews are transcribed and indexed and are available for use by students and researchers.

223

2 Elizabeth Roberts, *A Woman's Place. An Oral History, 1890–1940*, Oxford: Blackwell, 1984 and 1995, chap. 1; Elizabeth Roberts, 'The working-class family. Children and young people', in John Benson (ed.), *The Working Class in England, 1875–1914*, London, Croom Helm, 1984; Stephen Humphries, *Hooligans or Rebels. An Oral History of Working-class Childhood and Youth, 1889–1939*, Oxford, Blackwell, 1981, chaps. 2, 3 and 4.

3 Samuel Smiles, *Self-Help*, London reprint, Murray, 1908.

4 John Bartlett, *Familiar Quotations* (14th edition), Basingstoke, Macmillan, 1968, p. 76.

5 The respondents are given pseudonyms in the text to prevent confusion. In the notes they are given their code number in case their original transcripts need to be consulted. Mrs. M.1.P. b.1913. Father: fitter and turner; mother: weaver; 6 children. Mrs M. a tenter, widowed 1944. 2 children, 1 survived. p. 59.

6 Elizabeth Roberts, 'Working-class standards of living in Barrow and Lancaster, 1890–1914', *Economic History Review*, Second series, vol. 30, 1977, pp. 306–321; Elizabeth Roberts, 'Working-class standards of living in three Lancashire towns, 1890–1914', *International Review of Social History*, vol. 28, part 1, 1982, pp. 43–65; John Benson, *The Penny Capitalists – A Study of Nineteenth Century Working-class Entrepreneurs* (Dublin, Gill & Macmillan, 1983), *passim*.

7 Michael Anderson, *Family Structure in Nineteenth-Century Lancashire*, Cambridge, Cambridge University Press, 1971; Elizabeth Roberts, 'The working-class extended family, functions and attitudes, 1890–1940', *Oral History*, vol. 12, no. 1, 1984.

8 Elizabeth Roberts, *A Woman's Place*, chap. V, op cit.

9 Mrs M.3.P. b. 1898. Father: a dock checker; mother: a dressmaker and charwoman. 7 children, 3 survived. Mrs. M.: a worker in the Lamp Works. 5 children. pp. 20–21.

10 Elizabeth Roberts, 'Oral history investigations of disease and its management by the Lancashire working-class, 1890–1939', in John Pickstone (ed.), *Health, Disease and Medicine in Lancashire, 1750–1950*, Manchester, UMIST Occasional Publications, No. 2, 1980.

11 Mrs B.1.L. b.1888. Father: a labourer; mother: a weaver. 5 children, orphaned when very young and cared for by grandparents. Mrs B.: a weaver; 3 children. pp. 39–40.

12 Mr L.1.L. b.1896. Father: a docker; mother's occupation not known. 9 children, 5 survived. Mr L.: professional soldier, labourer, 6 children. p.12.

13 J.W. Cunningham, *A Few Observations on Friendly Societies*, London, Ellerton & Henderson, 1817, p. 22.

14 Mr B.1.B. b.1897. Father and mother: caretakers. 13 children, 11 survived. Mr B.: a baker, 2 children. p. 15.

15 These figures were calculated from annual reports on membership, published by the Friendly Societies in the local press.

16 Mr T.2.P. b.1903. Father: a labourer; mother: a weaver. 7 children, 3 survived. Mr T.: an engine driver, 1 child. pp. 18–19.

17 S.B. Rowntree, *Poverty: A Study of Town Life*, London, Nelson, 1901, p. 296.

18 Mrs P.1.P. b.1899. Father: a blacksmith; mother: a hawker after father's death. Mrs P. was brought up by foster-parents. Mrs P.: a weaver, 6 children, 4 survived. pp. 2–3.
19 *Barrow News*, 25 July 1909.
20 *Preston Guardian*, 28 December 1895.
21 Mr T.3.P. b.1886. Father: a labourer; mother: a washerwoman. 7 children, 4 survived. Mr T.: a mill worker, later, insurance agent. 3 children, 2 survived. pp. 2–3.
22 Mr L.1.P. b.1894. Father: a carter; mother's occupation not known. 12 children, 11 survived. Mr L. became a labourer, 2 children. p. 4.
23 C.L. Mowat, *The Charity Organisation Society, 1809–1913. Its Ideas and Work*, London, Methuen, 1961, pp. 1–4.
24 Mrs N.1.L. b.1899. Father: painter and decorator, but deserted the family; mother: a washerwoman. 9 children, 7 survived. Mrs N. became a textile worker. 8 children. p. 67.
25 Mrs A.2.B. b.1904. Father: a labourer but ill for long periods. Mother: a charwoman. 4 children. Mrs A. became a shop-assistant. 1 child. p. 62.
26 E. Sellars, 'Old Age Pensions and the 'belongingless' poor. A Workhouse census', *Contemporary Review*, 93, 1908, pp. 147–157.
27 Michael Anderson, 'The elderly, and changes in governmental income maintenance', in E. Shanas and M. Sussman (eds.), *Family Bureaucracy and the Elderly*, Durham, North Carolina, Duke University Press, 1977, p. 46.
28 *Poor Law and Relief of Distress, 1909*, Cd. 4499, xxxvii, pp. 731–732.
29 Standish Meacham, *A Life Apart – The English Working Class 1890–1914*, London, Thames and Hudson, 1977, p. 208.
30 Ibid., p. 210.
31 Mr T.3.P., p. 57.
32 Mr S.4.P. b.1915. Father: a pattern-maker; mother: no occupation after marriage. 2 children, 1 survived. Mr S. became a teacher; 3 children. p. 6.
33 Mr M.6.B. b.1892, Tyneside. Moved to Barrow as shipwright in 1912. 1 child. p. 42.
34 *Barrow Guardian*, 27 June 1925.
35 Mr B.4.P. b.1896. Father: a bleach-works labourer; mother: a fowl dresser. 10 children. Mr B.: a bleach worker, no children. pp. 23–24.
36 *Preston Guardian*, 31 December 1932.
37 *Committee on Unemployment Report to the Cabinet*, P.R.O. Cab. 23/27, Cabinet 76 of 1921, 6 October 1921; B. Bentley Gilbert, *British Social Policy, 1914–1939*, London, Batsford, 1970, p. 84.
38 Mr L.1.L., p. 6.
39 P.P. 1924–25 (200) v. 299, P.P. 1924–25 (238) v. 313 and P.P. 1930–31 (175) v. 609.
40 This confusion is frequently shared by the author. I am indebted to Dr Stephen Constantine of the University of Lancaster for his detailed and patient help in answering my questions about the insurance and unemployment benefit available during the inter-war period.
41 A.L. Bowley and M. Hogg, *Has Poverty Diminished?*, London, King, 1925, p. 37.

42 D. Caradog Jones, ed., *The Social Survey of Merseyside*, Liverpool, University of Liverpool Press, 1934, vol. 1, p. 150.

43 B.S. Rowntree, *Poverty and Progress: A Second Social Survey of York*, London, Longmans, 1941, pp. 28–29.

44 Mr M.6.B., p. 97.

45 In the period March 1921–September 1924, Barrow Guardians granted or lent £217,158, while those in Poplar during the same period granted £7,313, *Local Government Journal*, 18 October 1924.

46 Mrs D.1.B. b.1899. Father: a labourer; mother: no paid occupation. 9 children. Mrs D.: a domestic servant, munitions worker and domestic servant. 1 child. *passim.*

47 Mrs W.1.B. b.1900. Father: a moulder; mother: no paid occupation. 10 children. Mrs W. became a shop-assistant. 1 child. p. 87.

48 Statistics for Preston show rising figures for puerperal fever and maternal deaths which coincide with the increased number of hospital births. *Preston Medical Officer of Health Annual Reports*, 1911–1940; Jane Lewis, *The Politics of Motherhood: Child and Maternal Welfare in England, 1900–1939*, London, Croom Helm, 1980, pp. 35–38, 122–124.

10

HIV AND AIDS
TESTIMONIES IN
THE 1990s

Wendy Rickard

Despite the fact that, in real terms, HIV and Aids have directly affected only a relatively small proportion of the British population,[1] the epidemic has had a significant impact on the development of health and social welfare policy for a variety of complex reasons that are still unfolding. From the mid-1980s, the public aspects of this impact were well documented in an expansive specialist litera-ture, but as funding priorities changed in the early 1990s, work slowed considerably. This chapter assesses the role of oral history in documenting the epidemic in the first decade and draws on more recent oral history material to describe subsequent changes that emerged in the 1990s.

Important factors identified as affecting health policy in the first decade included the mix of hostile social reactions, the unpre-dictability of medical and psychological conditions associated with the virus, and the need to respond to the diversity of people infected and at risk, particularly those considered to be at the 'social margins'. The response was idiosyncratic in comparison with other client groups. As one of my interviewees pointed out:

> HIV is the only kind of disease that has had the kind of provision that it's had. There aren't drop-in centres in the same way for other people who have other sorts of long term, chronic, degenerative illnesses that are similar.[2]

With no traditional history of service provision to this group, there was room for significant innovation within the broader policy framework of Community Care.[3] In particular, since the service lead came initially from people infected and their lay supporters, important challenges for health and social care resulted from an active and articulate client group. Within this policy context, broader social issues have been raised. Aids emerged at a particular historic moment:

> when the reaction against social liberalism was gathering force, when the tocsins were sounding for the sexual freedoms of the 1960s and 1970s, when the New Right were mixing a potent brew of religion and familialism, when feminism and lesbian and gay rights were under challenge, and when welfare facilities were facing an unprecedented attack.[4]

Like other types of chronic illness such as multiple sclerosis and arthritis, HIV and Aids have played an important role in forcing health practitioners to acknowledge the social nature of problems faced by people with chronic disorders and to look outside a strictly medical arena in formulating a response.[5] It has also had a dramatic impact in reminding people about the constraints of life-threatening disease, early death and the associated insecurity which in modern times have largely been displaced by notions of a more predictable life-course in a relatively safe environment.[6]

Against this backdrop, my aim in this chapter is first to highlight the role that oral history continues to play in better understanding the historic and social impact of the virus. Second, I will draw on oral history material from people living with the virus to further explore and develop the interpretative framework of 'biographical disruption and reinforcement'. This includes consideration of the meaning of diagnosis in relation to disrupting a life narrative, particularly regarding experiences of non-Aids-related illness and the positive aspects of recomposing personal identities following diagnosis. Third, I will explore the contribution that life story accounts can provide to challenging social taboos and organisational rhetoric within institutions and communities. Finally, I will attempt to capture some aspects of the shifting nature of people's experiences in relation to HIV and Aids as the context changes over time, revealing new personal dilemmas, policy priorities and challenges that have relevance for the wider study of chronic illness. These focus on the way that, in the 1990s, there has been a policy impetus towards 'mainstreaming' the specialist health and welfare services that were set up and attendant equality concerns about parity of service provision for people with other chronic illnesses as new treatments bring the possibility of viewing Aids as a chronic manageable illness rather than a terminal condition. For those who have been diagnosed for some time, there is a mood of resignation to the unpredictability of the virus, mixed with cautious optimism about treatment options. For the newly diagnosed, learning to live with uncertainty is one of the key challenges.

The role of oral history in relation to HIV and Aids

HIV and Aids have presented a rich and complex opportunity to historians. Unlike the response to other contagious diseases in history such as tuberculosis and syphilis, for the first time, it has been possible to document the epidemic as it has been happening. Oral history interviewing has provided a key source of evidence that is perhaps unparalleled in the documented history of other health concerns. Although the epidemic is so recent, key texts have already emerged detailing its early history in the western world and these have relied significantly on personal testimony. For example, both Randy Shilts in *And the Band Played On*[7] chronicling the first five years of the unfolding epidemic in the US and Simon Garfield's *The End of Innocence: Britain in the Time of Aids*[8] are passionately intent accounts drawing on key public and private documents but relying primarily on interviews with people infected and affected. Similarly, Virginia Berridge's *Aids in the UK, the Making of Policy, 1981–1994*, draws significantly on personal testimony.[9] Newspaper columns and autobiographical accounts plus a proliferation of journal articles in the health and social welfare field looking at life narratives are further examples of the prominence of personal testimony in documenting and understanding the epidemic. Although a concern to identify the causes of infection through disease surveillance still dominates the social policy agenda in the 1990s, as new infections continue to be reported, prevention strategies have been found wanting. A trend towards examining the life-decisions and social contexts of people infected in greater depth has followed. One example is the work of Tony Coxon and his team at Project Sigma, Essex University, who conducted a five-wave longitudinal study of sexual behaviour in gay/bisexual men. The project used a range of qualitative methods including sexual diaries which linked risk and life histories. Life history approaches are also becoming an important feature in documenting the history of the epidemic in other non-western countries such as through the innovative work of Panos International. Panos produced a series of four fifteen-minute radio programmes on HIV/Aids and children as part of a UNAIDS campaign in 1997. Entitled *My Generation: Infected, Affected and At Risk,* the series showed children and teenagers from all over the world telling their own stories about how Aids has affected their lives. Further oral history work is planned by Panos for the future in the development context.

Yet inevitably it is media and professional concerns, especially those of medical practitioners and scientists, that have dominated the wider construction of Aids history. In her introduction, Virginia Berridge highlights how the history of Aids quickly acquired 'a type of media-induced "official history" that has become all-pervasive'. An example is seen in Channel 4's 1994 series 'with an almost "traditional" story of the US origins of the "discovery" of Aids, the role of the "disease detectives" at the Centre for Disease Control, the advent of the Haitian and African connections, a nod in the British direction and so on'.[10] So although oral history clearly continues to play an important role, the words of professional 'experts' and commentators have tended to outweigh the words of people who are themselves infected.

This chapter contributes towards redressing this imbalance by drawing on extracts from life story interviews with people living with HIV and Aids in the UK. These interviews form part of an ongoing oral history project entitled 'HIV and Aids Testimonies' that is being conducted in collaboration with the British Library National Sound Archive. It was set up in 1995 and so far, we have completed and archived more than thirty life story interviews, each ranging from three to ten hours in length.[11] The archive includes interviews with 'long-term survivors' (those diagnosed for over five years) or 'non-progressors' (those diagnosed for a long time who have not progressed to serious illness), people who are newly diag-nosed and those who fall between these temporal markers. At the time of writing, one of the thirty interviewees had recently died. For the project as a whole, we are selecting people to interview on the basis of broadly reflecting the range of epidemiological and demographic features evidenced by the wider pattern of HIV infec-tion in the UK.[12] Thus, interviews with gay men appropriately dominate the collection, but interviews with straight men and women are also included. Many, but not all, have borne other conventional 'HIV risk category' labels including drug-user, haemophiliac and ethnic minority. Unusually for oral history, because of the indiscriminate nature of the HIV virus the archive includes testimonies from the young and elderly alike.

Biographical disruption and illness histories

The meeting between health and social welfare professionals and recipients of care involves people with their own particular expectations. Among others, these expectations are about the meanings of health, illness, disability and death. Since the 1970s, increased attention has been paid to such meanings in relation to chronic illness more widely.[13] By considering life story accounts from people living with the virus, oral history brings into sharp focus the need to understand where the 'patient' role begins and how it is influenced by other life events. The people I have interviewed were all keen to emphasise the degree to which HIV and Aids affects their own and other people's perceptions of their identities following diagnosis:

> People, you know, they're not just HIV positive. They've had a life before and actually have a life afterwards as well.[14]

I'm a person, not just a virus-carrier.[15]

Interviewees suggested that pressure to document the pace of the epidemic and analyse the extensive public and social impact has meant that for people living with the virus, interest within health and social welfare debates has tended to focus only on their post-diagnosis experience. This is supported by other evidence suggesting that there has been an inclination among professionals to see HIV and Aids as the same thing, carrying the same meanings[16] and to conceptualise the experience of both these diagnoses as all-important and as defining a person and the response to them. The accounts of people infected suggest instead that HIV, like other chronic illnesses, is one thing that has happened to them: there are many others of significant diversity. Consider the following brief biographical summaries:

Reg lives in West London. Born in Breconshire in Wales, he was part of a large extended family and his early childhood was dominated by the war. Reg was educated at boarding school, but after being expelled from three separate schools for being 'a great prank player', he went on to a local grammar school. His working life included employment as a designer, a sales person in the menswear section of a big department store, time in National Service, amateur theatre and work as an interior decorator in Indian palaces. Reg had lived with an Aids diagnosis for two years when interviewed. He was sixty-two at that time.

Martyn is forty-five and lives in East London. He was brought up in Bristol by his mother and stepfather. A self-defined 'wimpy' child, he discovered his sexuality in his teenage years and rebelled in secret, flirting with male prostitution. During his life he has worked as a banker, an administrator, a youth worker and a business man. He has always been an active Bristol Rovers fan. Martyn and his long-term partner Colin were tested together in 1994 and both were HIV positive.

Alan was interviewed while living in the Special Unit of HM Prison, Peterhead, in Aberdeen. Brought up on a housing scheme in Dundee, Alan was involved in gang culture from a young age. He completed school and trained as a bricklayer before becoming a heroin dealer and addict. He has spent most of his adult life migrating in and out of prison, mostly for drug and violence related crimes. He was the first inmate to be diagnosed HIV positive in Perth Prison. He was married in a hospital ward, four months before his wife died of an Aids related illness. He was thirty-nine at the time of interview.

In the emergent sociological literature, the term 'biographical disruption' has been coined to describe the way in which the onset of a life-threatening illness fractures a person's social and cultural fabric, exposing him or her to threats to self-identity.[17] Treating it as a disruptive event in this way allows for its meaning to be situated in a life course context. This is a useful idea in relation to one of the key issues that emerges from the life story accounts: that HIV and Aids, although having a major impact on the life of people living with the virus, influence only a relatively small part of a life in chronological terms and in relation to the diversity of each individual's life experiences. It exists alongside other life events that create other significant sources of biographical disruption.

In a French study, Daniele Carricaburu and Janine Pierret looked at the way in which such 'biographical disruption' led to 'biographical reinforcement' for gay men and haemophiliacs. This is the notion that diagnosis leads to 'a reinforcement of the components of identity that, prior to HIV infection, had already been built around haemophilia or homosexuality'.[18] They reported that haemophiliac men interpreted their HIV positive status within an illness logic drawn from their efforts to live normal lives as persons with haemophilia. In contrast, gay interviewees did not consider being HIV positive to be an illness state, but a phase in a way of life that reflected a collective gay history. The authors suggest that identities were not simply reconstructed upon diagnosis, they were systematically reinforced through these different collective identities.

I wish to further explore this idea of 'biographical reinforcement' in relation to notions of illness identities and the reference points for these. Considering the wider experience of illness of the people I have interviewed suggests that such reinforcement is less specific to collective 'illness' identity than may be implied by the study described above. It has been well recognised to date that one of the only broad commonalities in the life experience of people living with the virus is in maintaining a level of compulsory consciousness about their own HIV related death and ill-health, and that of friends and others who are infected. But many of the people I interviewed also shared considerable experience of witnessing and coping with their own non-Aids-related illness and non-Aids-related illness and death in those they were close to. This influenced the way they reconstructed their own identities following diagnosis. These prior illness and death related experiences were diverse and not always linked only to a sense of collective illness history as in the case of the haemophiliacs described by Carricaburu and Pierret. For example, Martyn said:

> My granddad developed Alzheimer's disease, and we looked after him through all the stages and it was one of the saddest things to see someone who was so strong and so intelligent, become nothing more than a vegetable in the end. And I remember the day he died in Bristol, he was actually strapped to the bed he had become so violent through Alzheimer's.
>
> I fell in love when I was sixteen. . . . We did our growing up together, we were the same age . . . He was everything I could imagine . . . he was very much the kind of down-to-earth workman, you know garage mechanic, coupled with me being the banker . . . No-one caught on as far as I know. . . . But me and Kelvin were immensely

immensely close. . . . He died when he was eighteen and that broke my heart. . . . He apparently went out for a drive in the morning to his parents who lived just outside Bristol, and was killed in a car crash.[19]

While describing the way in which he told his mother about his HIV diagnosis, Alan spoke about his younger brother.

'I was not going to tell you', I says, 'because I was not wanting to worry you', ken. And she [*mother*] turned round and she says to us, 'John's got it as well.' She says, 'We were not wanting to tell you', ken. . . . So that was the two of us had it. My wee brother dealt with it totally different from me. He went away to London, he came off the drugs and started working . . . and drinking. He just blanked it. . . . And he lived his life as normal as he possibly could. He ended up having a bad accident at work. He fell off a scaffold and died, ken. He hit the bottom and was clinically dead.[20]

People's experience of major non-HIV-related illness prior to diagnosis was also revealing. Reg said:

I got cancer at one point, and they only gave me. . . . I had to go for an operation and if I didn't have that oper-ation I'd only have twenty-four hours more or less to live.[21]

Reflecting on his Aids diagnosis in 1994, he said: 'So really, you see, sickness wise, this is my second time round'. Daxa had two serious gynaecological operations prior to giving birth and was hospitalised for some time. For Martyn, a level of ill-health has always been present in his life.

I was in hospital for the first six months [*of my life*] virtually, with pneumonia and reversed stomach muscles, which I've had ever since. . . . I've always had problems that way, you know, in the stomach, been in and out a lot, you know, the convalescent homes and then the hospitals and it seems to have carried on all my life in its own weird way.[22]

Jonathan spoke of how experience of a condition of alopecia earlier in his life affected his own adjustment to being diagnosed and his decision to take a high public profile about living with the virus.

> I think part of me thought that people are just going to have to accept me as I am really. I'd been through that before with this whole alopecia business and having to be very concerned about what people would think about my experience. In doing something, to shave all my hair off, psychologically, I was saying 'well you're just going to have to accept me as I am' and this was slightly similar in a way. . . . I'd had the experience in a slightly different way before.[23]

Hence, experience of non-Aids-related illness and death among a significant number of my interviewees contributed to the way they viewed their identities and reinforced their biographies following HIV diagnosis, even though they cannot be said to have had a collective pre-diagnosis illness experience. No implication is made that this makes HIV any easier to deal with or that people with HIV or Aids are more likely to have had more non-Aids-related illness experience in their lives. Rather, this construction of a psycho-social identity represents a phenomenon that challenges medicine's tendency to reinforce the independent existence of patient identity purely around the virus itself or around issues of identity linked to conventional notions about risk category groups.

Recomposing personal identities

While the personal impact of HIV and Aids itself marks an appalling and continuing tragedy, life history accounts also capture the positive aspects of the way in which people recompose their identities following the disruption caused by diagnosis. Every individual interviewed has reported personal reflections of how HIV has in some sense had a positive impact on his or her life in subtle and interesting ways. Jonathan Grimshaw has written about the way in which many people with HIV or Aids have challenged traditional health and social welfare approaches by being proactive on a personal and political level:

> They are not fatalistically waiting to be helped and waiting to die and have contributed to a changing society. . . . Many people with HIV describe how the diagnosis in

some sense opens their eyes to things that are wrong, 'unjust', in the society or culture in which they live, often because they experience these wrongs and injustices personally, for the first time, as a direct result of their diagnosis or because their diagnosis adds a new dimension to social oppression or injustice they already experience.[24]

Many of the people interviewed have referred to the way in which HIV forced them to 'cut the bull-shit out of your life', becoming less tolerant of superficial conversations and unsatisfactory social relationships. This has been widely reported elsewhere in relation to chronic conditions more generally.[25] Reg talked about how the experience of HIV had accelerated his own personal development, making him take stock of the speed at which he was trying to live life:

> I don't have the energy to do all the things I'd like to do, or I used to do. But I never had a spare minute. My home was used for taking messages and sleeping in, that's all it was. And sometimes, I never saw it during the daylight, because I'd go to bed when it was dark and I'd get up when it was dark.[26]

Reg and Alan also spoke of the way they gradually adjusted to the need to keep themselves well informed about HIV-related issues and gained the time and the confidence to challenge people in authority:

> Go through history and the one thing about it, you know, when you are around the HIV, you know, like it gives you marvellous insight, you can turn round and you've got so much time to look things up, it's marvellous, you know like, I've thoroughly enjoyed it. The things that you can know. It's so easy to throw a spanner in the works of these professors.[27]

> I did not rely on the prison for help. I had to rely on getting that help myself, finding things out, which in the long run has benefited myself, after going through a lot of stages.[28]

Sociological work supports this notion. For example, Anthony Giddens describes it as a process of 're-skilling' that occurs as information is sought and absorbed, offsetting the feelings of powerlessness that encounters with medical experts may initially involve.[29] This has been characterised as changing the doctor–patient relationship to a form of 'meeting between experts'.

People also reported how reflective recomposition of their identities made them like themselves more. Martyn commented:

> It's changed me and I suppose the only worrying thing is when friends say to you, you know, that you are such a nicer person now than before you knew, and I mean it worries me because it makes you think: 'Well, God! What type of idiot was I, or arse-hole was I?', you know. But they said it has changed me and it has. I've forgotten about the age thing in the sense of, you know, acting my age: if I go out, you know, I've done the tattoos and other stupid things, like I've now beaten my fear of those white knuckle rides and that, I was even doing them yesterday, and I think all these years I wasted, you know, kind of worrying about an image: life's to be enjoyed not endured. And that is where it's moved me. As a couple, it's made us strong, even stronger. And yet I do have these days of worrying and being frightened, I dread to think what would happen if I lost Colin first. But we see the funny side of things as well, this is the awful . . . the sense of humour that comes in with this.[30]

However, interview evidence suggests that these positive attitudes are not universal. They develop only after a certain period of diagnosis and are less clear for people who are more socially isolated. Daxa, for example, was more cautious in her response:

> Yes, I think I have changed. I don't sort of think about things too deep in general . . . I sometimes wonder sort of, of asking somebody, to say to them, you know, if you knew you were going to die, what things would you want to do before you die, because to be honest I haven't really got any ideas. I feel like, I think visiting Disneyland with my son is the only thing that brings to mind. Apart from enjoying the time I have with my son, I don't really know.[31]

Alan described how his attitude to life had changed. He had stopped 'pressing the self destruct button' so often, but he found it

hard to separate how much of this was to do with growing older
and how much was to do with the impact of HIV on his life. His
reflections focused on more practical aspects, such as changing his
life in prison. He spoke of a profound impact arising from being
taken out of prison once every three months for hospital check-ups:

> You notice the seasons in here, as I say, notice summer
> and winter, that's obvious. You do not notice so much
> about like the spring and autumn because you've not seen
> plants and trees and all that so much. If I've got to go to
> hospital, and I get driven to the hospital, for instance, I've
> noticed sheep and when there's lambs around and that.
> I notice things like that, and I notice trees and I notice
> when the leaves are falling off, er, I would say I'm more
> aware of that now.[32]

People often ask how, as an oral history interviewer, it is possible
to cope with the level of trauma that HIV often brings. For me
and for many others working in the health and social care field,
witnessing the bravery and wisdom of people forced to recompose
their personal identities is rarely a depressing task. Oral historians
working in other traumatic contexts report similar experiences.
For example, in his work in Ukraine with victims of Communist
repression, Rob Perks commented:

> But although there was pain, there was also a strong sense
> (perhaps naive) of hope from those I interviewed: that
> freedom of expression and self determination can at least
> restore, perhaps not bread, but validity and dignity to
> individual memory.[33]

Challenging taboo

Throughout the 1990s, in relation to a range of chronic conditions including leukaemia and renal failure, increasing attention
has been given to modifying the organisation and culture of hospitals and clinics to better accommodate a proportionate increase
in hospital workloads related to chronic illness.[34] HIV and Aids
have also had a clear impact in this area with specialist hospital
provision such as the HIV wards developed at London's Chelsea
and Westminster Hospital becoming models of good practice. Less
attention has so far been paid to documenting the way in which

non-hospital institutions can better respond to people regarding the taboo subjects of sex, sexuality and illicit drugs, all issues that HIV and Aids bring into the foreground. For example, my interviewees highlighted some key challenges within residential homes for older people and in prisons. Reg spoke about undertaking HIV prevention activities in residential homes:

> And they get a shock, especially in the sheltered housing, you know, you say [*to the managers*] 'You know that quite a lot of sex is had in sheltered housing?' 'Oh no, we don't . . .' 'You leave some condoms out, just leave a few out here and there and see how they disappear.' Well they do. And then they ring up now and say, 'You're bloody right there, you know, I never thought of that.' She [*the housing manager*] was most concerned that they were able to have sex in their rooms. You know sit quietly, have tea and biscuit and a little fairy cake . . . that's all.[35]

Alan spoke at length about the way HIV was an important factor in challenging the Scottish prisons to face the drug problems of inmates:

> Years ago they would not acknowledge that there was a drug problem in prisons, but they've acknowledged it now. . . . You've only got to notice how the literature's changed over the years, ken. I mean, they started handing out sterilising tablets in Scottish prisons and, OK, they said it was for cleaning chamber pots and your knives and forks and all the rest of it. But it's also for cleaning out injecting equipment. So that's them admitting that there is injecting equipment in jails and they've got drug agencies coming in now, and support groups. You've got HIV support groups, Hep C support groups, drug support groups, all sorts. . . . You've got prison governors who are giving talks at conferences now about the drug problem in their prison. And you've got mandatory drug testing that's been introduced.[36]

As well as challenging taboos in institutions, considering the wider impact of HIV and Aids on gay men, much has been written about how it has given them a potent rallying point, increasing the visibility of gay men in organisations and rendering many of the demands of gay liberation more salient.[37] The life story accounts interestingly revealed that the recording of oral histories around the pivotal issues of HIV and Aids has also given gay men opportunities to speak out about issues that are in some sense taboo within gay 'communities'. For example, among the gay men interviewed, the existence and prevalence of gay domestic violence were highlighted many times. Martyn said:

> Despite the fact that he was smaller he was ten times more powerful than me, that's the frightening thing about it, and when he was in a rage he would be extremely violent. ... The fact is that you start to accept it as part of the relationship, and you live with it, and you can still love someone despite it, despite the violence and the pain, and trying to hide it as well you know.[38]

Reg's life was threatened by his partner who defrauded him of all his possessions. Martyn and Reg both eventually left their partners, but the repercussions were to affect their lives dramatically for many years to come. Martyn was imprisoned in 1994: a brief sentence for embezzling company funds to pay off his ex-boyfriend who after years of domestic violence then blackmailed him. For Reg, a long and painful court-case ensued. To date, it has been difficult for gay men to talk about these issues. Reg did not speak about his domestic violence until the very end of his interview when I asked him if there was any major issue of his life that we had missed out. He said:

> Oh, there is one, but it's too dirty. Yes, it's much much ... it involves gay people, and it would show gay people in a very bad light. Because they tried to kill me, they nearly succeeded.[39]

Martyn's silence resulted from a fear of prejudice from his employers:

> They were a really odd company. I couldn't come out as gay because I knew that would be totally unacceptable to them. And I think that was kind of accentuated, because we had most of a small office block, about five floors, and then one floor was available and the landlords wanted to rent to an organisation called Streetwise Youth which

works with young male prostitutes. But the board threatened to pull out of the lease and move if they allowed them in, because they didn't want to share toilets with gay people who might well have HIV or Aids you see. And actually it was recorded in the board minutes you know.[40]

Such issues have received scant acknowledgement in health and social welfare debates to date. HIV is starting to have an impact in inadvertently forcing issues such as this onto the health and social welfare agenda more widely.

The politics of changing policy agendas

The chronology of developments in knowledge about HIV and Aids and the policy response to it has been relatively well documented until the mid-1990s, although as will be highlighted later in this section, this has always taken place within a contested arena. Most commentators have identified a series of distinct stages in policy development. Virginia Berridge suggested that from 1981 to 1986 the HIV outbreak led to public alarm, social stigmatisation and scientific uncertainty. In policy terms there were no established mechanisms to frame the health and welfare response. Direct action relied heavily on 'self-help' initiatives that gradually became formalised voluntary sector projects, the earliest of which originated with gay men.[41] The setting up of organisations such as the Terrence Higgins Trust, London Lighthouse and Body Positive developed exciting models of self-help including, for example, the development of 'buddying' arrangements and telephone networks manned by positive people and other volunteers.

What the oral histories contribute here is details about other smaller, less well-known self-help groups that also proliferated in the late 1980s and early 1990s. Reg set up a local support group called ACE50+ for people with HIV and Aids who are over fifty years old. Martyn was director of The Globe Centre, a voluntary sector HIV/Aids support centre in East London. Alan set up the first HIV support group, the Phoenix Group, in Perth prison. In a broad sense, this evidence serves to demonstrate the extent to which a whole range of people living with HIV and Aids became involved in self-help activity on different levels. Yet, the oral histories suggest that while people initially saw such activity as reclaiming some power over their own lives, for many, in the course of time, this view became jaded and marred by political infighting and the gradual withdrawal of public funding.

Professionalisation in both statutory and non-statutory agencies followed and much criticism was voiced about the 'depersonalisation' that became apparent within the voluntary sector in particular, evidenced for example in describing people as 'service-users'. The years 1986 to 1987 signified 'quasi-wartime emergency' as the government responded. 'Normalisation' of the disease and 'Aids fatigue' followed, when panic levels began to subside, levels of new infection appeared to slow down and concerns about parity with other client groups gradually came to the fore.[42] The professional health and social welfare domain expanded to accommodate HIV, replacing much of the earlier voluntary activity and specialist provision. Fewer services and less specialist attention became available to people diagnosed in the 1990s. As Andrew Sullivan reflected in a recent media article, 'it must be hard to be diagnosed now . . . it's like you really missed the party'.[43]

The liberal consensus was challenged in the 1990s with a more terse, resource-restricted policy response, accompanied by what has been controversially identified as the partial repoliticisation or 're-gaying' of Aids.[44] This story is complex and has brought into sharp relief paradoxes about applying notions of empowerment within the self-help paradigm. This is well illustrated in Paul's comment:

> I remember one of the discussions at the Body Positive Gay Men's Group was led by a guy from [*a voluntary agency*] and he was excellent, he spoke very well. Except he was full of daft jargon about empowerment and so on and he had some very curious ideas about how people empower themselves and he seemed to think they do it by talking . . . anybody with even a half ounce understanding of politics knows that there are those in control and there are those who aren't and there are those moving either into or out of control and the question is who gets into which group and it's not just a question of 'I want to be in control, therefore I am . . . so what's really going on here?'[45]

Questions about whether specialist service development reached a natural peak and then became too prolific in key urban areas such as London were also raised by interviewees:

There has been some talk of the HIV and AIDS gravy train and, well, I have to say I've seen some evidence of it, you know. I've seen an awful lot of very, very necessary resources and I'm very, very glad that they're there. And I've seen some stuff which has made me think, 'Well, yes OK honey, but what do you actually do?'[46]

The recent trend towards the 'main-streaming' of specialist HIV service provision was stimulated largely by policy recognition of dramatic inequalities with other groups that increasingly became recognised by people living with the virus as well. Richard's partner, Mike, has Multiple Sclerosis:

Mike's MS has largely been in remission in the time that I've known him ... he gets buzzy legs every now and then and has problems with mobility. It's just been an interesting comparison. There's been times when I've been ill, there's been times when he's been ill. ... In the long term Mike's looking at being crippled by MS and probably dying along that way and, you know, I'm looking at pegging it with some sort of opportunistic infection linked to HIV in the indefinite future. Because so much is available to me as a person with HIV. ... It was relatively simple for me to get my benefits sorted out, relatively simple for me to get alternative therapies, conventional medicine ... the clinic I go to is so nice. The options for people with MS are just not there. The Immune Development Trust does actually treat people with MS as well as HIV, but unless your disability is sixty per cent of the time you can't get the same benefits. ... We've got to move to the stage now where we're looking at HIV in a broader context. ... One of the peculiar things is that because it has gone on so long [*the HIV epidemic*], things have actually changed a lot. I do see myself now with the degree of disability I have as being very similar to other sorts of disability. To say that I don't like a special case to be made for HIV is of course the wrong way of putting it. ... I see it as being very comparable with a lot of other things.[47]

However, others continue to argue that HIV is not like other chronic illnesses in important ways. Key issues identified by the interviewees included the fact that unlike many other chronic illnesses, with HIV and Aids, no medical prognosis can predict when people will actually fall ill, nor with what disease. The social stigma associated with the virus remains: Aids continues to be connected with ideas of contagious disease, promiscuity and irresponsible behaviour and this construction radically affects the lives of those concerned demanding continued specialist provision of services. Although this issue remains a contested area, there is broad agreement that change was inevitable and the most important issues in refocusing the health and social welfare service response is to continue to consult those infected about decision-making, to plan changes over time rather than simply cutting services at very short notice and to keep people informed of future plans.[48]

New hope for a cure?

In 1998, the message is that the search for a medical cure for Aids that has dominated the historical agenda for over a decade could be nearing fruition. With the arrival on the market of protease inhibitors and combination therapy, HIV, in the UK at least, is viewed as a manageable illness rather than a terminal disease. Specialist HIV hospital wards in Britain have been closed, but retained in case the new developments prove short term. Recent medical experiments in Philadelphia suggest that a vaccine may have been discovered – it worked on two monkeys.[49] However, other Italian research suggests that the virus has already mutated and newer strains that emerged in the 1990s are more virulent, attacking the immune system at a faster pace.[50] The climate is one of hope, marred by continuing uncertainty.

Oral history evidence gives particular insight into the reality of these advances and the pace of change as experienced by people already living with a diagnosis.

> There's a Steve Larson cartoon where there's a little dinosaur wandering around in these caves and all these caves have little signs outside saying 'Sorry. Extinct'. And I occasionally feel like that little dinosaur.[51]

> By agreeing to be on the [drug] trial, I am taking a calculated risk, an educated gamble, whatever you want to call it. I just didn't want to go full steam for the PIs [Protease

inhibitors] because we've seen it all before. You know, I was saying about Bob and AZT ... we put all our hope and expectations into one thing and in the paper this week there was something like fifty percent of people they reckon are failing. What we've got to do is build up the time before you fail. Because you're going to fail on all of them eventually. It's got to be a long term gain ... I described my condition on one occasion as creeping enfeeblement, getting progressively weaker. ... With the new treatments, ... yes I can get some of my strength back. Yes I can do other things. But I'm still not quite back where I was before it all happened. Twelve years now and they've had their toll.[52]

For those who are still being newly diagnosed other challenges continue. Paul described people's reaction to his recent diagnosis in 1996:

In HIV, illness is always a potential marker of your finitude. ... Something that people keep saying to you when you're first diagnosed is 'Oh well, it's really not that bad, especially now there are these new, wonderful drugs. You could just as well be hit by a bus tomorrow. ...' I was reading ... somebody was quoting an article that there were homophobic buses looking for gay men with Aids trying to run them down, just to prove it was true. It's not a helpful thing for people to say because nobody really expects to be hit by a bus. A bus always comes as a surprise, well unless you're about to make a suicide attempt. Serious disease progression with Aids is not a surprise, it's an expectation.[53]

Although it is too early to say what will ultimately come out of HIV and Aids, it is to be hoped that the illustrative accounts included here provide a vivid portrait of the way in which oral history evidence from people living with the virus continues to play an important role in documenting and understanding experiences. It also highlights the increased impact that the virus continues to have on the wider development of health and social welfare policies in relation to recomposing personal identity in the face of chronic illness and the impact of public service and treatment changes.

Notes

1 Epidemiological reporting began in the UK in January 1982. According to the CDSC report *Communicable disease report*, vol. 6, no. 3, 19 January 1996, by 1996 there had been 11,872 reports of Aids (69% of whom were known to have died). There were 25,689 reports of HIV-1 at this time. The most recent trends suggested by cumulative figures are that there has been a slight decrease in infected males and an increase in infected females, that gay and bisexual men remain the biggest UK group infected, and that there has been a steady rise in heterosexually transmitted infections, especially those acquired abroad. Transmission through intravenous drug use has now reached a plateau. Haemophiliac transmission peaked ten years ago. Mother to baby transmission is a key current concern.

2 Tape C743/18/02, National Sound Archive. Interview with Richard Desmond (born 19-06-64) Oct./Nov. 1997, recorded by Wendy Rickard.

3 Virginia Berridge, *AIDS in the UK: The Making of Policy 1981–1994*, Oxford, Oxford University Press, 1996.

4 Jeffrey Weeks, 'Post-modern AIDS', in T. Boffin and S. Gupta (eds), *Ecstatic Anti-bodies: Resisting the AIDS Mythology*, London, Rivers Oram Press, 1990, p. 133.

5 See, for example, Michael Bury's chapter, 'Chronic illness and disability', in M. Bury (ed.), *Health and Illness in a Changing Society*, London, Routledge, 1997, pp. 110–40.

6 P. Berger, B. Berger and H. Kellner, *The Homeless Mind*, Harmondsworth, Penguin, 1974.

7 Randy Shilts, *And the Band Played On: Politics, People and the Aids Epidemic*, New York, Penguin, 1987.

8 Simon Garfield, *The End of Innocence: Britain in the Time of Aids*, London, Faber and Faber, 1995.

9 Berridge, 1996.

10 Berridge, 1996, p. 5.

11 Everyone interviewed is offered the chance to restrict public access to their testimonies and/or anonymise their accounts. To date, about a quarter have closed access for up to 30 years, one for 50 years.

12 The extracts used in this chapter are chosen to be not representative, but illustrative.

13 For example, Mildred Blaxter's book *The Meaning of Disability*, London, Heinemann, 1976 and Strauss's book, *Chronic Illness and the Quality of Life*, St Louis, Mosby, 1975.

14 Tape C743/07, National Sound Archive. Interview with Martyn Pope (born 13-08-52), June/July 1996, recorded by Wendy Rickard.

15 Interview with Richard Desmond, 1997.

16 Neil Small, 'Living with HIV and AIDS', in B. Davey, A. Gray and C. Seale (eds) *Health and Disease: A Reader*, Buckingham, Open University Press, 1995, pp. 100–6.

17 Michael Bury, 'Chronic illness as biographical disruption', *Sociology of Health and Illness*, 1982, vol. 4, no. 2, pp. 167–82.

18 D. Carricaburu and J. Pierret, 'From biographical disruption to biographical reinforcement: the case of HIV positive men', *Sociology of Health and Illness*, 1995, vol. 17, no. 1, p. 85.

19 Interview with Martyn Pope, 1996.

20 Tape C743/15, National Sound Archive. Interview with Alan Shirkey (born 08-12-57), Jan. 1997, recorded by Wendy Rickard.

21 Tape C743/02, National Sound Archive. Interview with Reg Martin (born 01-06-35), Nov./Dec. 1995, recorded by Wendy Rickard.

22 Interview with Martyn Pope, 1996.

23 Tape C743/16, National Sound Archive. Interview with Jonathan Grimshaw (born 1954), 1997, recorded by Jean Jones.

24 J. Grimshaw, 'Life for a non-progressor', *AIDS Care*, 1995, vol. 7, supplement 1, pp. 5–9.

25 For examples, see Bury, 1997.

26 Interview with Reg Martin, 1995.

27 Interview with Reg Martin, 1995.

28 Interview with Alan Shirkey, 1997.

29 Anthony Giddens, *Modernity and Self Identity*, Cambridge, Polity Press, 1991.

30 Interview with Martyn Pope, 1996.

31 Tape C743/03, National Sound Archive. Interview with Daxa Volambiya (born 1959), Nov. 1995, recorded by Wendy Rickard.

32 Interview with Alan Shirkey, 1997.

33 Rob Perks, 'Ukraine's forbidden history: memory and nationalism', *Oral History*, 1993, vol. 21, no. 1, pp. 43–53.

34 Bury, M., 1997.

35 Interview with Reg Martin, 1995.

36 Interview with Alan Shirkey, 1997.

37 P.M. Davies, F. Hickson, P. Weatherburn and A. Hunt in the opening chapters of *Sex, Gay Men and AIDS*, London, Falmer Press, 1993.

38 Interview with Martyn Pope, 1996.

39 Interview with Reg Martyn, 1995.

40 Interview with Martyn Pope, 1996.

41 Berridge, 1996.

42 Ibid.

43 Andrew Sullivan, 'When plagues end: notes on the twilight of an epidemic', *Independent on Sunday*, 16 February 1997.

44 See for example the historical account given by P.M. Davies, F. Hickson, P. Weatherburn and A. Hunt in the opening chapters of *Sex, Gay Men and AIDS*, London, Falmer Press, 1993. Writing from the gay perspective, they directly dispute Berridge's interpretation regarding the policy impact of notions of 'gay plague'. See also Garfield, 1995.

45 Interview with Paul, 1996/7.

46 Tape C743/13/08, National Sound Archive. Interview with Paul (born 1962), 1996/7, recorded by Wendy Rickard.

47 Interview with Richard Desmond, 1997.

48 These messages were reinforced when in September 1997, the National AIDS Trust in association with two organisations repre-

senting people with HIV and Aids (the UK Coalition of People Living with HIV/Aids and the Network of Self-Help HIV/Aids Groups) organised the first national gathering of HIV and Aids organisations in Britain for ten years.

49 Tim Radford, 'AIDS cure hope raised', *The Guardian*, 30 April 1997.
50 Alessandro Sinicco, 'AIDS virus getting more aggressive', *British Medical Journal*, 1997, no. 314, pp. 1232–7.
51 Interview with Richard Desmond, 1997.
52 Interview with Richard Desmond, 1997.
53 Interview with Paul, 1997.

11

THE DELIVERY OF BIRTH CONTROL ADVICE IN SOUTH WALES BETWEEN THE WARS

Kate Fisher

Introduction

In 1938 Marie Stopes outlined the progress of her Cardiff birth control clinic in all local newspapers. 'Since opening last October the South Wales Mothers' Clinic at 60 Railway Street, Splott, Cardiff, has dealt with over 300 very touching, even tragic cases of South Wales mothers who until our coming had no one to turn to for the help they needed.'[1]

Marie Stopes is here typically over-enthusiastic about the successes of her own clinic and dismissive of other sources of birth control advice. The history of birth control in Britain in the twentieth century has similarly focused more on the gradual successes of the birth control clinic movement than on its failures, and created an image of birth control practice as involving a general shift away from allegedly 'unsatisfactory' birth control methods such as abortion and withdrawal, towards 'better' appliance ones including condoms, caps and eventually the Pill. Certainly birth control clinics were frequently very successful and for many women clinics were, as Marie Stopes emphasised, 'desperately needed'.[2] Certainly, too, it would appear that over the longer term there has been a shift towards appliance methods. However, in exploring the impact of birth control clinics in more detail I wish to highlight some of their limitations and failures.

The use of oral history adds a particularly important dimension to the study of birth control clinics. The documentary source material on their impact and success is limited. Little actual clinic data and few case records remain. Some information can be gained from the correspondence of those involved in setting up clinics: for example, a considerable archive has resulted from Marie Stopes' insistence on weekly reports from the nurses and doctors running her clinics, but these frequently featured colourful incidents rather than typical cases. A number of follow-up studies of birth control clinics were conducted and reports published.[3] However, here it is worth noting that such reports served as much to publicise and promote the need for clinics as to analyse the attitudes of patients. Moreover, no work has been done on the raw data compiled to write these scant reports (if the data still exist). Most fundamentally, such evidence rarely provides long-term analysis of the impact of birth control clinics. Women's attitudes towards birth control clinics were assessed on attendance and perhaps immediately afterwards. Whether their attitudes or contraceptive practices changed over the longer term remains unclear. Nor do such studies allow for the analysis of the impact of birth control clinics within a wider context of contraceptive practices and community attitudes. The voices of those who did not attend clinics remain lost. The great advantage of oral history is that it allows these silent voices and wider contexts to be revealed.

I have studied the impact of birth control clinics as part of a wider oral history of contraceptive use, using a sample of men and women married during the inter-war years from south Wales.[4] I have interviewed a total of fifty-nine people (forty-one women and eighteen men). Three of these also took part in a group interview which included twelve other women. Most were widows or widowers, but there were thirteen interviews with couples.[5] Interviews lasted up to four hours and covered various questions about marriage, family, courtship, sexual attitudes and concentrated, in particular, on birth control practices. Dates of birth ranged from 1899 to 1925.

Two people (who attended clinics) were interviewed as the result of a newspaper appeal. However, the response to this appeal was disappointing, and I was primarily interested in obtaining a more random cross-section of contraceptive practices. All but these two interviewees were located through visits to old people's homes, day centres and social clubs. All interviewees were guaranteed anonymity and interviews took place in private, generally in a respondent's own home. Very few of those I met declined to be interviewed.

'Wales presents ... very special need for our movement'[6]: birth control campaigns between the wars

South Wales had a high profile in the literature of inter-war birth control campaigners. Birth control propaganda, such as the *New Generation*, ran many articles about life in destitute mining districts, under headings such as: 'Huge miners' families'; 'Welsh destitution'; 'Teach the miners birth control'.[7] There were a number of groups and organisations agitating for information on the subject to be more freely available, from a number of different ideological standpoints. Birth control information, particularly for the working classes, was variously advocated as a solution to poverty, over-population, racial degeneration and maternal and infant morbidity and mortality. For all birth control campaigners, south Wales, seen as paradigmatic of deprivation in Britain, epitomised the need for municipal birth control clinics. Yet, most of the discussion of south Wales used the situation in the mining valleys simply as propaganda to impress upon the government the need for municipal clinics run as part of local authorities' maternity and child welfare services. During the 1920s, there were only a few concerted efforts to provide practical birth control assistance for Welsh women.

A number of prominent birth control campaigners such as Stella Browne, Richard Pennifold, Marie Stopes and Frida Laski lectured on the theory and practice of birth control to large and receptive audiences. A few clinics were also established in the 1920s. A clinic opened in Abertillery and District Hospital in 1925, although it closed, probably in 1926; Marie Stopes' caravan clinic spent a year touring south Wales between May 1929 and June 1930,[8] (not for three years as she was later to boast);[9] and in 1930 a clinic was opened in Pontypridd.

The strategy of birth control campaigners and the distribution of clinics in south Wales changed, however, after 1930, when the government issued Memo 153/MCW which stipulated that local authorities were permitted (but not mandated) to provide birth control advice in 'cases where further pregnancy would be detrimental to health'.[10] The main focus of the birth control movement shifted from the national to the local; the main aim became to persuade local authorities to implement the new government directive and south Wales was one of the areas particularly targeted by the newly formed National Birth Control Council (later the

National Birth Control Association, NBCA) which was an amal-
gamation of various birth control organisations. The NBCA
appointed Joyce Daniel, who had been instrumental in setting up
the Pontypridd clinic, as Area Organiser for south Wales. She
proved to be exceptionally active and dedicated. The executive
committee minutes of the NBCA frequently noted the amount of
unpaid overtime she put in. She tirelessly approached councils
and lobbied Medical Officers of Health, health committees and
maternity committees in the attempt to persuade local authorities
to set up birth control clinics alongside their maternity and child
welfare clinics, frequently revisiting areas where she did not meet
with immediate success. It was easy for local authorities to ignore
birth control especially given that the government did not initially
publish the new memorandum, supplying copies only to authorities that asked for it.[11] Joyce Daniel thus forced those authorities
which were either unaware of their new powers or reluctant to
implement them to discuss the establishment of birth control
clinics. Her achievements were impressive.[12] In September 1932,
after only two years' activity, Joyce Daniel reported that she had
succeeded in getting eight clinics established. By 1939 fourteen
local authorities had set up clinics (Aberdare, Barry, Caerphilly,
Gelligaer, Llanelli, Llantrisant and Llantwit Fadre, Mountain Ash,
Ogmore and Garw, Pontardawe, Pontypridd, Port Talbot and
Rhondda), Maesteg was in the process of setting up a clinic,
Glyncorrwg urban district council had made arrangements to send
women to the clinic at Pontypridd and financially desperate
Merthyr had opened a clinic in co-operation with the NBCA. A
private clinic was set up by the NBCA in Pontypool as the
Monmouthshire County Medical Officer refused to set up any
birth control clinics in that county. Marie Stopes, who left the
NBCA because, as she told Helena Wright, they did not run clinics
her way and according to her instructions, also set up a private
clinic, in a run-down area of Cardiff – Splott – in 1937.[13]

These clinics were appreciated and used by a significant number
of women. However, in this chapter, I shall concentrate on two
common failings of birth control clinics. Firstly, clinics failed to
spread information adequately about their existence and purpose.
Secondly, they failed either to convince many potential patients
to accept their particular attitudes towards the use of birth control,
or, alternatively, to tailor their clinics to make them more attractive to the working-class communities they targeted. Both oral
history and clinic documents suggest that clinics had a limited

impact on working-class communities. I argue that many working-class people were put off, not by the principle of family limitation, but by the social and moral beliefs that underpinned the delivery of birth control advice in birth control clinics.

'I had great difficulty in obtaining information about the clinic'[14]

Clinic records give some indication of the difficulties faced in informing women of clinics and inducing them to attend. Many clinics suffered from poor attendance, and this can, in part, be put down to a lack of knowledge of clinics on the part of potential patients. Sometimes, innovative measures were taken to attract attention to birth control clinics. In 1925 Marie Stopes wrote to Nurse Naomi Jones enclosing 'some *Chimes of the Times* which have just been published as Christmas cards and if you could get any Abertillery people to send them round, it might make a good form of propaganda'.[15] When clinic attendance dropped in Abertillery Nurse Jones had 6,000 pamphlets printed and 'went from house to house. ... I walked miles and distributed them myself also Cwm, Ebbw Vale, Beaufort, Blaina, Nantyglo and as far down as Newport.'[16] In Barry and in Merthyr advertising was also adopted when attendance dropped to worrying levels. Generally, however, clinics were only rarely advertised. Marie Stopes informed Nurse Gordon that 'We simply cannot afford to advertise'[17] and local authority clinics were hampered from appearing to court all women in a community by Memo 153/MCW which stipulated that only mothers whose poor health justified the use of birth control could be advised.

Consequently, birth control clinics depended on local doctors and health visitors to inform patients of their existence. The clinic at Caerphilly was 'excellently attended', and this was largely because, as Joyce Daniel reported, 'the co-operation of the Caerphilly general practitioners is stronger than that in any other place hereabouts, no less than nine having already sent us patients' (after only five sessions).[18] Margaret Pyke replied, over a year later: 'How very good that there are still so many patients. This just shows what can be done if local doctors are really helpful.'[19] However, many doctors throughout Britain were opposed to birth control and were unwilling to co-operate with the new clinics, or send patients.[20] Joyce Daniel complained about 'the apathy or antagonism of the local doctors'.[21] Similarly, Marie Stopes vehemently criticised

Cardiff doctors, providing examples such as 'Mrs C – five times pregnant. . . . Asked doctor for advice and was told that withdrawal (very bad, unwholesome and unsafe) was the only method he could suggest.'[22] In fact, many doctors (and other health professionals) were also unaware of clinics as Medical Officers of Health frequently failed to inform them when a birth control clinic was set up in their district. Joyce Daniel reported, for example, in 1937 that 'the promise he (Dr Greenwood Wilson, of Cardiff) gave me last year to instruct his assistants to send suitable cases to Penarth Clinic was never carried out'.[23] In Monmouthshire the letter written by the Medical Officer of Health, Dr Rocyn Jones who was adamantly opposed to birth control, explaining that birth control advice could be given out in 'dire necessity' at five designated ante-natal centres, was not received by many doctors.[24] Campaigners such as Joyce Daniel resorted to sending details of clinic times to doctors, midwives and health institutes so that they might refer their patients. Thus, clinic nurses reported the continued ignorance of birth control clinics on the part of women and the difficulties many faced in locating them. As Nurse Gordon told Marie Stopes: 'a patient who came this week had also searched for weeks and then her husband discovered it by accident'.[25] She lamented, 'It is a great pity that we cannot make it more widely known.'[26]

Such evidence of the limited impact the existence of clinics had on local communities is underscored by oral history testimony. The vast majority of the people I have interviewed about their contraceptive use were totally unaware of birth control clinics, even when one existed in their own small town, and even though they went regularly to the premises for other sorts of welfare services – ante-natal clinics, dentists, etc. Only six interviewees actually attended a birth control clinic. Many also experienced the ignorance, antagonism or embarrassment of local doctors who tended 'to advise couples to have no more children for health reasons, without giving any suggestions as to how this could be accomplished'.[27] Joyce is one of many of my interviewees who experienced this. 'I wasn't suppose to have any more . . . but he didn't tell me what to do, I had to figure that out myself.'[28] As Eva found: 'It took a lot of courage to even ask the doctor [sc. how to limit births]. And the doctor was as embarrassed as I was. So I wasn't satisfied with what he told me, but I didn't have the nerve to go to another doctor or anything.'[29] In such circumstances only chance and perseverance led to the discovery of birth control clinics:

We started hearing vague talk about family planning, and when they were having meal breaks where he worked sometimes they would talk about the babies, because they had babies about the same age as mine. And he came home one day, full of excitement, he said, 'Well, I understand that there's a family planning clinic out in Splott and you can just go there – you don't have to be sent by the doctor or anything – you just go there.' So, we had a little talk about it, and I said, 'well I'll go out on the bike and scoot around', because it wasn't advertised in any way. And I went into Railway Street and went up and down and I did spot it.[30]

'That's the last time they poke me'[31]

The limitations of the success of birth control clinics were not due, solely, to ignorance on the part of working-class women of clinics' existence and availability and the failure of welfare providers to inform them of such services. The evidence from clinic records tends to underestimate and make little of more fundamental difficulties faced in attracting patients and persuading them to adopt methods of birth control favoured by clinics. Not only do clinic records detail the reactions of those already disposed to favour birth control clinics by dint of the fact that they were willing to attend, they also reflect only the immediate post-attendance reactions of patients and the opinions they were prepared to voice to clinic nurses.

Oral testimony indicates that the attitudes and approaches of birth control campaigners towards birth control were in many respects very different to those of the women they were attempting to assist. Attending a clinic required a significant shift on the part of the woman patient away from familiar methods of birth control generally accepted or trusted in favour of a novel appliance method. This was not an easy transition for many women. Oral testimony reveals the attitudes to all forms of birth control and highlights the need to understand clinic encounters in relation to wider cultures of contraceptive use.

Birth control campaigners were convinced that 'birth control was easy and simple, and that we only had to make appliances accessible to women to solve the difficulties of unwanted pregnancies'.[32] The documentary material is full of similar optimism and a general failure to appreciate how burdensome their regime was. When clinic worker Sylvia Dawkins was interviewed she cheerfully remembered the elaborate fitting procedure without hinting at the implicit difficulties in the consultations.

> If you gave a barrier method you had to instruct the people how to use it. You fitted them with, say a diaphragm, instructed them, asked them to go home and practice putting it in and out, come with it in, so that we could be sure they got it right, you see, and knew what they were doing. Then we gave them the cap, and we didn't fit on the first occasion because you couldn't fit them properly the first occasion, they were tense. When they'd come back with the cap in they were relaxed and you found the size wasn't anywhere near right.[33]

Although many clearly showed great patience in trying to teach these methods, Marie Stopes appears to have been exasperated by some of the difficulties faced by clinic nurses, blaming instead the 'extremely stupid and unreliable women whom it is difficult to instruct'.[34] Although simpler methods such as condoms were sometimes provided, clinics were often determined to teach women to use female barrier methods if at all possible. Patients were refitted on several occasions, sent away to practise, sometimes with written instructions.[35] Few concessions were made. Mrs Jones 'finds it rather difficult to place as she is very stout, but perseveres'.[36]

Ironically, in clinics which ostensibly provided advice to women for whom further pregnancy would be dangerous, the preferred methods, caps and diaphragms, were frequently unsuitable for those with internal damage. Clinic records are dotted with examples of women such as Mrs Davies who was 'too tender to use the sponge' and Mrs Williams for whom a 'sheath was given' due to a 'severe prolapsed uterus'.[37] Nurse Williams commented as she toured south Wales in Stopes' caravan clinic that 'the uterine conditions of the mothers on the whole is not good. The sponge and the sheath being practically the only suitable methods'.[38] Yet there is evidence that even in such cases condoms appear only to have been given as a last resort after all efforts to fit a female method failed. Such indication is underscored by the experience of Gertrude who was sent to a local authority clinic in Aberdare.

> Um, for yourself. I had it for myself. But in the end I couldn't, I couldn't fit it because I should have been

stitched when my daughter was born, see, and I couldn't wear mine. . . .

And I couldn't wear what the woman did, I couldn't hold it. I went, I don't know how many times they tried to fit me, and you had to go on the table and be examined and all that, see, before they would, err. But I couldn't, I wasn't, I should have been stitched and I wasn't, so I couldn't hold it.[39]

'Did not bother to use method'[40]

Patients were also required to revisit the clinic for regular check-ups. Lapsed attendance was a significant problem for birth control clinics, partially solved in Caerphilly where 'each patient is written to and given an appointment, not only for her first attendance, but for her second visit, which is of such importance.'[41] A reminder to attend this second time was also sent, and a patient who failed to turn up would be visited.[42] In Pontypridd in 1932, however, 43 women were found to 'have lapsed from attending' (there were 184 revisits that year, and 96 new cases). Dr Severn (the Medical Officer of Health) reported that 'efforts are being made to get in touch with these women, and as a result 11 have renewed their attendance'.[43]

Gertrude clearly illustrated the difficulties of keeping up regular attendance. To travel to the clinic involved a considerable journey, on foot, with children in tow. In addition, if she met anyone in the waiting room she would leave.

Oh, and we used to have to take the babies up to Aberdare to the clinic see, didn't have a place near 'ere, had had to go, had to take the pram and walk up and back. . . .

Were there many people in the clinic?

Oh, there was a lot, well yes there'd be a lot there, but you'd be in a little room and they'd take all your notes, privately, you wouldn't be among those people and then you'd go in [the waiting room] and you wouldn't go back in there! You'd go home! . . .

I had the shock of my life when I seen this one woman [an acquaintance], and I went out and I tried to hide until she'd gone, 'cos I know she was there before me and of course you'd go in the waiting room, see.[44]

For many, such as Mrs Walters, attending a clinic and using a female method of contraception was 'too much trouble'.[45] Birth control campaigners were exasperated to find women in 'a state of apathy . . . many were too indifferent to make the effort'.[46]

Clinic records provide only limited information on the success with which women put the methods taught at birth control clinics into regular practice. Frequently clinics paraded success stories rather than failures. For example, Marie Stopes assumed that all those who did not return to her clinics with problems were using the method regularly and successfully.[47] There were no reports on the longer-term use of methods provided at clinics. However, some important sources do exist. The assessment of Lella Secor Florence on the success of her clinic in Cambridge is notably honest. Of 247 patients, 155 were reported to have found the method provided 'too difficult, too painful, or too uncertain to continue'.[48] With regard to Wales, particularly informative are the detailed reports the nurse sent to Marie Stopes when she decided to visit those who had attended the birth control caravan six months after their first consultation to see whether they were still using the method provided. While the majority told her they were using the method 'successfully', there were not insignificant numbers who were not.

Many were not following instructions. Mrs Jenkins was one such woman: eager to help friends who had not attended the caravan clinic she adapted the principle involved and created her own version of the method provided. She told the nurse: 'many around here who did not come to the caravan got their own sponges or crocheted nets and are being helped'. Similarly, when Mrs Phillips was visited it was found she had used olive oil instead of the recommended chinosol and 'became pregnant. . . . Says she has learned her lesson'.[49]

Many women were unhappy with the novel appliances provided. A number of people were suspicious that the devices provided by clinics were not safe or efficacious and would not trust them. Clinic workers found a number of patients such as Mrs Thomas who was 'too nervous to use sponge. I discussed things with her but failed to assure her.'[50] Similarly, Mrs Heard simply 'couldn't fancy the idea'.[51] Other common worries included fears that a cap or sponge would be impossible to remove or that it might be harmful. As Lella Secor Florence also found, 'even after instruction at the Clinic, a patient will write in great anxiety to know whether it is possible for the pessary to get lost inside, or whether this or that story she has been told about the ill-effect of contraceptives is true'.[52] Similar dislikes and suspicions of weird new appliances were also revealed by interviewees. Leslie, for example, explained that his wife would not go to the clinic in Pontypridd that his sisters went to:

Ooh, my wife never went to any like that. Oh no, no, no. But she didn't believe in anything like that.
Why was that?
Oh well, she don't know, she didn't believe in it. Perhaps, I was so much of a dead nut against it, causing cancer, things like that.[53]

Gwen 'didn't like it at all'. 'You didn't have intercourse until you put it in – so long – and then take it out and all that business. It was horrible, really.'[54]

'Just used our own methods'[55]

It is clear from both clinic records and oral testimony that central to such rejections were existing beliefs about contraception. Clinic records indicate that traditional methods of birth control, especially withdrawal, were still popular. Many patients refused to reject traditional methods completely in favour of the clinics' preferred 'scientific' and 'modern' alternatives. Clinic workers found a lot of people, such as Mrs Jones, who 'did not bother to use' the method she had been given as she 'felt quite safe with coitus interruptus'. Traditional methods were often used in conjunction with the methods provided by clinics. Many revealed that they were using the method 'successfully when husband goes all the way, other times coitus interruptus'.[56]

The importance of traditional cultures of contraceptive use is particularly revealed by oral history, where almost all of those I interviewed used some form of birth control while only six attended birth control clinics. These six also used other methods, and four of them rejected clinic advice in favour of alternative methods. Those who attended clinics were not necessarily participating in a shift away from traditional towards more modern methods of birth control. Rather, most gave up using female appliance methods in favour of tried and trusted ones at some time during their contraceptive careers. Elizabeth used a cap during her first marriage; her second husband, however, took it upon himself to withdraw – this was how she answered when I asked her which of these methods she preferred:

> 'Withdraw, oh yes, you knew you were safe then, you know.
> 'Cos it was a worrying time though they got protection.
> *So would you trust withdrawal more than caps?*
> Definitely. Oh yes, yes, yeah.
> *Why was that?*
> I don't know. You felt safer, you know. Not so messy, no.[57]

Oral history allows one to examine birth control clinics' appeal from within the wider culture of contraceptive use, and over the whole of respondents' contraceptive histories. Eva, for example, was initially very enthusiastic about birth control clinics and appears to have been a committed cap user. She first went to Marie Stopes' clinic in Splott, Cardiff, in 1937 when she was 20. She found the method 'easy as anything, no trouble' and felt it was the safest option. Initially she attended regularly whenever she felt it was 'time I had a new one'. However, 'after a while we stopped going [to the clinic] so often. I stopped using it after the war.'[58]

Oral history thus reveals a dominant preference for traditional methods. I argue that it is the presence of extensive, alternative cultures of contraception which explains many of the comparative disadvantages of clinics and the methods they promoted. I shall now explore two areas in which traditional approaches to birth control were particularly at odds with clinic principles.

'Get some gin down you, they used to say'[59]

A striking example of the continuation of preferences for other methods and one that illustrates the gap in attitudes between clinics workers and working-class people is that of abortion. Those running birth control clinics were vehemently opposed to abortion. Women attending clinics and the women I have interviewed, on the other hand, did not always share their objections. Clinic campaigners presented their methods as an alternative to criminal abortion, yet many potential patients refused to draw a moral distinction between controlling their fertility before rather than after conception. To their horror, clinics found themselves inundated with demands for abortions. Nurse Gordon reported: 'We have had two requests for abortion this week and both seemed to think that the clinic existed for the purpose. The unlawful side of it had not struck them at all. The other said, 'surely you are going to do something for me.' I had to explain to her very plainly that we did not teach how to destroy life. She had douched with very hot Lysol, taken salts, Beechams pills and female pills.'[60] One of the women I interviewed was similarly convinced that Marie Stopes used knitting needles to 'bring her friend on'.

Had you heard of a woman called Marie Stopes?
Marie Stopes. She was in London, I think, yeah a lot of people used to write to her and she used to send them pills and things like that, Marie Stopes.
And what were the pills for?
To try and bring your periods back on, you know. I'm sure there was a Marie Stopes in Splott somewhere.
There was.
There was! I thought, too, yeah. There was a Marie Stopes in Splott, she had an old shop made into a clinic, aye, aye, yeah . . .
And did you know anyone who went there?
Yeah, friend of mine went there, I don't know, she never had any children, so she must have come on . . . .
I know she used to give tablets to the people, like. I think she used a knitting needle and all, yeah, I'm sure my friend had a knitting needle, come to think of it.[61]

Patients did not prefer contraceptive measures advocated by clinics or find them 'morally' more satisfactory than abortion. One woman thought the cervical cap she was given was 'disgusting'; she had 'got rid of things regularly for years', which was 'much easier'.[62] Most of the women I have interviewed have not suggested that they felt that abortion was 'morally' wrong, or, in principle, any less acceptable than any other form of birth control.[63] Many respondents gave no indication that they were aware of the existence of arguments condemning abortion on the grounds that a foetus has a right to life; no-one seemed to feel the need to defend their actions against such 'moral' objections. Methods of abortion were presented very straightforwardly as were decisions whether or not to abort a pregnancy – consideration of general moral principles concerning the rightness or wrongness of destroying an unborn foetus were usually completely absent. Decisions to attempt an abortion involved little moral agonising and could be reached somewhat casually as is well illustrated by Iris' memory of her conversation with a friend when they were both pregnant:

> I can tell you a funny bit. Um, my neighbour next but one, she had, three children I think, and she went in for a fourth, and she'd read somewhere that there were these tablets, 2 and 6 each, which was a fortune then, half a crown like, so she said, 'Do you want one Iris?' I said, 'No,' I said, 'I don't think I'll bother,' 'cos we were pregnant at the same time. 'Oh, I'm going to have one.' They were great, big, dark green jellies, like a jelly sweet like, oval sweet. So, anyway, she took it. Done nothing for her. She was still pregnant. We used to laugh and do things like that. Then she'd take blue, she took a square of blue in a glass. Stupid things she used to do, you know, because she didn't want any more children like. But, err, it's funny looking back at it, but she could have killed herself couldn't she?[64]

'She thought it was my duty'[65]

There was a further principle which underpinned all birth control clinics which came into conflict with existing working-class traditions of fertility control. The emphasis in all clinics was to give women the responsibility and power to control contraceptive use. Clinics were for mothers only, and the methods provided were for female use (except in unusual circumstances). Clinics presented themselves as battling against men and their propaganda portrayed them almost as refuges where women who had been mistreated by either male doctors or husbands could go. Such stories of suffering were prominent in clinic literature, as were arguments in favour of female methods such as cervical caps: vaunted because they could be used without the knowledge of the husband (although in practice in cramped working-class homes this must have been nearly impossible). Although many women benefited from this approach, such as Mrs James, who said on leaving the Splott clinic, 'Thank God, I can keep myself safe now and not have to trust to him',[66] there is reason to believe that this anti-male stance may have alienated a number of other women from attending, and done nothing to encourage husbands to send their wives. My oral evidence suggests that husbands played a very significant role in all aspects of contraceptive use: in initiating discussions about birth control, in determining which methods to use, in making sexual advances and in deciding how frequently contraception would be employed, in finding out about methods, and in obtaining any appliances used. A great many of those I have interviewed, both women and men, have asserted that men were expected to take 'responsibility' for birth control. Ernest, for example, was adamant that it was 'the man's duty':

> Oh well, we used, we used to use the err french letters we used to call em, I don't know, what's the official thing call? What was the expression? Sheaths. The sheath, that's right. It was the man's option. . . . It was the man, it was the man's job.[67]

Doris, was typical in emphasising her husband's role:

> *So what did you use, in order not to get pregnant, during those 12 years?*
> Oh, he used something. Not me.
> *What did he use?*
> Well, the usual, whatever you call 'em, french letters we used to call them.
> *And where did you first find out about those?*
> Oh, that was up to him. In the army I suppose. Oh, well, no, he hadn't been in the army then, had he? Um, well, he had been in the army between the two kids, kind of thing, you know, but, um, oh, men knew all about those things long before they got married, don't worry.

She later revealed that she had, in fact, used a female method, but she preferred leaving it to her husband.

> Yeah, I did use some sort of pessary in the beginning. I forget what they were, so long ago. Gosh. But um, he started using something then, see, didn't bother.
> *So which did you prefer, you preferred french letters to pessaries?*
> Oh, yeah.
> *And why was that?*
> I thought it was safer. He had all the stuff then, I didn't (laughs).

Such a woman would not have been easily wooed by birth control clinics which wanted women to take control of their own fertility and promoted female methods such as the cap. Indeed, she attested that she had not been interested in attending her local clinic, because, she and her husband 'just used our own methods'.[68] Clinic methods demanded action on the part of women that ran counter to their expected marital and sexual roles. They demanded that women challenge male responsibility for the regulation of sexual behaviour. They required women to subvert traditional sexual roles and anticipate or prepare for sexual activity instead of responding to male initiative. Clinics' requirement that women upset traditional gender roles was, I argue, one of the clearest reasons why many women rejected birth control clinics and the methods they promoted.

Such an argument appears initially to challenge the dominant historical image, largely drawn from the documentary evidence of birth control clinics' cases, of unco-operative husbands unwilling to restrain their sexual expression in any way at all and opposed to 'male' methods of birth control such as condoms or withdrawal. However, it is important to understand that such cases were emphasised in clinic literature precisely because they were unacceptable or against the norm (and also because they supported birth control campaigners' advocacy of contraceptive methods that did not require male co-operation, and served to highlight the need for clinics). Lesley Hall has criticised the 'unflattering picture of the average male' presented by much of the material in the historiographical literature and much of the contemporary sexual advice literature and surveys.[69]

> The problem of birth control is and was often seen as something concerning women alone. The notion that men were reluctant to use birth control or even opposed to its use as diminishing their control over their wives has often been advanced. The idea of men as indifferent, if not wholly hostile, to the use of reliable methods of birth control, or at least methods which did not leave control in their own hands, cannot be substantiated.[70]

A careful reading of the clinic records provides further striking evidence to support the conclusion that men were far from opposed to the use of birth control and indicates the centrality of their role in contraceptive decision-making. Lella Secor Florence's report on the achievements of her birth control clinic in Cambridge concluded that 'a word must be said on behalf of the working-man whose alleged excesses and lack of self-restraint have been the subject of so much indignant moralizing on the part of birth control opponents. The great majority of men whose wives have visited our Clinic are extremely moderate and self-controlled.'[71] Only one of 234 husbands whose wives went to a Liverpool clinic disapproved of the visit.[72] The 'Letters from struggling parents', a regular column in *The New Generation,* was dominated by earnest enquiries from men anxious to acquire better knowledge of birth control methods.[73]

The evidence of unfortunate women who did not have co-operative husbands, should be interpreted, not simply as evidence of women's desire and need for methods of contraception that did not require male co-operation, but also as evidence of the widespread assumption that a husband's expected role was to take the initiative with regard to contraceptive use. Evelyn Faulkner stresses the role played by women in contraception during the inter-war years. She quotes one woman who wrote to Marie Stopes. This correspondent explained that her husband was 'very shy regards getting advice on this matter I thought I would try myself.' This surely implies that men were generally expected to take a more pro-active role and that her husband was unusual, just as much as it betrays evidence of 'how women were taking the initiative'.

Male roles in the use of birth control appear, then, to have been crucial and it is essential that we acknowledge this role and revise any tendency to assume that men were, by and large, opposed to the use of birth control, or that women must have been the sole driving force behind family limitation. Clinic records do not support this view. Rather, although clinic evidence highlights the predicament of a minority of women whose husbands were opposed to birth control, for whom clinics provided a valuable service, we must remember that such women were the minority and that for many women attendance at a birth control clinic meant challenging contemporary gendered cultures of contraception.

Conclusion

Oral history is uniquely capable of seeing the impact of birth control clinics from within the context of contraceptive practice more generally. I have argued that it is the presence of developed, alternative cultures of contraception revealed by oral testimony which illustrates the comparative disadvantages of clinics and the methods they promoted. While clinics were appreciated by many patients, oral testimony particularly uncovers the hidden voices of the unconvinced, unsatisfied and indifferent. The principles that underpinned birth control clinics were largely at odds with the attitudes of many working-class people in south Wales. Attending a clinic meant not just accepting the principle of using contraception, but accepting a new approach to the practice. It meant rejecting traditional methods of birth control, particularly withdrawal and abortion; it meant accepting medical intervention in decisions about family size; and it meant leaving the woman in charge of using contraception. This proved too difficult a shift for many couples, who preferred, like Iris, to ignore the establishment of birth control clinics.

> *But you never knew there was a birth control clinic in Pontypridd?*
> No I didn't, no I didn't. Not that it would have interested me much, because I knew what I was doing, like.[74]

Notes

1 'Some Facts about the Cardiff Clinic', 5 July 1938, letter sent to various newspapers, Marie Stopes Papers in the Contemporary Medical Archives Centre at the Wellcome Institute for the History of Medicine (hereafter, CMAC, PP/MCS), C25.

2 Stopes to Ingledew, 4 April 1938, CMAC, PP/MCS C.25.

3 See e.g. Lella Secor Florence, *Birth Control on Trial*, London, George Allen & Unwin, 1930; Marie Stopes, *The First Five Thousand*, London, John Bale & Co. 1925; Norman E. and Vera C. Himes, *Birth Control for the British Working-classes. A Study of the First Thousand Cases to Visit an English Birth Control Clinic*, offprint from Hospital Social Services, 1929, vol. 19, 578.

4 The bulk of the research for this paper was conducted as part of an Oxford University D.Phil. study supported by the Wellcome Trust. See, Kate Fisher, 'An Oral History of Birth Control Practice c. 1925–50. A Study of Oxford and South Wales' (D.Phil., 1997).

5 All had been married.

6 Stella Browne, 'How the Fight Goes', *The New Generation*, January 1930, vol. IX, no. 1, p.5.

7 *The New Generation*, December 1927, vol. VI, no. 12, p.133; April 1928, vol. VII, no. 4, p. 38; January 1929, vol. VIII, no. 1, p. 1.

8 *Daily Herald*, cutting in CMAC, PP/MCS C.15; *The New Generation*, October 1924, vol. III. 'The Welsh Tour', *Birth Control News*, February 1930, vol. VIII, no. 10, p. 154.

9 'Behind the Scenes', *Birth Control News*, December 1937, vol. XVI, no. 5, p. 54.

10 Ministry of Health: *'Birth Control,'* Memo *153/MCW*, London, HMSO, July 1930.

11 See e.g. R. A. Soloway, *Birth Control and the Population Question in England, 1877–1937*, Chapel Hill, University of North Carolina Press, 1982, p. 311.
12 On the establishment of birth control clinics in South Wales and the activities of Joyce Daniel, see, Kate Fisher, '"Clearing Up Misconceptions": The Campaign to Set Up Birth Control Clinics in South Wales Between the Wars', *Welsh History Review*, vol. 18, no. 1, June 1998, pp. 103–29.
13 See June Rose, *Marie Stopes and the Sexual Revolution*, London, Faber and Faber, 1992, p. 205.
14 Eva bc1#1. All names have been changed.
15 Stopes to Jones, 16 December 1925, CMAC, PP/MCS D.16.
16 Jones to Stopes, 14 September 1926, CMAC,: PP/MCS C.16.
17 Stopes to Gordon, 7 November 1937, Marie C. Stopes papers in the Department of Manuscripts at the British Library (hereafter BL) Add. Mss 58624.
18 Joyce Daniel report, April 1936, Family Planning Archive in the CMAC, SA/FPA A11/9.
19 Margaret Pyke was the secretary of the National Birth Control Association (NBCA); Margaret Pyke to Joyce Daniel, 23 June 1937, CMAC, SA/FPA A11/9.
20 See e.g. Angus McLaren, *A History of Contraception from Antiquity to the Present Day*, Oxford, Blackwell, 1990, p. 223; Elizabeth Roberts, *A Woman's Place. An Oral History of Working-class Women 1980–1940*, Oxford, Blackwell, 1984, p. 94.
21 CMAC, SA/FPA A11/2.
22 'The New South Wales Clinic. Open Every Day and Busy all the Time', *Birth Control News*, November 1937, p. 1.
23 Joyce Daniel to Margaret Pyke, October 1937, CMAC, SA/FPA A11/9.
24 CMAC, SA/FPA A11/65. (Joyce Daniel also reported that a woman sent by her doctor to one of these centres was 'laughed at' and turned away.)
25 Gordon to Stopes, 18 March 1938, BL Add. Mss 58625.
26 Gordon to Stopes, 5 November 1937, BL Add. Mss 58624.
27 See also, Lesley Hall, '"Somehow very Distasteful": Doctors and Sex Problems Between the Wars', *Journal of Contemporary History*, 1985, vol. 20, p. 558; Lesley Hall, *Hidden Anxieties, Male Sexuality, 1900–1950*, Oxford, Polity, 1991, pp. 161–4.
28 Joyce, bc1#2.
29 Eva, bc1#1
30 Eva, bc1#1.
31 Claris, bc2sw#10.
32 Lella Secor Florence, *Birth Control on Trial*, London, George Allen & Unwin, 1930, p. 14.
33 Derek Jones and Sharon Goulds, eds., *In the Club? Birth Control This Century*, London, Television History Workshop in Association with Channel Four, 1988.
34 Marie Stopes to Victor Roberts, 12 December 1924, CMAC, PP/MCS C.15.

35 Deborah A. Cohen, 'Private Lives in Public Spaces: Marie Stopes, the Mothers' Clinics and the Practice of Contraception', *History Workshop Journal*, 1993, vol. 20, p. 105–6.
36 BL Add. Mss 58622.
37 BL Add. Mss 58622.
38 Nurse Williams to Marie Stopes, 6 May 1929, BL Add. Mss 58621.
39 Gertrude, bc3sw#27.
40 BL Add. Mss 58622.
41 Joyce Daniel to Margaret Pyke, April 1936, CMAC, SA/FPA A11/9.
42 Joyce Daniel to Margaret Pyke, July 1936, CMAC, SA/FPA A11/9.
43 Pontypridd Urban District Council, Medical Officer of Health, Annual Report, 1932.
44 Gertrude, bc3sw#27.
45 Fowles to Stopes, 10 January 1930, BL Add. Mss 58622.
46 Joyce Daniel, 'The Wind of Change', *Family Planning*, July 1964, cutting in CMAC, SA/FPA A14.19.
47 Marie Stopes, *The First Five Thousand*, London, John Bale & Co., 1925 p. 51.
48 Lella Secor Florence, *Birth Control on Trial*, London, George Allen & Unwin, 1930, p. 72.
49 Fowles to Stopes, 10 January 1930, BL Add. Mss 58622.
50 BL Add. Mss 58622.
51 Fowles to Stopes, 22 March 1930, BL Add. Mss 58622.
52 Lella Secor Florence, *Birth Control on Trial*, London, George Allen & Unwin, 1930, p. 144.
53 Leslie, bc3sw#1. Marie Stopes also declared that caps caused cancer, excepting her own 'pro-race' version. See Ruth Hall, *Marie Stopes. A Biography*, London, Andrew Deutsch, 1977, p. 260.
54 Gwen, bc3sw#18.
55 Doris, bc3sw#6.
56 Fowles to Stopes, 10 January 1930, BL Add. Mss 58622.
57 Doris, bc3sw#6.
58 Eva, bc1#1.
59 Elizabeth, bc3sw#12.
60 Florence Gordon to Marie Stopes, 10 December 1937, BL Add. Mss 58624.
61 Elizabeth, bc3sw#12.
62 Gordon to Stopes 21 July 1939, BL Add. Mss 58625.
63 See Kate Fisher, '"Didn't Stop to Think, I Just Didn't Want Another One": The Culture of Abortion in Inter-War South Wales', in Hall, Hekma and Eder, eds., *Sexual Cultures in Europe: Volume II, Studies in Sexuality*, Manchester, Manchester University Press, 1999, pp. 213–32.
64 Iris, bc2#8.
65 Fred bc2#14.
66 Gordon to Stopes, 29 April 1938. BL Add. Mss 58625.
67 Ernest, bc3sw#2.
68 Doris, bc3sw#6.
69 Shani D'Cruze, also acknowledges the importance of seeing the evidence of exceptional 'violent' men within the wider context of expectations and norms of 'good' husbands. Shani D'Cruze, 'Women

and the Family', in June Purvis, ed., *Women's History. Britain 1850–1945. An Introduction*, London, UCL Press, 1995, p. 62.

70 Hall, *Hidden Anxieties*, p. 91.

71 Lella Secor Florence, *Birth Control on Trial*, London, George Allen & Unwin, 1930, p. 119.

72 Norman E. and Vera C. Himes, *Birth Control for the British Working-classes. A Study of the First Thousand Cases to Visit an English Birth Control Clinic*, offprint from Hospital Social Services, 1929, vol. 19, 578, p. 612.

73 More generally, Margaret Loane argued that the working-class father was not 'as black as he is painted' and that philanthropic 'prejudice against him is so strong that all evidence in his favour is unread or misread'. M. Loane, *From Their Point of View*, London, Edward Arnold, 1908, p. 144.

74 Iris, bc2#8.

12

MIDWIVES AS 'MID-HUSBANDS'?

Midwives and Fathers

Robin Dixon

The subject of this paper is the changed relationship between the maternity services and fathers (or expectant fathers). The underlying hypothesis is that the maternity services now provide fathers with a context of opportunities in which to behave in ways which may be linked to the phenomenon of the couvade. In turn, this suggests that midwives have become, in part, 'mid-husbands' too.

The couvade

The term couvade was introduced into English in 1865 by Edward Tylor.[1] In Old French the word meant to hatch or to brood. Tylor borrowed it, to refer to behaviours of men at the times their wives were pregnant or parturient, or for a period after the birth. For example, in some societies, immediately after the birth, the father takes to his bed, nurses the infant and receives the felicitations of visitors, while being fed titbits, prepared by – guess who? Generally, in early anthropology, a society in which the couvade was practised was seen as a primitive society, characterised either by a belief in magic, or by its recent development from matriliny to patriliny. Where instances of couvade behaviours were found in Europe, they were explained as a trace of an earlier stage of civilisation, or as a mistake or joke. Around the middle of the twentieth century, medical psychiatrists developed the concept of the couvade syndrome, and the earlier couvade became known as the ritual couvade. The syndrome referred to pseudo-maternal symptoms among European males – male 'morning sickness', for example – and various other ailments and categorised them as (mildly) pathological.[2] A third main area of interpretation is the psychoanalytic, where the key concept is ambivalence (unconscious hatred and conscious love of the father towards his infant and/or his wife) or envy (male parturition envy).[3] All of these interpretations are open to question and may be seen as socially constructed.

Methodology

The interviews with fathers and midwives which provide the raw material for this chapter were conducted as part of work for a doctorate in which the couvade is reinterpreted in the light of a theory about fatherhood. In brief, this is that all men have a latent need to reduce a psycho-biological distance that they feel to exist between themselves and their infants, arising, rather obviously, from their inability to bear children or feed them from their own bodies. Whether or not this latent need finds expression and, if it does, how it does, is culturally mediated. The purpose of the interviews was to see how far it might be said that this need finds expression in modern society.

The methodology of the interviews was drawn from oral history. Twenty-six midwives, one of whom was a male midwife, were interviewed. They were of varying seniority. Fifteen worked on the labour wards, ten were community midwives and one worked in special care. Table 12.1 provides summary information about their ages and experience.

Interviews were discursive where informants wished; every interview was conducted in private between the author and the respondent. All the midwives worked at one of two maternity hospitals in Essex, and were chosen for interview by the senior staff on a day-to-day basis, from among all the midwives employed there. As it is very hard to predict when a midwife will be able to spare time in her working day, the criterion of choice was availability at the times arranged for the author to visit. Each midwife was told in advance that the interviews were in connection with research into how men react to becoming fathers. Later in the interview, midwives were invited to discuss the couvade. Midwife interviews were held in the last three months of 1994.

The fathers were found individually by the author, in various ways. A few were known to him in advance, others were approached by a third party, or occasionally opportunistically by the author. The principal criterion of choice and a sine qua non was that a man had had children; the only other, and subsidiary, criteria were age

Table 12.1 Age and experience of midwives interviewed

Ref.	Birth year	Year qualified	Years of experience
A	1934	1960	33
B	1938	1952	33
C	1941	1962	32
D	1941	1965	30
E	1942	1966	28
F	1942	1967	25
G	1943	1975	18
H	1946	1981	16
I	1946	1970	14
J	1946	1985	9
K	1946	1984	10
L	1946	1969	15
M	1947	1970	15
N	1948	1971	25
O	1949	1990	4
P	1951	1974	17
Q	1952	1984	10
R	1953	1977	10
S	1953	1985	10
T	1958	1982	12
U	1959	1982	10
V	1960	1987	7
W	1962	1988	6
X	1963	1990	4
Y	1965	1989	5
Z	1965	1990	4

and occupation, in an attempt to get an approximate spread of both. Summary information on the fathers is provided in Table 12.2.

Those approached were simply asked if they would be prepared to be interviewed on the subject of becoming a father. Care was taken to ensure that, in the case of those known to the author, the subject of fatherhood had never previously been discussed between us. Nothing was said, either in advance or during the interviews, about the couvade or the theory underlying the questions. Interviews took place in 1994 and 1995 in various locations in southern England.

The historical context

Earlier in this century, only a minority of men in our society were present at their partner's labour and the birth of their children.

Table 12.2 Summary information on fathers interviewed

Ref.	Birth Year	No. of children	Occupation
1	1906	2	Roadman (retd)
2	1929	3	H.E. teacher
3	1931	3	H.E. teacher
4	1933	3	H.E. teacher
5	1935	3	Electrician
6	1935	3	H.E. teacher
7	1941	2	Probation officer
8	1943	3	Scientist
9	1951	2	Bank worker
10	1954	1	H.E. teacher
11	1955	2	Civil engineer
12	1958	3	Insurance agent
13	1958	3	Market trader
14	1958	2	Solicitor
15	1959	1	Plasterer
16	1959	2	Minister of religion
17	1960	1	Journalist
18	1960	1	H.E. teacher
19	1960	1	F.E. administrator
20	1962	3	Honey farmer
21	1962	2	Army N.C.O.
22	1962	1	Systems analyst
23	1963	1	Retailer
24	1964	1	Photographer
25	1967	2	Actor

These two comments are by retired midwives interviewed by Leap and Hunter:

> It was very rare for the fathers to be there, but they came in and out with anything you wanted. The men didn't want to be there and the wives didn't want them there either.
>
> Oh, no, no, no! The husbands were never there when the babies were being born. I remember the fight I had with one dirty old devil. . . . This creature, what he used to do was pull the cloth across to see what was going on when she was having the baby – the dirty old dog! . . . Oh no, you didn't want them there.[4]

A man born in the same year as Josephine M., the second midwife quoted, had children who were born at home in 1938 and 1944.[5] Asked if he was present, he said he wasn't, that he went to work as usual and added that in his opinion in those days women in labour 'got on better without the men.' A man with three children born in 1957, 1960 and 1963[6] made no attempt to attend the first two births but was encouraged to be present at the third. Although glad to be there, he nevertheless thought it wasn't really the father's business, because he was otiose and just an observer. But another man of a similar age, and with children born in the same years, was enthusiastic about his presence at the home births of the second and third, while he still resented being 'banned' from the birth of the first, in hospital in 1957.[7] A father, whose first child was born in 1961,[8] said that, to get him into the labour ward, a case had to be made out that his wife was 'a neurotic wreck', which would mean that, in turn, he would be seen as 'a kind of persona the medical profession could accept'. He was given a letter permitting his presence, 'but I was warned periodically that if I showed the slightest signs of male hysteria at all these female things going on, I would be dismissed forthwith ... but I behaved, and they did let me in the delivery room.' Another father remembers that he said he would like to stay for the birth of his second child in 1965,[9] but was physically ejected from the labour room by a senior nurse. And a midwife recalls her experience of the attitudes of the senior midwives with whom she trained in London in 1969–70, attitudes which carry echoes of the view of Josephine M.:

> *Can I just ask you now to cast your mind back to when you trained, and tell me if there was anything included in the training at any sort of level of training, whether in lecture room or by what people said to you when you were out on the community with a more senior midwife or whatever, about the role of the father?*

Well, at that stage fathers weren't included in delivery. We did attend a few home deliveries, even home deliveries fathers didn't attend. Their mothers did, their mothers were there and their sisters were there, and the husband or the par– they were husbands at that stage, we weren't into partners, they would disappear, with dad, into another room, or they would go out, to have a drink and they would come back later. It was still very much that situation. But fathers weren't encouraged to be there, people didn't think they needed to be there, it wasn't their place. And certainly, within hospital, I saw they were actively discouraged from being there. They could stay if it was visiting time, but if the lady was labouring and it wasn't visiting time, no one would call her husband. It was felt by the senior midwives, and they had great power at that stage and were often single ladies that quite ruled the hospital area, that 'Why would you take a man off a day's work?' You know, that was his place, to be at work. You shouldn't be encouraging him to have a day off work, that wasn't considered. I mean, we thought that was unkind, but we were children of the '60s and we thought that was, you know, a bit hard. But they were the bosses and they didn't encourage it.[10]

Most of the older midwives offered similar accounts of that time, when men were beginning to be admitted to hospital births. One pointed out how difficult it was to practise midwifery at such a time:

When they first started letting fathers into the labour, how was it then?
Very frightening, very – I mean, we're going back possibly 25 or 30 years, because it was not long after I came here that they started it, so there was a whole debate 'They Shouldn't Be There', especially with the old school of midwives. So it was quite threatening, because you had someone taking notice of what you were doing . . . it had always been just our domain, and now we'd got people looking over our shoulders.[11]

Of course, there are other accounts of that period, mainly in the context of home births. The history of the movement, starting mid-century, from home birth to hospital birth (and now, very slowly, back to home again) is a subject there is insufficient space to discuss here,[12] except to say that there is evidence suggesting that a significant minority of the men whose children were born at home in the 1950s, 1960s and 1970s were likely to be present at the delivery, while fathers were very rarely present at hospital births in those years. There were clearly some midwives who, in the domestic context, allowed, even encouraged, the involvement of fathers, but not all. A father, with children born at home in 1964 and 1967, contrasted the two midwives who attended. Of the first, he said:

Miss A. was a classic professional midwife of the old type.
... It was a very nice experience, actually. Everything
went smoothly. Miss A. was very pleasant. We did our
work, I was stroking C. and helping her breathe and all
that kind of thing. I thought it was great. It was a totally
positive experience, actually. Really wonderful, in fact.[13]

Then, of the second, whom he described as much the worst type
of traditional midwife:

The midwife arrived and she was like a kind of police-
woman with huge boots and went poom-di-poom! Made
humming sounds. She said to me first of all: 'Now, you
do something really useful, just go out and boil some of
these old cloths.' Or something like that. 'We'll need
those!' And she kept making totally unpleasant remarks.[14]

Although this father faced down the midwife and stayed for the
birth, which he said was spoilt by her attitude, it is clear from
other remarks by him that the midwife did not want him there.

Fathers' increased involvement in birth

Generally, the fathers who were present at home births in the 1960s
tended not to be involved; they were spectators or they fetched and
carried for the midwife. The first men who were let into the delivery
room were mostly told to sit in a corner, out of the way. But, by the
time of this research, hospital midwives were almost unanimous, and
quite strongly so, in their objection to men simply as spectators.
There may have been a special reason for the earlier practice of
restricting the father's role. This may have been due to fear of infection; that was the time when, as one midwife put it, 'we were into
sterility'.[15] But there has now been a marked change in attitude.

The evidence from the midwives and fathers interviewed for
this chapter does not confirm the impression conveyed by some
of the literature. For example, Charlie Lewis, in 1986, argued that
men were considered only when they reacted pathologically,[16] and
endorsed Richman and Goldthorpe's 1978 conclusion that 'there
has been this cultural conspiracy against fatherhood in modern
times'.[17] Similarly, in 1984, Jackson wrote of men treated as if
marginal, while feeling central.[18] By these accounts, there seems
to have been little change since the 1930s, when it was possible

276

to refer to the father-to-be as 'the forgotten man of propagation'.[19] And in a 1997 work on fatherhood, Adrienne Burgess speaks of 'our blindness almost to the very existence of fathers during pregnancy' and argues that 'the average expectant father is killed off through lack of interest, his concern tolerated at best (and discouraged at worst) by health professionals completely out of touch with paternal experience.'[20]

Changing attitudes of midwives

Of course, change has taken place neither universally, nor uniformly. Just as one father found a great contrast in the attitudes of the two midwives at the home births of his children in the 1960s,[21] another found a similar contrast between two NHS hospital births in 1990 and 1991.[22] The first hospital was 'a very enlightened place' and the second 'like this extraordinary 1950s idea.' At the second, 'it seemed to be much more as if I had made the decision to be there,' whereas, at the first 'the attitude was "of course you're here."' At the second, 'I was definitely surplus to requirements.' But, overwhelmingly, the interpretations of Lewis, Richman, Jackson and, most recently, Burgess are not borne out by the evidence from the younger fathers interviewed, whose children were born in the 1990s, nor are they by what the midwives say when talking about the present.

Initially, the father's role was largely passive. Or, with the introduction of psychoprophylaxis, he would be encouraged to help in 'the fierce counting that they used to do, in order to try and relax: "one, two, three, four, five" or "Baa, baa, black sheep"' (a midwife recalling practice in the late 1960s).[23] And he would be told to wait outside on almost any medical pretext.[24] Increasingly, the father has now become more involved. The birth plan often states what it has been agreed that the father will do; e.g. cut the cord, be the first to take the baby, whether wrapped or not, and so on. In addition, fathers now often become involved ad hoc in other ways:

I wasn't made to feel like a spectator. I think the midwife was very good at consciously involving me: you do this, and you hold this, and you mop her brow, and things like that. . . . When the birth was happening I was holding her leg. That was a real sort of job, somebody had to hold her leg and I was doing it, so that was quite nice. . . . There was a midwife and me holding a leg each. And

277

I seem to remember that she was not engineering it, but she was encouraging me to do things, and I was wanting to get involved anyway.[25]

Today, the only circumstance in which the father will be routinely excluded is when his partner has to have an unplanned caesarean and general anaesthetic.

In making this rapid transition from an attitude of hostility or indifference to one of willing acceptance, many midwives, just a few years back, went through a period in which they were vigorously encouraging fathers to be present, even, according to one midwife, being 'very forceful in getting a man to do a thing that he doesn't really want to do.'[26] And it may have caused a few mistakes:

> *When you started, fathers were already there, or only a few, or what?*
> I think it was the change-over. We were encouraging the fathers to stay.
> *Right.*
> I can actually tell you a funny story about a colleague of mine.
> *I'd like to hear it.*
> The girl came in with a man and he brought the girl up to the delivery suite, it was in Chelmsford. And he was encouraged to stay and he held her hand and everything. And it actually turned out he was the taxi-driver. He was there at the birth. Because we all encouraged the men to stay, she had trapped this guy in a corner. And he was actually the taxi driver! We were encouraged to – you know. And there was wonderful bonding between the three of them with this baby. But he was actually the local taxi driver.[27]

So men are now there and midwives are aware that their presence has become necessary to the way the maternity hospital is organised on a day-to-day basis. At its simplest, the father is shown the emergency bell, the couple are left alone and the midwives relieved of the need to look in on the mother as much as they would otherwise. Generally, the picture is one of reliance on any husband who shows himself to be able and willing. This is from a father recollecting the births of his second and third children, born in 1988 and 1992:

Did the midwives give you anything to do?

Perhaps I looked more experienced, they were saying, right, come on then, do this, do that, bossing me about, as if I was one of the staff there! 'Come on, you should be holding her now! You should know that by now, come on!' You know, that sort of thing.[28]

But midwives have thought beyond the practical value of the men's presence, and considered more deeply the possible reasons they are there and the consequences:

What do you think the men are doing there, I don't mean in literal terms 'What are they doing there?'

Why do they want to be there?

Why do you think they want to be there? You said that people feel they have a right to be involved, etc., but is there any more to it than that?

Well, I mean, it's their baby as well. You get different viewpoints. Some men will say they want to be there because they want to support their wife, she wants them there, and I'm always a little bit worried then. Do they really want to be there? I mean, at my parentcraft classes I always say to the men: 'Right, who's going to be there at delivery?' And I say: 'Are you being coerced into it, or do you want to be there?' And you get the odd one who says: 'Oh, she wants me there'. And I say: 'But do you want to be there?' Because I think it does make a difference.

What do they say?

Well, they say 'I feel I have to support her', and the wife will say: 'I want him there, I want him there.' And I think that is one reason. The other reason is because it's part of them, they want to be part of it. It's just as much their baby as their wife's.[29]

A father, asked why he was present at the births of his children in the 1990s, confirms this view:

Perhaps it sounds like a somewhat simplistic question, but why were you there?

Partly to support N, partly because I guess I'm fond of classing myself as one of these 'new men', who, of course, are always present at childbirth. Partly because I would have been ridiculed by my peers had I not been there.

And partly because it was a major life-changing occasion, and I wouldn't have been anywhere else. And it's that last thing which is the largest of them, by far.[30]

The presence of fathers in the labour room has changed the midwife's perception of her duties, partly for the practical reason that now the couple can be left alone for long periods, but also partly for a very different reason, an emerging obligation to the father, which is additional to the obligation to the mother and baby. Two midwives talked about the responsibility that midwives now have, to do their best to ensure that the men will subsequently feel good about the experience:

> I really feel, as professionals, we've included them, haven't we, into the birth scene now, but I do feel it is our duty, we have a responsibility towards them, to prepare them well, so they don't go away feeling that they've let themselves down and that they've let their partner down. . . . If I have a man in the delivery room, I always give him plenty to do. Never take over, be the one, you are not doing the couple a kindness. It's far better to say: I would like you to do this and this and this. And he feels part of it then, he feels involved, and at the end he will have a great sense that he has achieved a lot.[31]

> I think there are things that have to be suggested, because a lot of fathers just wouldn't think of saying: can I do this, can I do that, even if they had thought of it. What they get involved in is partly up to what they want to get involved in, because they are never forced to do anything. A lot of them have some knowledge, but I really think it needs the midwife who is looking after them to help them have the confidence to do things and to suggest other things they might like to do to get involved with the birth of the child.[32]

Although they have some reservations about some men, the midwives are mostly warmly enthusiastic about the fathers' participation, even, in some cases, to the point of willingly conceding part of their role:

> Some midwives like to keep it all to themselves. But I like to involve the parents. I sit there in the rocking chair and

rock myself, and the mother gets on with it in her way. I let her do whatever she wants to do. She can be in whatever position she wants to be, I don't like to intrude into the partners' activities until I need to. She knows I'm with her and I'm there when she needs me, when they both need me, but unless they do need me, I let it just happen. . . . I do a lot of water births and that's in a room where you don't get interrupted by other people. And the lights are dim and it's all very nice. . . . I've had one father who actually got in the water with his wife, and that was a lovely delivery. He just got in, and she relaxed a lot more when he got into the water. She just lay on her side and had her baby. It was lovely.[33]

They've taken part of our role, which is good. I think it is more satisfying as a midwife to sit back and watch a couple working together . . . I'd rather step back out of the picture and watch them, and then I'm there if they want me. I think that's real job satisfaction then.[34]

Cutting the cord: a ritual act?

When midwives were asked what they had observed of fathers' involvement with their partners' pregnancies, with the birth and the new-born infant, they produced, between them, a very long list of behaviours and attitudes. The interviews with fathers produced several more. This chapter cannot discuss all of these; in any case, it is about midwives and many of the behaviours and attitudes do not entail the involvement of the midwife. So I have chosen to discuss the cutting of the umbilical cord by the father, partly because it was the subject most often raised by the midwives, when asked 'what do fathers do?', and partly because it could not happen without the midwife's active agreement.

In the modern anthropological literature there is an example of a society in which the cutting of the umbilical cord by the father is standard practice. This is among the Siriono people of Eastern Bolivia, where it is part of the ritual observed by the father of a newly born baby.[35] It is interesting that this same practice is currently developing in British maternity hospitals, where it does not seem unreasonable to describe it as a nascent ritual of modern childbirth. When midwives were asked how they could account for the introduction of the practice, they made various suggestions. No one seemed sure.

In 1994, in the two Essex hospitals in which midwives were interviewed, some 30–40 per cent of fathers cut the cord. Each midwife has autonomy to determine her practice in such a matter; some offer the possibility to all or most fathers and say that for the most part the fathers like to do it. Here are three midwives who normally offer the scissors to the father:

Could you say a bit more about what they do, how they behave, through the labour and delivery?
Yes, well I think that they've obviously gone to parent-craft classes with their partners, they all seem to know what's going on. They are very supportive at home. When the woman arrives in here they are very good at all the support roles, the back-rubbing, the sips of water. She might want to go and have a bath or a water birth, and they sort of act the hand-maiden role, and do it very well. I don't mean getting involved down the sharp end, as I call it, except, having said that, yes, I do like to involve them at the end, when the baby's born. I do invite the father to cut the cord. I think it's more an involvement, an emotional involvement, really. Just being there for her, if she's not happy, making the right sort of soothing noises.
When you invite them to cut the cord, what proportion of them – Do it?
Nearly all. I never ask before, I'm not a planner. I think you can't plan for how somebody is going to feel. Yes, I would say nearly all. I wait until the baby has arrived. I usually put it straight on mummy's tum and then I just offer the scissors and say, 'Do you want to separate this couple?' And they might look a little bit taken aback at first. But usually not. Yes, they are happy to do it, very rarely do they say 'Oh no, I wouldn't want to.'
When did that, how could I call it, custom, practice – Come into being?
Probably when I was bringing up my family, I don't know. We certainly didn't do it before, because if I can call it in the olden days, in the '60s, we were very much into masks and gowns and sterility. And offering a father a pair of sterile scissors would have filled me with horror. I would think: What would I have done with those sterile scissors afterwards, I don't know? So I think it all happened while I was busy being a mother myself, yes.[36]

A lot of them have some knowledge, but I think it needs the midwife that is looking after them to help, help them have the confidence to do things, and to actually suggest other things they might like to do to get involved with the birth of the child.

To what extent do they get involved, can they get involved, not routinely, of course, with the birth of the child? For what aspects of the actual birth would you allow them to be, as you might say, hands-on?

The actual delivery bit, where the baby's being born? There's no reason why they can't put their hands on their baby's head, with your hands over the top, which is how you teach a student midwife to deliver a baby, and help to deliver their baby. You can do that, there's no reason why not. … And, obviously, afterwards, cutting the umbilical cord, a lot of fathers like to do that now. I think they feel that it is the final transition, obviously, from being part of the mother to being an independent person.

You, as a qualified midwife, you're allowed quite a degree of latitude, from what you told me earlier on, when you said it depends on a number of factors, and you said one of them is the attitude of the individual midwife?

That's right, yes.

From your own practice, your own views about how you think, do you kind of routinely offer them these possibilities?

Yes, I do.

Do you make some kind of an assessment of them, before you –

I think you, obviously, you must make some sort of assessment, I think it's humanly impossible not to. You know whether a father is motivated or not, you can pick it up, the verbal and non-verbal communication, you can just tell. And obviously, I think that's going to affect how much you actually offer. But I think there are certain things, like cutting the umbilical cord, that I would offer to every father.[37]

You said that you offered to them that they'd like to cut the cord. What proportion of them would take up the offer, or say, 'no, you do it, please'?

I'd say about half. They say: Oh yes, oh yes, I'll do that. They really think it is something special (laughs). They can tell everyone: I cut the cord.

Do they ask you anything about it?

Not usually, because it's such a — because the baby's just born and it's all so — everything's happening, they are usually all fingers and thumbs.

They aren't worried about doing it the wrong way?

Yes, they are, and we just reassure them, and say, oh, come on. In fact, we encourage it, I think, really.[38]

Of course, some midwives do not offer fathers the opportunity to cut the cord, or say that fathers recoil from the idea:

You mentioned that the father sometimes cuts the cord. Do you offer that, or do you respond positively when it's asked?

I'd say that in my practice it's very new, don't actually ask the father if he wants to. If he says he wants to, that's fine. But when it comes to it, they don't always want to do it. It's not a very nice thing, the cord, is it? It's very squidgy.[39]

Another said she couldn't cope with what she saw as an extreme example of the romanticising of childbirth.[40] Nevertheless, it seems likely that in the maternity hospitals in which I interviewed most midwives have now taken up the idea, and often with considerable enthusiasm.

Among the Siriono, the ritual cutting of the cord by the father is explained as a laying of claim to parenthood.[41] No midwife volunteered such an explanation of cord-cutting by the father in Britain today, although a few talked about bonding. And, although no one used the word 'ritual' in describing it, it is, of course, an ideal ritual act, because it is of little immediate practical consequence and at the same time most obviously symbolises the separation of the child from the mother. That symbolism is, of course, open to various interpretations. The hypothesis adopted here is that it is one way in which a man may symbolically express his sense of fatherhood.

Conclusion

The argument of this chapter is that changes in midwifery practice and midwives' attitudes have brought about a new situation in which men are provided with opportunities to express their sense of fatherhood, in ways which may be seen as couvading. As the midwives make clear, they too have changed, with attitudes that are different from those of most midwives of the previous generation. Most important in this respect is the fact that the midwives have different backgrounds, many more of them have families of their own and work part-time:

> We are mothers, most of us are mothers ourselves, we're part-time, we've come back into hospital and we do twenty hours a week, and we've got families at home. It's a far more balanced view, we are dealing with the public in a far more sensitive manner, because we are of the public ourselves. The people who ran hospitals thirty years ago were like an order of nuns.[42]

Most of the midwives interviewed would probably think of themselves as instrumentalist in their approach to the involvement of fathers: 'He's there to help his partner.' That is the role they prioritise. But there seems little doubt that, intentionally or not, they are now, and increasingly, also ministering to the emotional needs of the father. I would argue they are therefore, again intentionally or not, helping him to express his sense of fatherhood. To this extent, they might now be described as 'mid-husbands' as well as midwives.

If the midwives' attitudes are analysed further, three general tendencies are apparent. The first of these is that the minority of midwives who are cool towards the idea of fathers' participation are the same midwives as those who say that men don't really want to be involved. By contrast, the more enthusiastic majority are also committed to the belief that most men want to be there and want to take part.

The second general tendency is for only a minority of midwives to be able to relate the men's behaviours to the couvade, even when the phenomenon is explained and where the midwife is an enthusiastic supporter of men's involvement.

The third tendency is for the midwives to act so as to encourage fathers to behave in couvading ways, without, of course, and for the most part, recognising that that is what they are doing. The encouragement of cord-cutting is a good example of this. In the recent history of fatherhood in our society in the context of childbirth there is little to suggest an overt attempt by men to acquire the opportunities which will enable them to couvade. What we mostly see, instead, is the taking of opportunities, not by all men, but by many, some apparently consciously, some not, and as and when those opportunities present themselves. These opportunities have become available for a complex of cultural reasons, one of which is the social change that has opened the labour ward to fathers.

So the changes in midwifery have provided men with opportunities to express their sense of fatherhood, opportunities that were not previously available. This does not mean that men did not find such opportunities in the past; perhaps they did, perhaps cultural imperatives concerning what it was to be a man in Western society prevented them, at least in their publicly observable behaviour. Perhaps the pathologies of the couvade syndrome were a consequence of a lack of positive, socially accepted ways to express fatherhood. Lewis noted in his 1982 chapter that private reactions by fathers to pregnancy and birth are much better defined than their public roles suggest.[43] But fifteen years later this was no longer so obvious; it had become easier to relate their public behaviour, in the labour ward and otherwise in the context of pregnancy and birth, to their private feelings.

Notes

1 Tylor, Edward, *Researches into the Early History of Mankind and the Development of Civilisation* (London, John Murray, 1865), second edition.
2 See, for example, Trethowan, W.H. and Conlon, M.F., 'The couvade syndrome', *British Journal of Psychiatry*, 1965 111: 57–66.
3 See, for example, Reik, T., 'Couvade and the Psychogenesis of the Fear of Retaliation', in *Ritual/Psychoanalytic Studies* (London, Hogarth Press and Institute of Psycho-Analysis, 1931; first published in German, 1914) and Bettelheim, B., *Symbolic Wounds* (Glencoe, Illinois, Free Press, 1954).
4 Elizabeth C., midwife, born 1905, trained 1930 (first quotation) and Josephine M., midwife, born 1906, trained 1928 (second quotation), from Leap, Nicky and Hunter, Bille, *The Midwife's Tale* (London, Scarlet Press, 1993), pp. 61 and 62.
5 Father 1.
6 Father 2.
7 Father 5.
8 Father 4.
9 Father 3.
10 Midwife M.
11 Midwife D.
12 See, for example, Campbell, Rona and Macfarlane, Alison, *Where to be born? – the debate and the evidence*, National Perinatal Epidemiology Unit, Oxford, 2nd edn, 1994; Department of Health Report of the Expert Maternity Group, *Changing Childbirth* London, 1993; and Kitzinger, Sheila and Davis, J.A. (eds), *The Place of Birth*, Oxford, OUP, 1978.
13 Father 6.
14 Father 6.

15 Midwife E.
16 Lewis, Charlie, *On Becoming a Father*, Milton Keynes, Open University Press, 1986, p. 21.
17 Richman, J. and Goldthorpe, W.O., 'Fatherhood: the social contruction of pregnancy', in Kitzinger and Davis (eds.), *The Place of Birth*, op. cit., pp. 157–8.
18 Jackson, Brian, *Fatherhood*, London, Allen and Unwin, 1984, p. 78.
19 Victor, David, *Father's Doing Nicely; the expectant father's handbook*, Indianapolis, Bobbs-Merrill Company, 1938, p. 15.
20 Burgess, Adrienne, *Fatherhood Reclaimed*, London, Vermillion, 1997, p. 113.
21 Father 6 (see pp. 275–6 above)
22 Father 25.
23 Midwife F.
24 There is a brief but helpful study of two English maternity hospitals in a state of transition with respect to father participation in the later 1970s by Elizabeth Perkins in *Men on the Labour Ward*, Nottingham, University of Nottingham Press, 1980. She concludes that 'midwives may have some difficulty in focussing on husbands' (p. 25). This, on the evidence of my interviews with midwives, has, by the 1990s, proved not to be the case.
25 Father 25.
26 Midwife N.
27 Midwife U.
28 Father 12.
29 Midwife L.
30 Father 14.
31 Midwife M.
32 Midwife Y.
33 Midwife X.
34 Midwife U.
35 Holmberg, A.R., *Nomands of the Long Bow*, Garden City, N.W., Natural History Press, 1969. The general acceptance of the ritual in Siriono society is indicated by a story of the consternation caused in one village when a man refused to cut the cord. He said that he wasn't the baby's father, that he had 'divorced' the mother some time earlier. Under protest, eventually, he cut it (Holmberg, op. cit., p. 74).
36 Midwife E.
37 Midwife Y.
38 Midwife R.
39 Midwife A.
40 Midwife F.
41 Holmberg, op. cit., p. 73.
42 Midwife M.
43 Lewis, C. '"A Feeling You Can't Scratch"?: the effect of pregnancy and birth on married men' in Beaill, N. and McGuire, J. (eds.), *Fathers: a psychological perspective*, London, Junction Books, 1982.

13

THE MODERN HOSPICE MOVEMENT

'Bright lights sparkling' or 'a bit of heaven for a few'?

Neil Small

Introduction

This chapter considers the origins and development of the modern hospice movement. This began as an 'unashamedly reformist' movement[1] outside the formal structure of the NHS. Its development, generally accepted as a considerable success story, has seen it both expanding and moving into the mainstream of service provision.

The chapter is divided into three parts. The first considers the context within which the modern hospice movement developed. This includes necessary, but not sufficient, background factors; the shifting pattern of need as population structures changed and disease patterns modified; development in the essential area of pain control; a recognition of the shortcomings of existing services and a change in the way death and bereavement were discussed and understood. But this context did not, in and of itself, produce change. The necessary catalyst was a combination of personal vision that things should be better for those at the end of their lives and a tenacity to translate the resulting discontent into action. Here the work of Dame Cicely Saunders, her team at St Christopher's Hospice in Sydenham, south London, and some of its closest supporters will be introduced.

Part two shifts focus, and is concerned with processes of change. Conflicts occurred as hospices sought to become established. In its early days a hospice must win friends. Its establishment is something that has to be fought for, it prompts opposition. I will consider the personal impact of being an innovator and of the challenges to those who follow. I continue by identifying the changing challenges hospices have faced, in part the challenges of success.

Part three considers some of the outcomes of hospice development. Even the rapidly expanding hospice movement is a veritable minnow next to the leviathan of the NHS and, as such, had to be hugely influenced by the latter's development. But the history of hospices does show how work in one discrete area can have an impact wider than the apparent boundaries of its institutional development. I will also be concerned to examine, as is implied by my title, how far one can see the development of hospices as offering an example of excellence for others to look to and emulate, or how far it is a much more limited history of an elite service developed for the few.

Throughout I will reflect on the relationship between the hospices and the National Health Service. I will address some of the institutional aspects of that relationship but will also consider the extent to which there was a shared philosophy. Would the hospice pioneers have recognised Bevan's credo:

> It is no answer to say that things are better than they were. People live in the present, not in the past. Discontent arises from a knowledge of the possible, as contrasted with the actual. There is a universal and justifiable conviction that the lot of the ordinary man and woman is much worse than it need be. That is all I need to have admitted for my present purposes.[2]

The chapter utilises material gathered via oral history interviews with key figures in the history of hospices. As such it constitutes a small part of an ongoing study.[3] There are histories of the hospice movement.[4] There are also histories of particular units,[5] works by pioneer figures[6] and works of biography.[7] The development of hospices has prompted sociological and historical analysis; for example James and Field in a much-cited article[8] borrow from Max Weber the idea of a shift from charisma to bureaucracy and James[9] develops this picture in presenting a shift from vision to system in the maturing of the hospice movement.

What the oral history approach offers, as we seek to develop a wide-ranging, thematic, approach to interviewing many people from the hospice movement,[10] is the capacity to add to the extant histories and analyse an approach that allows us to engage further with the interface of personal experience and the broader social and cultural context. The words of the protagonists in this history expand the breadth of contextualisation, at various levels and in different domains,[11] and also give a sense of the way protagonists reflecting on their own experience helped to shape subsequent developments.

This is a multi-faceted history in which hospices were at one and the same time welcomed by some and feared by others, where their structure changes while their focus and character remain more fixed. The reality of the development both of individual units and of the movement more generally is messy, edges are blurred, individuals change the practice of others but their practice is also changed as they move from ideas to engage with operational imperatives. The oral history approach offers a way into this rich confusion.

Starting up

Four background factors contributed to shaping the development of hospices. First was the changing demographic and morbidity picture in the UK. Second came emerging treatments that impacted on the typical client group of the hospices. Third was a growing body of research and anecdotal evidence that was critical of existing practice in the care of the elderly and of the dying. A fourth factor was a shift in the way we understand death and bereavement in society.

By the beginning of the 1960s life expectancy in the UK had increased to 66.2 years for men and 71.2 for women and has continued to increase. Death from infectious disease had almost disappeared and most deaths were from circulatory or respiratory disease or from cancer. By 1960 two in ten of the population died before the age of 65 (a reversal in one hundred years of the mid-nineteenth-century figure of eight in ten).[12] While most terminal care took place in the home, 62 per cent of deaths occurred in hospital in 1960, and the figure was rising.[13]

The ability to understand and respond effectively to pain both contributed to the development of hospices and then, in turn, was much enhanced by the research, practice protocols, and understandings of pain developed in them. Building on an accumulating body of work from the 1950s clinical pharmacology and pain research were able to make considerable advances. Important articles on pain were published in the late 1950s and early 1960s. Subsequently a comparative study of oral morphine and diamorphine was based at St Christopher's Hospice in Sydenham, south London.

From its opening in 1967, as well as offering an environment for research, St Christopher's was a setting in which the holistic philosophy of offering 'total care' for 'total pain', that is care for physical, psychological, social and spiritual pain, could be put into practice.[14] As such it became, in effect, the prototype of a modern hospice – one that incorporated science and education alongside this holistic understanding of care.[15] It built on a tradition of hospice care then evident in a number of long-established hospices – St Joseph's Hospice in Hackney, east London, for example. But at its opening the philosophy of care it would exhibit was well developed and had been refined over at least ten years of work by Dame Cicely, her colleagues and supporters, and a worldwide network of interested and expert individuals.[16] St Christopher's was established with funds raised from charities, foundations and individuals and was quickly supported by the National Health Service which provided a grant to support the Home Care Service which began in 1969. Other hospices followed in the early 1970s: St Luke's in Sheffield, St Ann's in Stockport near Manchester and St Barnabas' in the south coast town of Worthing were early modern free-standing hospices.

While there was the pull towards improvements that came from medical and other advances there was also the push from the identification of the shortcomings of existing services. A series of studies identified the poor quality of care for the elderly and for people with cancer and continued revelations, from the early 1950s until the 1980s, underlined the intractability of the problem. These studies included a Marie Curie Memorial Foundation study which found many cancer patients 'living on their own, or with equally old or infirm relatives, often in appalling housing conditions and often short of the right sort of food, warm clothing and bedding.'[17] Sheldon[18] described geriatric services in Birmingham using phrases such as 'human warehouses' and 'storage space for patients'. Other reports by Hinton,[19] Townsend,[20] Robb[21] and Martin[22] all identified shortcomings in institutional care and highlighted the suffering this caused.

Kastenbaum[23] has argued that every society works out, more or less formally and explicitly, a system which it interposes between death and its citizens. This system intervenes to help a society and its citizens deal with death and its implications and interpret death to the members of the society in socially approved ways. This societal death system in the years since the Second World War in the West has been changing and one can identify hospices, and the range of services they provide, both as a contributory cause and as one manifestation of this change.

The range of critical scholarship about the death system expanded.[24] Gorer described society as manifesting an increasing distance from death as a natural reality.[25] Feifel's 1959 book, *The Meaning of Death*, was an important spur to the developing academic profile of thanatology.[26] Glaser and Strauss[27] looked at 'awareness contexts' of the dying person. They went on to look at the differing trajectories of dying and how, in some, death can be predicted and anticipated.[28] Aries[29] identified five basic patterns in attitudes towards death in Western society from the middle ages to the present. He categorised the last of these as 'forbidden death' in which the subject is perceived as socially unacceptable or forbidden and is to be removed or hidden from social view, for example into institutions. There is some recent work that claims a 'revival of death'[30] or which argues that we need to consider dying and death as separate systems.[31]

At a recent 'Caring for Cancer' Conference in London (20 April 1998) Dame Cicely Saunders reminded people that the hospice movement 'grew by listening' and embodied the basic philosophy that 'You matter because you are you' and that people should 'be helped to live until they die'.[32] A contribution from Japan complements this approach:

> Regardless of the differences in the concept of death, socioeconomic and religious backgrounds, and medical and nursing situations, a common hope of people all over the world is to die peacefully.[33]

By the early 1960s there were a few long-established hospices run by religious orders, in the UK, Ireland, the United States and Australia. Cancer Care Inc. had been established in New York by social workers, the Marie Curie organisation had ten homes in the UK and there were nineteen beds for the care of the terminally ill at the Royal Cancer Hospital (now the Royal Marsden) in London.[34] But the genesis of the modern hospice movement is widely linked with the opening of St Christopher's Hospice in 1967. Its establishment was manifest at a time when the NHS had been with us for almost twenty years, but the origins of what was to become St Christopher's might be more properly aligned with the Second World War and the years immediately following it. The opening of St Christopher's was not the beginning of the story but only a significant milestone on the route.[35] Dame Cicely Saunders, then a hospital almoner, identifies the origin of her ideas that came to fruition in St Christopher's in her clinical work in the 1940s and in an encounter with a patient, David Tasma, whom she visited in Archway Hospital in London until his death on 25 February 1948.

> He was forty and he had an inoperable cancer . . . he was an agnostic Jew who'd come originally from the Warsaw Ghetto. . . . I think I visited him twenty-five times in the two months he was in Archway Hospital . . . and it was while we were talking together that the idea [came] of somewhere that would have helped him more than the very big, sixty bed I think it was, surgical ward, with an excellent sister but very busy. And the idea of somewhere that could have been more appropriate for him sort of came as we were talking . . . we would be better about controlling symptoms, but the most important thing for him was to find someone who would listen.[36]

Indeed, each year at St Christopher's the anniversary of David Tasma's death is remembered as the real starting point. He died just a few months before the appointed day on which the NHS came into operation, 5 July 1948. By this measure both modern hospices and the NHS celebrated their fiftieth anniversary in 1998.

By the mid 1990s there were over two hundred in-patient hospices in the UK. In addition there has been a rapid expansion in the modes of care offered to those people for whom the intent of treatment is no longer cure. Palliative care is offered in day care centres, through domiciliary care services, specialist hospital teams and in-patient care. Many thousands are treated within the palliative care paradigm. Indeed by 1997 it was possible to identify 223 in-patient units in the UK and Ireland, 56 operating as NHS managed units and the remainder in the voluntary and charitable sector. In total, 3,253 beds were available. In addition there were 408 home care teams, 234 day care centres, 176 hospital support nurses, 139 hospital support teams and 60 home respite services.[37]

But the spread and impact of hospices goes wider. Its enthusiasts would have it identified as 'a philosophy not a facility'.[38] If we accept this, influences can be identified in a wide range of activity, from palliative medicine and bereavement care to a propagation of multi-professional working and a holistic approach to responding to need.

The years between Dame Cicely's conversations with David Tasma and the opening of St Christopher's in 1967 were ones of refining ideas, developing skills and building support. One important element was Dame Cicely's concern to stay outside the NHS 'so that the ideas could move back in'. These were years when, within the Department of Health, powerful supporters including Dame Albertine Winner (Principal Medical Officer) were attracted by the hospice idea. It was seen as very important that St Christopher's was established:

> not as a competitor with the NHS, but as an organisation which was working with the National Health Service. It's easier to innovate, isn't it, if you are working slightly to one side and you don't have to go through quite so many hoops. . . . I think it was important for St Christopher's and for other hospices to feel that they weren't seen as being competitive with the NHS; that there was space for such a thing to happen in the voluntary sector. And we're talking of several governments of different political persuasions but all being able to give this developing movement a fair wind. And it must have helped to have people in the Department who knew what it was and were practically supporting it in various ways.
>
> (Dr Dougan)

The opinion of civil servants at the time of the early development of hospices was supportive:

> The mandarins' thinking, I think the political view of hospice, hospices as being community commitment, voluntary effort going into them, a kind of good works which were quite tangible, really meant that they were popular, and it wasn't seen as being threatening to the NHS, indeed it was supporting it.
>
> (Dr Dougan)

But if there was important support from central government, and a recognition that this was a welcome addition and not a threat, the reaction from elsewhere was more mixed.

> We met enormous opposition, opposition yes, opposition, not scepticism, cynicism, caution. . . . It was frank opposition by the establishment – not by the public, not by patients. A lot of bewilderment on their part . . . what exactly is it? What do you do? Why do you have to be here, and I don't want to talk to you about dying. It wasn't that. I think it was very much the medical profession were aghast that anybody should imply criticism, imply that standards were not all they might be. And that has all, just about gone, but that's the story of palliative care.
>
> (Dr Cook)

This account relates to the early and mid 1970s but is a familiar story, and a further example from the late 1970s to early 1980s from another part of the UK shows similar problems. There was clear support from local people for the establishment of a hospice (manifested by their financial commitment), from the local Health Authority and from the National Society for Cancer Relief. But once more there was opposition from doctors:

> There was a great deal of local opposition for all sorts of reasons. A lot of people didn't understand what it was about. Other people felt that, however little it cost, it would be taking away from their slice of the cake. And it was very sad, because people who had been my friends and colleagues for years in General Practice, now shunned me or virtually ignored me. . . . A lot of people did their utmost to undermine the service when we first started and we were constantly having to look over our shoulder.
>
> (Dr Edwards)

Occasionally things went more smoothly.

> From the launch of the appeal to a service that was offering day care, home care and an in-patient unit, we were only two and a half years . . . on average within Britain at that time it was taking between five and seven years to set up a service.
>
> (Administrator Albery)

The hospice movement wanted things to change. But it also had to listen to what others saw as its shortcomings. We can see how there was, in the main, approval from some sectors – the Ministry of Health, and its successor government departments and the public – and a mixed reaction which included suspicion and hostility from the medical profession. Opposition appeared to be caused by a sense that the establishment of hospices in itself implied criticism of established practices. There was also a concern that limited resources might be diverted into these new services, an important local dimension to the nature of reaction to hospices. The experiences in different parts of the UK varied considerably and particular local circumstances – an enthusiastic supporter or a vociferous opponent in a key position, for example – could make a considerable difference.

But it was not just the reaction of others that counted. The hospices and their supporters also had a part to play in shaping the public and professional responses they encountered. Looking back on this part of the history Dr Cook sees mistakes made and lessons learned:

> It was a philosophic move, it was a medical threat, it was a massive nursing threat, and all that I think combined . . . we did not sell ourselves originally. I think the original hospice world promoted itself as a response, as indeed it was to some extent, a response to public demand, to need, to things that were wrong. This was a protest movement, but it was a look at things and saying, 'God, things could be better, you know we've got a little section of people here at the most painful, critical, heart-breaking time of their lives and they're being badly looked after, what are we going to do about this thing?' And which we now know has changed to a much bigger thing than that. And I think we did not sell ourselves to the profession. We said to the public. 'We're here, we'll respond' and to the profession, 'Do like this and you'll be all right'. And I don't think there was nearly enough research done then and the result is, I think, that we didn't, at the time, earn the credibility and the respect that we believed that we were due. And I say that quite carefully because I don't think we deserved it. I think we thought we deserved it, but we didn't work for it. That has changed . . . several things have brought it about . . . a pretty toughly, strictly

refereed, journal, the very name of a medical speciality, *The Oxford Textbook (of Palliative Medicine)*. We have really gone out in the last fifteen years and said to our colleagues: 'We are not asking to be accepted just on the basis of here we are, the public loves us why do you not love us?', but, 'Do you want to check my credentials, do you want to check our credentials because I have them?' That was a vast leap which I don't think many people have given credit for or recognised. . . . In short, I think we probably deserved the opprobrium and the criticism, and everything else that we got in the original days, because I think we were probably a little bit bumptious, a little arrogant . . . a little bit of conceit . . . a certain smugness, you know. 'Thank God we're all right.'

Keeping going

I have concentrated so far on the organisational and policy relationship between hospices and other health services. But there was also a sense in which staying outside the NHS had a personal appeal. It made possible a degree of independence some people did not think they could find elsewhere. As with the institutional history we again encounter a range of reactions and now, as well as local differences, a marked shift in attitudes from the originators of hospices to those who would carry on the work.

> In my mind I knew that if I didn't work on the Mission field 'till I either dropped dead or retired I would come home and do hospice work. One thing became abundantly clear to me over the years in (Africa), was that I would never fit into the National Health Service because out there you have a tremendous amount of responsibility, we didn't even always have a doctor in the hospital, we might have a month or two with no doctor, so we did carry an enormous load of responsibility and we had to do procedures that, you know, I would have been sacked if I'd have even contemplated under the National Health Service.
>
> (Nurse Bolton)

And:

I was becoming quite disillusioned with the way medicine
had gone in Britain whilst I had been away (in Africa)
and not seen it first hand.

(Dr Cook)

Hospices offered a morally acceptable alternative. Dr Cook was
relieved that he could move,

out of the Health Service, thank God not into private
medicine, but into hospice medicine.

But those drawn towards hospice work had to balance an attraction to the job with concerns for the career implications:

I spent a year going round different hospices and the joke
was, I was drawn in screaming really, because the joke
was: every one I went to, I'd come back and say, 'This
is fantastic, you know, terrific, you know, I really could
do this job', and I'd wake up the next morning . . . (you
can see I'm very decisive), wake up the next morning and
think, 'You're nuts', you know, 'You've got . . . children,
. . . this is ridiculous, you know, you can't take a chance
like this, it's lunacy'.

(Dr Green)

As I have described, hospices developed with charitable funding
and outside the financial and administrative structures of the NHS.
But from the early years of St Christopher's NHS money was
forthcoming for specific services, home care from 1969 for
example. Partnerships between the NHS and charities emerged,
so that, for example, between 1976 and 1982 twelve continuing
care units were developed with funding from National Society for
Cancer Relief and local NHS authorities.[39] This allowed the possibility of adopting the hospice method within the context of an
NHS that also seemed worthy of support.

It was certainly appealing to me because, you know, I've
grown up with the NHS. OK I was born pre NHS but
I've, you know, from early years I've been NHS as a
patient and I heartily approve of the NHS. I believe in
socialised medicine and I think being within an NHS Unit
would have a natural appeal to me.

(Dr Flynn)

Hospices within the NHS offered, for some, the chance to engage with an agenda they felt was not within the remit of the independent hospices:

> For me being in what I call the rough and tumble of what I call the real world ... we were actually trying to offer a service to an area, rather than offering a bit of heaven to a few.
>
> (Dr Green)

Despite the development of hospices within the mainstream NHS, potential staff recruits still felt vulnerable because of the apparent absence of a career structure and of an acceptable level of academic respectability for the area. The professionals contributing to hospice care were operating in areas that had not yet been recognised by their respective professional hierarchies. Hence there was not a clear way of professional advancement within the hospices, nor was there a sense of the wider recognition of the care and treatment innovations being developed by professional hierarchies outside the hospices. Hence the pioneers' pressure to have palliative medicine accepted as a specialty, something achieved in 1987 when the Royal College of Physicians granted palliative medicine sub-specialty status:

> we're inundated with people saying if it was a specialty we would come and do it but we don't really feel like pioneers like you who would give up our career and move into this, we've got wives and children and what is the security for the future?
>
> (Dr Cook)

The twin agendas of wanting to do better than the inadequate care delivered inadequately that had been evident in many establishments and also wanting to make available the best advances in symptom control set the scene for much early hospice practice.

One thing that was required was a different relationship between carer and cared for. Listening to the patient and seeking to understand need as something beyond the narrowly physiological was at the heart of the nascent hospice contribution to better care regimes. Talking of his pre-hospice experience in the 1950s and 1960s Doctor Adams describes how:

Consultants were handling obviously very distressed patients by distancing from them, or rather by not handling them. I became aware, fairly early on in my medical career, that there was this sort of distancing process, and the very thing that I'd learned in medical school as a means of thinking about what goes wrong in the body – that's a sort of detachment from the human being and thinking about what's going on under the skin – was being used as a defence to prevent the doctor from actually getting too emotionally involved, getting too close to his patients.

Doctor Barnes sees this as a continuing agenda item as he comments on a concern that has continued through his long career, from the 1950s to today:

Doctors and nurses, as part of their professional training, medicalise inaccurately the needs of their patients because they are the needs as they see them. If they listen to the patients they will see that there's much more social need than the purely medical/nursing need. And the social need of dying, while you're playing bingo, or listening to music, or playing cards, or having chums to talk with, is much more important than the rather myopic, blinkered vision of the professional doctor, the professional nurse.

The initial need for symptom control provided a focus, but the relationship between service and need is a dialectical one. As services develop, so too does the focus of need:

it was a time when we were feeling our feet . . . we knew that hospices were there for symptom control, and in those days it was mostly pain control, because most patients who came in were on nothing stronger than paracetamol. . . . But from those days to now the type of patient that we have seen has gone through different phases. It began to change, because of the education that we were inputting to district nurses, general practitioners, hospitals; as that expertise in symptom control increased then we saw fewer patients who were actually coming in for symptom control because they could be managed at home

or in the hospitals. So we saw a change in that we were
getting more patients who were coming in just to die.

(Nurse Austin)

While the nature of demands on the hospice changed so too
did the organisational structure of services. There was a proliferation of new ways of responding to those with palliative care needs.
Multi-disciplinary teams were recognised and supported.
Recognition of specialty status for constituent professional group-
ings followed.

The growth of hospices and specialist palliative care has generated new agendas both for hospices and for the health service.

With the development of our services now I even have to
keep reminding our Trustees that, you know, our role as
an independent voluntary organisation is to identify gaps.
. . . There is a real danger that we almost feel that we
have to fit in with the Health Board's strategic and business plan. And I think we have to be very, very, careful
that instead of providing what, at one point, would have
been looked on as the extras, the services that might not
come if we depended on the NHS, that we're almost, if
we're not careful, providing services that should be
provided within the NHS.

(Dr Hughes)

I don't think anybody ever envisaged the whole of the
nation being as well served as it now is, and we certainly
never thought that there would be competition between,
perhaps, home care teams working on more or less the
same patch but with different specialist palliative care
units in their backgrounds. So the variety, the diversity,
the need for co-ordination and collaboration; all those
things hadn't, in my view, been envisaged. I rather think
they were thought of as being bright lights sparkling.

(Dr Dougan)

Later on . . . the grants which were then being made to
hospices were thought, perhaps, to be promoting their
establishment; because there was money for it, and I know
that Mrs Bottomley (Secretary of State) was concerned
about that. She said, 'the more money we put in, the

more new ones develop'. And how, you know; how can this be? Are we really needs-based?

(Dr Dougan)

As well as the new questions raised by the growth in the number and range of services, the shift from hospice to palliative care and the development of professional specialisms raised others:

When it comes to the crunch, I think that the professionalisation has actually been enabling. I think that there are more people, certainly more with cancer, who are having better symptom control, are able to live quality lives, are able to be up and about ... even if that sort of cosy, rather slow sort of aspect of some of the hospices is threatened. I think, I think in the end, the benefits are there and can be counted.

(Dr Dougan)

Looking back

The hospice as something wider than its organisational boundaries is evident in a number of ways. One can look at the impact, and subsequent activities, of people working in such places:

A lot of people come for training to a hospice, work in a hospice for a few years and then go off and do something else. And that's because they may find that what they have learned in hospice is relevant when they are working with amputees, is relevant when they're caring for people in other settings. And, you know, the clergyman who, having worked as a hospice chaplain, goes and works in the community and meets people who are suffering the effects of divorce and other losses in their lives, again, has opportunities to use the lessons that he's learnt in one setting to improve care in another. I hope I'm not being romantic in suggesting that there are, the long term influences of hospice may well extend far beyond the medical care system, and maybe have important implications for the entire social structures that we live in.

(Dr Adams)

Some influence comes from the organisation reaching out:

I think we see our future work here, and our development, more about being a resource centre and enabler
for others. And I think that fits in with what people are
looking for nationally, but although we have been able to
help hundreds of patients we have to acknowledge that
only a small portion of the patients have actually received
palliative care (in the region). And so what we hope in
the future is, more and more for our team, specialist team,
to use their skills to improve the knowledge of other
people, I think, is the way we'll be going in the future.

(Administrator Albery)

The wider impact is also evident in the way the hospice has
been shaped, and in turn has shaped, the debate about the social,
psychological and spiritual context of death, dying and bereavement in contemporary society. By the mid 1970s some at
St Christopher's, Dame Cicely, Dr Colin Murray Parkes and
others, had begun an involvement in the International Work
Group on Death, Dying and Bereavement (IWG). This was 'a
group of individuals who were concerned with the care of the
terminally ill and the bereaved, and with issues of research, education and values in health care'.[40] Others in the St Christopher's
team were also encouraged to contribute their experience although
there was sometimes a sense that the gap between practical experience and theoretical speculation was still wide:

It was quite a culture shock. I'd never thought of death
in terms of thanatology and Institutes and it was all dedicated and frightfully serious, about the whole business,
and, yes, well, of course, one should be, but I mean it
was really a culture shock for me to see their approach
as it must have been a culture shock for them to see our
approach here.

(Volunteers Organiser King)

The developing hospice movement has been accompanied by a
considerable amount of political and public support. For example,
the degree of charitable giving is such that if all money given to
hospices were aggregated it would constitute the biggest sum of
charitable giving in the country. But there are critics, some of whom
might be best described as critical friends, often commenting from
'inside'. While others are more overtly hostile. Of this second group

the 1992 paper by Douglas summarises many of the most generally made points. He argues that hospices had been worthwhile in that they had drawn attention to earlier inadequacies in the care of the dying, they had been the base for the development of aspects of nursing skill and service innovation, in particular home care, and they had provided a home for the emerging specialty of palliative medicine in its infancy. But the charges against them were formidable: why should it assume that care at the end of life should be separate from care that goes on before?; why should collective dying be a good idea?; why should only a minority of a minority (those with cancer) be singled out for special treatment?; and finally why should a large and general need for end of life care be left to the 'scanty and scandalously choosy efforts of a patchwork of local charities'?[41] Other commentators have pointed to the disproportionately large number of middle-class hospice patients[42] and the absence of people from minority ethnic communities.[43]

Friends from within, Hillier for example, point to dangers in 'overzealous growth' and an undue concern with cancer.[44] Others ask about potential elitism. Has the hospice movement created 'a bit of heaven for a few'?

> It occurred to me that this multi-million pound institution, this ghetto of excellence, was incredible and certainly where I wanted to die. On the other hand it wasn't just, it was not cost effective, because the fantasy that you could duplicate St Christopher's enough times to meet the needs of the 80 per cent of the Western culture who die in institutions, with our shrinking, even then, health care budgets, just seemed to me to be untenable and unlikely, unreasonable.
>
> (Dr Kershaw)

But if the hospice is more than bricks and mortar we need to consider if it has had an impact wider than that evident within its institutional boundaries. If it has, then perhaps the hospices have become 'bright lights sparkling' leading the way for others. In the early days there were problems:

> The St Christopher's model, I suppose, was adopted almost wholesale in the early days because there was no other model. And I was quite embarrassed in sort of going to far distant corners of the world and finding that they'd

304

built hospices that looked exactly like St Christopher's, and behaved exactly like St Christopher's, and seemed to take very little account of major cultural differences that might exist. Over time things have changed . . . America has been the first big change. . . . The thing that caught on in America . . . was hospice at home. The idea that you could care for dying patients in the community instead of admitting them to hospitals.

(Dr Adams)

We have seen that the recent history has been one of expansion and diversification. But while the history of hospices is undoubtedly a story of growth and influence this, of itself, should not serve as a proxy for success. More appropriate measures might include how far hospices retain their reformist drive, and how far their institutional form helps or hinders their ability to improve care for the sick and dying.

The same critical questions can be directed at the NHS, whose establishment was not just to do with a package of specific reforms. At least for some of its founders it was something with an end goal, something in which one could act on one's aspirations and combine utopianism and militancy. Writing about the socialist tradition, Eley has observed that at:

rhetorical and motivational levels, the sense of an end goal was crucial to the staying power of the tradition, not only to the movement's élan, but to the sustained commitment that ultimately allowed the civilising of capitalism to occur.[45]

Similar questions can be asked both of the NHS and of the hospice movement. If what each has achieved has been a series of procedural changes and institutional reforms then they have gone part way only. More fundamentally we might judge them according to how far they continue to seek a goal best summarised by Aneurin Bevan's maxim that 'Preventable pain is a blot on any society.'[46]

Notes

1 James, N., Field, D. 1992. The routinization of hospice: bureaucracy and charisma. *Social Science and Medicine*, 34, pp. 1363–75, at p. 1363.

2 Bevan, A. 1952. In Place of Fear, London, Heinemann, at p. 2.

3 Interviews were conducted as part of the Hospice History Project. This began in 1995 and is based within the Sheffield Palliative Care Studies Group, Sheffield University. The project is funded by the Wellcome Trust (Grant No. 043877/Z/952); the Sir Halley Stewart Trust and the Royal Society. The team comprises Professor David Clark and Dr Neil Small (who have undertaken the majority of the oral history interviews), Paul Lydon who has led on archival and preservation work, Gilly Pearce who manages the processing of the oral history interviews and Clare Humphries who is studying the role of religious orders in hospice development.

4 Stoddard, S. 1979. *The Hospice Movement: a Better Way to Care for the Dying*, London, Jonathan Cape; Taylor, H. 1983. *The Hospice Movement in Britain: its role and its functions*, London, Centre for Policy on Aging.

5 Lack, S.A., Buckingham, 1978. *First American Hospice: Three years of care*, New Haven, CT: Hospice Inc.

6 Saunders, C. 1992. The Evolution of the hospices. *Free Inquiry*, Winter, 19–23.

7 Du Bouley, S. 1984. *Cicely Saunders*, London, Hodder and Stoughton.

8 James, N., Field, D. op. cit.

9 James, N. 1994. From vision to system: the maturing of the hospice movement, in: Lee, R., Morgan, D. (eds) *Death Rites. Law and ethics at the end of life*, London, Routledge, 102–30.

10 Thompson, P., Perks, R. 1993. *An Introduction to the Use of Oral History in the History of Medicine*, London, National Life Story Collection, 5–6.

11 Monks, J., Frankenberg, R. 1995. Being ill and being me: self, body, and time in multiple sclerosis narratives, in: Ingstad, B., Reynolds Whyte, S. (eds) *Disability and Culture*, Berkeley, University of California Press, 107.

12 OPCS 1985. *Mortality Statistics, 1841–1980*, Series DH1 No. 15, London, HMSO.

13 Cartwright, A. 1991. Balance of care for the dying between hospitals and the community: perceptions of general practitioners, hospital consultants, community nurses and relatives. *British Journal of General Practice*, 41, 271–4.

14 Saunders, C. 1993. Foreword, in: Doyle, D., Hanks G., Macdonald, N. (eds) *Oxford Textbook of Palliative Medicine*, Oxford, Oxford Medical Publications, v–viii.

15 Stoddard, S. op. cit.

16 Clark, D. 1998. Originating a movement – Cicely Saunders and the development of St Christopher's Hospice 1957–1967. *Mortality*, Vol. 3, No. 1, pp. 43–63, at p. 58.

17 Marie Curie Memorial Foundation. 1952. *Report on a National Survey Concerning Patients Nursed at Home*, London, Marie Curie Memorial Foundation, p. 18.

18 Sheldon, J.H. 1961. *Report of the Birmingham Regional Hospital Board on its Geriatric Services*, Birmingham Regional Hospital Board.

19 Hinton, J.M. 1963. The physical and mental distress of the dying. *Quarterly Journal of Medicine*, 32, 1–21.

20 Townsend, P. 1964. *The Last Refuge*, London, Routledge and Kegan Paul.

21 Robb, B. (ed.) 1967. *Sans Everything – A Case to Answer*, London, Nelson.
22 Martin, J.P. 1984. *Hospitals in Trouble*. Oxford, Blackwell.
23 Kastenbaum, R. 1972. On the future of death: some images and options. *Omega*, 3, 307–18.
24 Corr, C. 1993. Death in modern society, in: Doyle, D., Hanks, G., Macdonald, N. (eds) *The Oxford Textbook of Palliative Medicine*, Oxford, Oxford Medical Publications, 28–36.
25 Gorer, G. 1955. The pornography of death. *Encounter*, 5, 49–52.
26 Feifel, H. (ed.) 1959. *The Meaning of Death*, New York, McGraw Hill.
27 Glaser, B., Strauss, A. 1965. *Awareness of Dying*, Chicago, Aldine.
28 Glaser, B., Strauss, A. 1968. *A Time for Dying*, Chicago, Aldine.
29 Aries, P. 1974. *Western Attitudes Toward Death: From the Middle Ages to the Present*, Baltimore, Johns Hopkins University Press; Aries, P. 1981. *The Hour of Our Death*, New York, Alfred A. Knopf.
30 Walter, T. 1994. *The Revival of Death*, London, Routledge.
31 Small, N. 1997. Death and difference, in: Field, D., Hockey, J., Small, N. (eds) *Death, Gender and Ethnicity*, London, Routledge, 202–21.
32 NCHSPCS. 1998. *Information Exchange*, 25 June. London, National Council for Hospice and Specialist Palliative Care Services, 6–7.
33 Kashiwagi, T. 1991. Palliative care in Japan. *Palliative Medicine*, 5, 165–71.
34 Lamerton, R. 1980. *Care of the Dying*, Harmondsworh, Penguin.
35 Clark, D. op. cit.
36 Respondents are identified by their professional affiliation and by a pseudonym except where they are discussing subject areas, or are expressing views that have been previously attributed to them in published work. Many of these respondents are still actively involved in the hospice world, hence my use of pseudonyms. I have also changed some details when they specifically refer to individual hospices or places, to help preserve anonymity. The early tranche of interviews for the Hospice History Project, which this chapter draws on, concentrates on figures considered to be of national and international importance in hospice development. Subsequent interviews will consider in more detail the role of people from a wide range of professional, and non-professional, backgrounds in national and local developments. They will also include dissenting voices, individuals critical of both the philosophy and practice of hospices. We will also seek to record patient and carer views of hospice in so far as this is possible. The very circumstances of their admission, of course, creates problems for gathering any retrospective reflection on the experience of hospice for its users. About half the admissions to hospices are followed by the patient's death. These patients, and others admitted, are likely to be in considerable need of urgent symptom control. All patients and carers are likely to be under stress. This scenario does not make oral history impossible but it does create challenges and we hope to report our response to these in subsequent work.
37 Jackson, A., Eve, A. 1997. *Directory of Hospice and Palliative Care Services in the UK and Ireland*, London, Hospice Information Service.
38 Corr C., Corr D. 1983. *Hospice Care: Principles and Practice*, London, Faber and Faber.

39 James, N., Field, D. op. cit., p. 1374.
40 Corr, C., Morgan, J.D., Wass, H. 1994. *Statements on Death, Dying and Bereavement*, London, Ontario, IWG, p. 1.
41 Douglas, C. 1992. For all the saints. *British Medical Journal*, 304: 29 Feb., 579.
42 Cartwright, A. 1992. Social class differences in health and care in the year before death. *Journal of Epidemiology and Community Health*, 46, 81–7.
43 Smaje, C., Field, D. 1997. Absent minorities? Ethnicity and the use of palliative care services, in: Field, D., Hockey, J., Small, N. (eds) *Death, Gender and Ethnicity*, London, Routledge, 142–65.
44 Hillier, E.R. 1983. Terminal care in the United Kingdom, in: Corr, C.A. and Corr, D.M. (eds) *Hospice Care: Principles and Practice*, London, Faber, 319–34.
45 Eley, G. 1998. Socialism by any other name? Illusions and renewal in the history of the Western European Left. *New Left Review*, 227. Jan./Feb., 97–115, at p. 113.
46 Bevan, op. cit., p. 75.

INDEX